THE CHETNIK
MOVEMENT
AND
THE YUGOSLAV
RESISTANCE

THE CHETNIK MOVEMENT
&
THE YUGOSLAV RESISTANCE

Matteo J. Milazzo

THE JOHNS HOPKINS UNIVERSITY PRESS
BALTIMORE & LONDON

This book has been brought to publication with the generous assistance of the Andrew W. Mellon Foundation.

The John Hopkins University Press, Baltimore, Maryland 21218
The Johns Hopkins University Press Ltd., London

Library of Congress Catalog Card Number 74-24383
ISBN 0-8018-1589-4

Library of Congress Cataloging in Publication data will be found on the last printed page of this book.

CONTENTS

:

PREFACE

:

Historians of World War II have devoted enormous efforts to the highly sensitive themes of popular resistance to and treasonous collaboration with the Axis occupation order. In virtually all the socialist countries and in some Western nations, like France and Italy, research and publishing on the wartime resistance movements have developed into something of a scholarly industry. In spite of this, however, we are probably just beginning to arrive at an understanding of these problems which is relatively free of the immediate postwar political disputes and clashes over ideology.

Yugoslavia, one of the few nations of Fortress Europe in which a broad-based resistance did contribute significantly to the obstruction of the Axis military effort, is a good example. Yugoslav historians have produced a vast amount of monographs and articles and a highly useful collection of documents, but practically all this material deals with the growth, development, and triumph of the Partisans. Other questions, such as the realities of the occupation system, movements of collaboration of one sort or another, and, finally, the non-Communist resistance, have received inadequate treatment. For obvious reasons, Mihailović and the Chetniks were subjects of intense controversy from the beginning, and until now virtually everything written about the officers' movement either dismisses it as collaborationist or represents it as the legitimate alternative to Titoism.

The first and most immediate aim of this book, then, is to fill a gap in our knowledge of wartime Yugoslavia. By focusing on the Chetnik movement we can gain a more clear understanding of the wide variety of ways in which important segments of the population, especially most of the Yugoslav officer corps and large numbers of the Serb civilians, perceived and responded to the occupation. The Partisans' ultimate success does not conceal the fact that during the greater part of the war several armed groups, owing a least some sort of allegiance to Mihailović, chose very different courses of resistance.

It is unavoidable that a study which deals with a movement whose leaders' long-haul anti-Axis goals all proved abortive and whose short-term arrangements involved a number of tactical accommodations with the occupation order must attempt to clarify the extremely difficult issues of resistance and collaboration. The overriding question is how a movement whose leadership was in no sense pro-Axis found itself progressively drawn into a hopelessly compromising set of relationships with the occupation authorities and the native Quisling regimes. What was it about the situation in occupied Yugoslavia and the Serb officers' response to that state of affairs which prevented them from carrying out serious anti-Axis activity or engaging in effective collaboration? The question is phrased that way because the tactic of collaboration not only discredited the Chetniks with the Yugoslav civilian population and the Allies but also, largely because it was never more than tactical collaboration, failed to increase Mihailović's standing with the occupation authorities.

How was it, then, that the officers' collaborationist tactics actually worked to undermine the effectiveness and cohesion of the movement? To what degree did Mihailović and his coterie of delegate-officers direct this whole effort? Was the officer leadership responding to developments more than initiating them, and was Mihailović ever actually the effective head of a Chetnik movement?

Evidently, the focus of this book is on the situation in occupied Yugoslavia rather than on the diplomacy of the resistance movements. Particular attention is given to the emergence, organization, and failure of the Chetniks, the regional peculiarities of the movement, and Mihailović's efforts to establish his own authority over the widely scattered non-Communist armed formations. The following chapters discuss the domestic opposition to Tito and the complex reality of the national and political civil war in Yugoslavia. The argument will be developed that the failure of the Mihailović movement was basically internal, and that the collapse of their relations with the British was of secondary importance.

This overall focus was made possible by relying very heavily on source materials dealing directly with the resistance and the Axis occupation rather than on external diplomatic materials. In addition to the multitude of Partisan documents and the Chetnik trial materials, the operations and intelligence reports of the Axis occupation authorities have been particularly useful. Special mention should be made of the records of the Italian Second Army and its civil administration in Montenegro, available to researchers only since 1967. These made possible a careful examination of the growth of the Chetnik movement in the western parts of Yugoslavia and also included some invaluable intercepted Chetnik radio transmissions. With the records of the German Foreign Office and Balkan commands, these sources constitute the large bulk of unpublished evidence for this study.

During two trips to the National Archives, Robert Wolfe and his staff saved me a great deal of time working with the German records and the Mussolini papers. I would also like to thank Jean Owen of The Johns Hopkins University Press for kind assistance in preparing this manuscript for publication.

When writing about wartime Yugoslavia, it is virtually inevitable that interpretations will offend one side or another. As I have tried to arrive at an explanation of the Chetnik movement which neither condemns it as strictly collaborationist nor idealizes Mihailović as the rightful defender of a "Western" and democratic Yugoslavia, neither the officers' detractors nor their apologists will be satisfied. In any event, the judgments expressed here are exclusively the author's own.

THE CHETNIK
MOVEMENT
AND
THE YUGOSLAV
RESISTANCE

I

THE AXIS POWERS AND THE DESTRUCTION OF YUGOSLAVIA

:

The resistance and civil war in wartime Yugoslavia never would have assumed the dimensions they did had it not been for the Axis Powers' establishment of an occupation system which fostered rebellion and anarchy. Instead of creating political order, it produced rival "states" and zones of influence. Instead of being based on a common occupation policy, the "new order" was at best a temporary arrangement which no one thought would last. Playing on prewar political and national tensions, Berlin and Rome tried to solve the Yugoslav problem through a policy of divide and rule. Instead they encouraged a reign of terror in half the country which only fed the ranks of the rebellion and soon got totally out of hand.

Unlike countries like Poland and the Soviet Union, where a brutal occupation regime was the result of German expansionistic policies and long-range planning,[1] the Axis Powers almost stumbled into the war

[1] For these themes, see Martin Broszat, *Nationalsozialistische Polenpolik (1939–1945)*, Schriftenreihe der Vierteljahrshefte für Zeitgeschichte 2 (Stuttgart: Deutsche Verlags-Anstalt, 1961); and Alexander Dallin, *German Rule in Russia (1941–1945)* (London: MacMillan, 1957).

against Yugoslavia and, with other priorities in mind, dismembered the country in haste and without adequate consideration of the likely consequences of their decisions. In the spring of 1941 Hitler was interested primarily in preparing for the invasion of the Soviet Union by securing his flank in southeastern Europe through an expansion of the Three-Power Pact to include Yugoslavia and Bulgaria. The short-term goals were to eliminate Soviet influence in the Balkans and to lay the groundwork for a quick campaign in Greece.[2] In Belgrade, the Cvetković-Maček government had few alternatives; overcome by tremendous diplomatic pressure, the threat of German attack from Bulgaria, and the British refusal to offer concrete promises of military support, they signed the pact on 25 March 1941.

As it turned out, Prince Regent Paul and his ministers had next to no options at all. Had they refused to sign the agreement, they would have had to face Germany on impossible terms. Instead they decided to join the Three-Power Pact but could not bring the rest of the country with them. The Serb nationalists were motivated primarily by a desire to defy Hitler but perhaps also by opposition to the concessions made by the Cvetković-Maček government[3] to the Croats' demands for increased administrative autonomy, and they resented Yugoslavia's ostensible entry into the Axis camp. On 27 March a military coup in Belgrade overthrew Prince Regent Paul, and the leader of the conspiracy, Air Force General Bora Mirković, declared the maturity of the seventeen-year-old Prince Peter and installed a fellow Air Force general, Dušan Simović, at the head of government.

The Simović government was in an even worse predicament than its predecessor. It needed time to consolidate its authority, to patch up relations with Maček's Croat Peasant party, and to appeal for guarantees from the Allies. Accordingly, it refused to ratify the Three-Power Pact but did not reject it openly. This strategy failed: Hitler flew into a fury at the news of the coup and the anti-German incidents at Belgrade[4] and

---

[2] For the diplomatic background, see P. W. Fabry, *Balkan Wirren 1940–41* (Darmstadt: Wehr and Wissen Verlag, 1966); and J. B. Hoptner, *Yugoslavia in Crisis (1934–1941)* (New York: Columbia University Press, 1962). For the coup of 27 March, see Ferdo Culinović, *Dvadeset Sedmi Mart* [March twenty-seventh] (Zagreb: Jugoslavenska Akademija Zvanosti i Umjetnosti, 1965).

[3] Franjo Tudjman, "Društveni Aspekti Narodnooslobodilačkog Pokreta u Jugoslavije" [Social aspects of the Yugoslav national liberation movement], *Putovi Revolucije* 7 (1966): 14.

[4] Von Heeren to Aus. Amt, "Telegramm N. 276 vom 27.3.1941," 27 March 1941, *National Archives Microscpy No. T-120* (hereafter all German and Italian microfilmed materials are cited by microscopy number, for example, *T-120*), roll 1687, frame 3569H/E02321; von Heeren to Aus. Amt, "Zusammenfassende Darstellung der Vorgänge in Jugoslawien," 27 March 1941, *T-120*, roll 1687, frames 3569H/E023719, 3569H/E023720; von Hereen to Aus. Amt, "Telegramm N. 274 vom 27.3.1941," 27 March 1941, *T-120*, roll 359, frame 3569H/E023715.

on the same evening ordered that Yugoslavia be crushed militarily "as quickly as possible." [5]

The action against Yugoslavia was, then, a "rushed" campaign which the Germans wanted to end quickly and with the smallest possible commitment of permanent occupation forces. At the end of March O.K.W. (Oberkommando der Wehrmacht) was planning to station only six divisions in the German spheres of Yugoslavia and Greece [6] and to carry out the invasion with the greatest possible participation of allied Italian, Hungarian, and Bulgarian units.[7]

The Italians, too, despite their long-standing desire for a Balkan sphere, were totally unprepared for a war with Yugoslavia. Fresh from another unsuccessful offensive against the Greeks in Albania and therefore already overcommitted in the Balkans, they were stunned and horrified by the coup in Belgrade. Only about five divisions were stationed along the Alpine Italo-Yugoslav border, compared with thirty-seven in the fall of 1940,[8] and the Italians were still pinned down by the Greeks. Mussolini even feared a Yugoslav attack against the Italian rear on the Albanian front.[9] At the end of March, after Hitler had already decided on invasion, the Italian foreign minister, Ciano, even briefly attempted to act as an intermediary in improving relations between Germany and Yugoslavia.[10]

The invasion began on 6 April and, although the Germans prepared it at the last minute, the Yugoslav army was in a hopeless position and was routed in a matter of days (see the map). It was outflanked by German forces in former Austria and Bulgaria, and, in view of recent events, the military commanders could not count on the allegiance of their Croat troops. On the eve of the attack about 400,000 of their 700,000 soldiers were recent inductees, and the large bulk of the units were strung out along the 1,860-mile frontier according to a "cordon" defensive strategy. Furthermore, the final operational plan, which Yugoslav army leaders worked out immediately after the Germans en-

[5] OKW/WFSt/Abt. L., N. 44379/41 g. K. Chefs., "Weisung N. 25," 27 March 1941, in Germany, Wehrmacht, Oberkommando der Wehrmacht, *Hitlers Weisungen für die Kriegführung (1939–1945)*, ed. Walther Hubatsch (Frankfurt am Main: Bernard und Graefe Verlag für Wehrwesen, 1962) (hereafter cited as *Hitlers Weisungen für die Kriegführung*), p. 106.

[6] Germany, Wehrmacht, Oberkommando der Wehrmacht, *Kriegstagebuch des Oberkommando der Wehrmacht* (hereafter cited as *KTB/OKW*), ed. Hans-Adolf Jacobsen (Frankfurt am Main: Bernard und Graefe Verlag für Wehrwesen, 1965), 1: 371.

[7] OKW/WFSt/Abt. L., N. 44395/41 g. K. Chefs., "Weisung N. 26," 3 April 1941, in *Hitlers Weisungen für die Kriegführung*, pp. 108–9.

[8] Mario Roatta, *Otto Milioni di Baionette* (Verona: Arnoldo Mondadori, 1946), p. 161.

[9] Leonardo Simoni [Baron Michele Lanza], *Berlino: Ambasciata d'Italia 1939–1943* (Rome: Migliaresi, 1946), pp. 216–17.

[10] Giorgio Perich, *Mussolini nei Balcani* (Milano: Longanesi, 1966), p. 88.

Axis invasion of Yugoslavia, April 1941 (arrows show movements of German troops and their allies). *Source: The War in Maps* (New York: Oxford University Press, 1943), no. 27.

tered Bulgaria, did not reach the army commands until 31 March. After only a week of fighting, German units had already marched on Zagreb and Sarajevo and were rather well received by the Croatian and Muslim civilian populations.[11] General Simović therefore decided on an armistice.[12]

Less than two weeks after the war had begun, on 17 April 1941, the rout was complete and the Yugoslav High Command was compelled to sign an unconditional surrender. The striking fact about the events of April, however, is that the Germans failed to follow up their military victory. Hasty preparations for Operation Barbarossa prevented the Wehrmacht from completing mopping up actions and forced the withdrawal of the crack German units from Yugoslavia as early as late April. Therefore, only 344,162 officers and troops, or about half the Yugoslav armed forces, were captured. After most of the Croats and Macedonians were released, about 200,000 prisoners, largely Serbs, remained in camps in Germany,[13] and over 300,000 officers and troops, again Serbs for the most part, disobeyed the capitulation order and escaped capture.[14]

Even more important, the Germans, largely because they lacked clearly defined plans for Yugoslavia's postwar disposition and were unable to make a large permanent military commitment there, had to turn over the administration of the country, or a large part of it, to their allies and to native collaborators. Rump Serbia was the only important area of exclusive German influence. Part of Macedonia would probably go to Bulgaria, and the Adriatic littoral would fall in the Italian zone, but the overriding question of predominant political influence in the central parts of the country was still undecided. Hitler was rather disinclined to see Croatia, Bosnia, and Herzegovina become an Italian satellite and even thought briefly of turning over the area to the more pliable Hungarians.[15] As for native political elements in Croatia, the Germans attempted to influence Maček but got nowhere.[16]

[11] Generaloberst von Vietinghoff (XXVII. Army Corps), "Balkan Campaign 1941," p. y, 14–15. This is a special study, numbered MS#B-334 and catalogued in U.S. Army, European Command, Historical Division, *Guide to Foreign Military Studies*. The Germans' warm welcome in Zagreb is even granted by Vladko Maček, *In the Struggle for Freedom* (New York: Speller, 1957), p. 230.

[12] For the Balkan campaign of 1941, see Josef Matl, "Jugoslawien in Zweiten Weltkrieg," in Werner Markert, ed., *Jugoslawien* (Cologne: Boehlau Verlag, 1954), pp. 99–119; L. Hepp, "Die 12. Armee in Balkanfeldzug 1941," *Wehrwissenschaftliche Rundschau* 5 (1955): 199–216; E. Rohricht, "Der Balkanfeldzug 1941," *ibid.*, 12 (1962): 214–26.

[13] Václav Král, *Prestuplenia protiv Evropy* [Crimes against Europe] (Moscow: Izdatel'stvo "Mysl'," 1968), p. 208.

[14] Helmut Heiber, "Der Stand der Partisanenbewegung in Jugoslawien Ende September 1941," *Gutachten der Instituts für Zeitgeschichte* 2 (Stuttgart: Deutsche Verlags-Anstalt, 1966), p. 292.

[15] Szotay to Bardossy, 6 April 1941, in Lajos Kerekes et al., eds., *Allianz Hitler-Horthy-Mussolini* (Budapest: Akademijai Kiado, 1966), no. 102.

[16] Woermann to von Grote, 29 March 1941, *T-120*, roll 1369, frame 2548H/D523310;

The Italians, far more than the Germans, had major territorial ambitions in the western half of former Yugoslavia. Recognizing that no Croat political figure would be happy about them, they looked for someone in their debt. The choice fell on the Croatian-Ustaši terrorist and separatist Ante Pavelić, a veteran of over a decade of political exile in Italy and one of the chief conspirators behind the assassination of King Alexander in Marseilles, France, in 1934.[17] Mussolini offered to sponsor a Ustaši regime in Croatia in exchange for Pavelić's support of the Italian annexation of the Dalmation coast. Pavelić agreed, and even proposed an Italo-Croat union under the House of Savoy, arguing that there would "no longer exist any political and administrative differences with the Italians . . . and that the Dalmatian problem will no longer have any meaning." [18]

By early April the Germans, having failed with Maček, were also talking to Pavelić through his principal agent in Zagreb, Colonel Slavko Kvaternik,[19] and less than a week after the invasion Hitler approved the Pavelić movement's assumption of power.[20] Thus the Ustaši leader, who only days before had an armed following of about 230 Croat separatist émigrés, based in Pistoia, Italy, and outfitted with uniforms from the Ethiopian campaign, marched on Zagreb and was proclaimed *poglavnik* ("chief") of the Independent State of Croatia.

Italy's diplomatic triumph, though, proved more apparent than real. Hitler gave in, accepted Pavelić, and professed relative lack of interest in Croatian affairs, probably because he recognized that a falling out between the Italians and the Ustaši was inevitable. Pavelić was even more open: he told the German minister in Zagreb that he was relying on the "later disintegration" of the Italian army to reassert Croatia's rights on the Adriatic.[21] In the meantime, German agents in Zagreb worked assiduously to encourage the Ustaši regime's growing anti-Italian orientation.

Practically all the German diplomatic efforts had the effect of undermining Italy's territorial designs. First the Germans delayed approval

Maček, *Struggle for Freedom*, pp. 220–22; Franjo Tudjman, *Okupacija i Revolucija* [Occupation and revolution] (Zagreb: Institut za Historija Radničkog Pokreta, 1963), p. 50.

[17] Martin Broszat and Ladislaus Hory, *Der Kroatische Ustascha Staat (1941–1945),* Schriftenreihe der Vierteljahreshefte für Zeitgeschichte 8 (Stuttgart: Deutsche Verlags-Anstalt, 1964), p. 43.

[18] Filippo Anfuso, *Da Palazzo Venezia al Lago di Garda* (Rome: Capelli, 1957), p. 160.

[19] Broszat and Hory, *Kroatische Ustascha Staat,* p. 50.

[20] Ribbentrop to Veesenmeyer, 13 April 1941, *Documents on German Foreign Policy, 1918–1945* (hereafter cited as *DGFP*), ser. D, vol. 12 (Washington, D.C.: U.S. Government Printing Office, 1962), no. 328.

[21] Kasche to Aus. Amt/Pol. IV, "Telegramm N. 123 vom 25.4.1941," 25 April 1941, *T-120,* roll 212, frame 161808.

of Pavelić's public statement announcing the transfer of Dalmatia to Italian sovereignty; [22] then, on April 21, Ribbentrop opened talks with Ciano by supporting Croatia's absorption of Bosnia and Herzegovina and "considerable portions" of the Dalmatian coast.[23] On the following day the German foreign minister announced that Berlin had decided to maintain an occupation force in "a strip of Croatia running from northwest to southeast in order to safeguard the railroad communications with Serbia" and to preserve certain economic privileges in the Italian zone, particularly with regard to bauxite mining operations.[24]

These tactics forced the Italians to reduce their territorial demands from all to most of the Dalmatian coast and gave Pavelić the courage to defy Rome at almost every turn.[25] By 25 April he had gone so far as to insist on all of Dalmatia, as defined by the Treaty of London, Split (Spalato), Dubrovnik (Ragusa), and several islands in the Adriatic. As a result of prolonged negotiations, during which Zagreb continuously appealed to Berlin for support,[26] the Italians finally got most of Dalmatia (with the exception of Dubrovnik), an area inhabited by about 280,000 Croats, 90,000 Serbs, and 5,000 Italians.[27]

The territorial arrangements finally agreed upon on 18 May solved the problem in a formal diplomatic sense but only marked one phase in the progressive estrangement between the Italians and the Ustaši government. Although they had acquired the southern half of Slovenia, a large share of the Adriatic coast, and a protectorate over Montenegro, the Italians' "puppet," Pavelić, defied them openly, and they grew increasingly suspicious of German intrigue in Zagreb.[28] Rome had dramatically underestimated the strength of Croatian nationalist aspirations along the Adriatic [29] and the *poglavnik*'s capacity for independent action.

During and after the negotiation of the territorial settlement a virtual administrative war went on between the Italians and the Zagreb government. Rome tried to reinforce its foothold along the Adriatic by

---

[22] Anfuso, *Palazzo Venezia*, p. 102.

[23] Galeazzo Ciano, *L'Europa verso la catastrofe* (Verona: Arnoldo Mondadori, 1948), p. 652.

[24] RAM, "Record of the Conversation between the Reich Foreign Minister and Count Ciano at the Hotel Imperial," *DGFP*, ser. D, vol. 12, no. 385.

[25] Kasche to Aus. Amt/Pol. IV, "Telegramm N. 123 vom 25.4.1941," 25 April 1941, *T-120*, roll 212, frame 161808.

[26] Kasche to Aus. Amt/Ha Pol., "Telegramm N. 141 vom 3.5.1941," 3 May 1941, *T-120*, roll 1127, frame 2120H/461867; memorandum of Weiszäcker, 3 May 1941, *DGFP*, ser. D, vol. 12, no. 440.

[27] Mackensen to the foreign minister, 1 May 1941, *ibid.*, no. 428; Broszat and Hory, *Kroatische Ustascha Staat*, p. 67.

[28] Anfuso, *Palazzo Venezia*, p. 142.

[29] King Victor Emmanuel was a major exception. In late April he told Ciano that "the less of Dalmatia we take, the fewer problems we'll have." Ciano, *Diario II (1941–1943)* (Milan: Rizzoli, 1946), entry for 30 April 1941.

Dismemberment of Yugoslavia, April 1941. *Source: A Short History of Yugoslavia: From Early Times to 1966*, ed. Stephen Clissold (Cambridge: Cambridge University Press, 1966), fig. 37.

demanding that Croatia enter a monetary and customs union with Italy, but Pavelić remained firm and refused.[30] Zagreb countered by erecting a high customs barrier around Split to obstruct the flow of agricultural products into the port and urged civilians everywhere to boycott Italian goods.[31] Increasing numbers of Croat civilians refused to exchange Yugoslav dinars for lire.[32]

Economic rivalry spilled over into the political sphere. Pavelić at once

[30] Kasche to Aus. Amt/Ha Pol., "Telegramm N. 141 vom 3.5.1941," 3 May 1941, *T-120*, roll 1127, frame 2120H/461867.

[31] Comando VI. Corpo d'Armata, "N. 1325 del 21.6.1941," 21 June 1941, *T-821*, roll 232, frame 172.

[32] Comando VI. Corpo d'Armata, "N. 631 del 15.5.1941," 15 May 1941, *T-821*, roll 232, frame 20.

sent Ustaši agents into Dalmatia to oversee the "discipline and behavior" of the heavily Croat population [33] and to establish contacts with local nationalists.[34] In Zagreb a Dalmatian Ustaši set up an office for the occupied coastal territories, where they attempted to direct the relations between the Croats and the Italian authorities.[35]

The growing mutual intransigence on the Dalmatian question had the far greater effect of undermining Italo-German cooperation on all matters regarding policy in former Yugoslavia. Certain knowledge that the Germans at least tolerated Zagreb's policies and reports that German officers were promising the war minister, Slavko Kvaternik, arms supplies from the Reich [36] only exacerbated the situation. Hitler hardly helped matters by appointing the former Austrian officer and outspoken Italophobe Edmond Glaise von Horstenau as plenipotentiary general in Croatia.[37] In a more general sense, Croatia, although falling in a vaguely defined Italian sphere, looked more and more like a German satellite in fact if not in name. Pavelić gave this relationship concrete expression when he permitted the Germans to recruit freely among Croatia's 150,000 *Volksdeutsche* for the S.S. "Prinz Eugen division." [38] Consequently, by June, Mussolini was railing against the German invasion of Zagreb, and Ciano and Giuseppe Bastianini, governor of Dalmatia, saw a concerted German effort aimed at undermining Italian influence in Croatia.[39]

The significance of all these rivalries and disputes over territory and spheres of influence is that they generated a mood which militated against the effective coordination of policy. The Italians, the Germans, and the Zagreb government were not satisfied with existing political arrangements, nor were they very enthusiastic about upholding them. The Italian military authorities were increasingly anti-Ustaši [40] and anxious

[33] Veesenmeyer to the Foreign Ministry, 11 April 1941, *DGFP*, ser. D, vol. 12, no. 356.

[34] Comando VI. Corpo d'Armata, "N. 793 del 23.5.1941," 23 May 1941, *T-821,* roll 232, frame 17.

[35] Comando VI. Corpo d'Armata, "N. 601 del 13.5.1941," 13 May 1941, *T-821,* roll 232, frame 14.

[36] Comando VI. Corpo d'Armata, "N. 917 del 30.5.1941," 30 May 1941, *T-821,* roll 232, frame 73.

[37] Glaise von Horstenau served with the Austro-Hungarian liaison staff with the Germans during World War I; in 1925 he became director of the Austrian War Archives and served in Schussnigg's cabinet from 1936 to 1938 as minister without portfolio. From the Anschluss to March 1941 he was vice-chancellor, then interior minister under Seyss-Inquart, and from April 1941 to August 1944 he was German plenipotentiary general in Croatia. He committed suicide in 1946.

[38] Broszat and Hory, *Kroatische Ustascha Staat,* pp. 70–71.

[39] Giuseppe Bastianini, *Uomini, Cose, Fatte* (Milan: Vitagliano, 1959), p. 152.

[40] This was granted even by the Italian Fascist party delegation at Zagreb. "Delegazione del PNF presso il Partito Ustascia to Segretario del PNF," 21 August 1941, *T-821,* roll 295, frame 80.

to extend their occupation zone further into Croatia; the Ustaši were openly revisionist on the Dalmatian issue, and Berlin tried to feign an impartial attitude while in practice using the Ustaši state as a buffer against Italy's Balkan pretensions.

The occupation system was weakened from the very beginning by differences between the occupying powers. Mussolini's and Hitler's decision, made for very different reasons, to support Pavelić only compounded the problem. The émigré Ustaši group had very little domestic support and was utterly unfit to rule a Greater Croatia. Even according to members of the Ustaši organization, the movement had at most about 40,000 "followers," or barely 6 percent of the population.[41] The largely rural Croatian population was traditionally loyal to the Peasant party; several efforts of the Ustaši leaders to win Maček over to some sort of collaborationist posture failed.[42] When they annexed Bosnia and Herzegovina and absorbed almost two million Serbs it was almost certain that the Ustaši would have to govern by strong-arm methods, but Zagreb immediately went far beyond that and decided to solve the "Serb problem" with a policy of unrestricted terror. By the end of the summer at least a third of Independent Croatia's population, practically all the nearby Italian occupation authorities, and even several Germans were irreversibly opposed to the Ustaši regime.

The cession of the Serbs in Bosnia and Herzegovina to a Greater Croatia does, however, illustrate one of the overriding motives of the Axis Powers, especially the Germans, as far as the Yugoslav territorial settlement was concerned. Hitler, in particular, singled out the Serb military leaders and nationalists as responsible for the events of 27 March and thought in terms of a Yugoslav "new order" which would dismember the Serbs even more than the Yugoslav state. As Ribbentrop explained it to Ciano, the Reich's aim was "to reduce Serbia to the smallest limits to prevent . . . conspiracies and intrigues." [43] Accordingly, the Serbs in Bosnia and Herzegovina were sacrificed to the Ustaši, those in parts of the Vojvodina to Hungary, and the Montenegrins to the Italians. Probably less than four million Serbs remained in rump Serbia, which for all practical purposes lacked the very rudiments of a political existence.

The Germans maintained the large part of their weak occupation forces in Serbia and at the end of April set up a fictitious multiparty Commissar Administration in Belgrade, headed by Milan Aćimović. Originally, Berlin was neither willing nor able to work with well-known

[41] [Capt.] Arthur Haeffner to Glaise von Horstenau, "Bericht über die vordringlichsten Probleme des selbstständigen Staates Kroatien," 14 June 1941, *T-501*, roll 265, frame 335.

[42] Broszat and Hory, *Kroatische Ustascha Staat*, p. 88.

[43] Ciano, *L'Europa verso la catastrofe*, p. 654.

conservative collaborators. During the April war, the Serb political elite had almost vanished. The young King Peter and the Simović cabinet had left the country, and practically all the political leaders of a rightist stripe, with whom the Germans conceivably could have made a deal, were also in exile. Stojadinović, for example, spent the war under British guard in Mauritius.

It is possible that the military administration in Serbia could have made this arrangement work if O.K.W. had been able to commit more than a weak army corps there and if the disastrous course of events in Independent Croatia had not taken place. What Germany was attempting, however, was the imposition of a Carthaginian peace on Yugoslavia's Serb population which it lacked the strength to enforce.

During the summer of 1941, a revolt in Montenegro temporarily wrested a large part of the province from Italian control. In Serbia, the Germans recognized that the authority of their military occupation barely extended beyond the few large cities,[44] and in Independent Croatia Ustaši policies quickly threw whole areas of Bosnia and Herzegovina into a state of almost continual anarchy and national war. These simultaneous upheavals were interrelated: Serb rebels from Herzegovina fled south and played a major role in the Montenegrin uprising; Ustaši terror caused a growing influx of desperate and embittered refugees into rump Serbia. By August probably about 100,000 Serbs had fled east from the Ustaši state, and at the end of September the number of refugees in Serbia was estimated by the Germans at over 200,000.[45] With half the Yugoslav army at large and many of them remaining in the hills, the Ustaši government and Axis occupation authorities faced a nearly impossible situation.

[44] Benzler to Aus. Amt, 23 July 1941, *T-120*, roll 200, frame 230/152287.
[45] Wehrmachtbefehlshaber Südost (AOK 12)/Ic, 26 July 1941, *T-312*, roll 460, frame 8046565; Broszat and Hory, *Kroatische Ustascha Staat*, p. 108; Jovan Marjanović, *Ustanak i Narodnooslobodilački Pokret u Srbiju 1941* (The uprising and national liberation movement in Serbia in 1941) (Belgrade: Institut Društvenih Nauka), p. 50.

II
THE MIHAILOVIĆ
MOVEMENT IN SERBIA,
1941

:

The Yugoslav High Command, which exercised almost no control over the Croatian troops during the two-week war, wielded just as little authority when it concluded the formal capitulation of 17 April 1941. While large numbers of the Croats were reluctant to fight and welcomed, or at least tolerated, the new order, dismay and bitterness were widespread among the Serbian detachments, where many refused to accept defeat and German capture. Rather than obey the orders to capitulate, several of them broke up into small, straggling bands, especially in the interior provinces of the country, like Bosnia, where German supervision was minimal.

Colonel Dragoljub-Draža Mihailović's behavior during the confused days of April and May 1941 was probably very similar to that of several members of the Serbian officer corps. Mihailović, who had held a number of General Staff positions in the interwar period,[1] acted as the chief of

---

[1] Dragoljub "Draža" Mihailo Mihailović was born on 27 April 1893 in Belgrade, attended a military academy from 1910 to 1912, became a private in 1911, and served as platoon leader in an infantry regiment during the Balkan Wars of 1912–13; as a

staff of the Second Army in Bosnia for a short while in early April before taking over a far smaller and hastily formed motorized "Rapid Unit" (*brzi odred*) on April 13.[2] His formation reconnoitered the situation along the Second Army's collapsing front, had a brief clash with an Ustaši unit, and, on 15 April, moved toward the area around Doboj, Bosnia, where they skirted a German armored column and received first word of the Yugoslav High Command's decision to capitulate. With only part of his followers, Mihailović immediately withdrew into the surrounding hills and, shortly after, began his journey to the east with a few dozen loyal officers and troops.[3]

After a march of a few weeks, during which the small group of about eighty men attempted some minor sabotage activity and clashed with a local armed Bosnian Muslim band, Mihailović reached and crossed the Drina River on 29 April.[4] Now in rump Serbia, they began to receive rumors and reports, probably from Serb refugees or other escaping troops, on the situation in other parts of the country, and, at a meeting in early May, word circulated that there were "strong, armed illegal bands in Serbia," that Chetnik *Vojvoda* Kosta Pećanać was moving toward the

lieutenant, Mihailović again served as a platoon leader during World War I. After the war he was promoted to the rank of captain (1920), attended officers' schools, and began serving as a staff officer in the late 1920s. By 1930, now a lieutenant-colonel, he served with the chief of the General Staff of the Royal Guard; in 1935 he moved to the General Staff section of the War Ministry and was advanced to the rank of colonel. In the following year he was stationed in Sofia and in Prague as Yugoslav military attaché. From 1937 to 1939 Mihailović was in Yugoslavia, where he held a number of lesser General Staff positions. A detailed summary of his prewar military career, based on the records of the Yugoslav War Ministry, may be found in Auswertestelle Ausland, "Zusammenarbeit der Tschetniki mit dem jugoslawischen Generalstab u. deren heutiger Führer Mihailović," 5 November 1941, *T-314*, roll 1457, frames 1203–6.

[2] This account of Mihailović's activities during and immediately after the Axis invasion is taken from Radoje L. Knezević, ed., *Knjiga o Draži* (The book on Draža), vol. 1 (Windsor, Canada: Srpska Narodna Odbrana, 1956), especially the articles by Knezević, Major Mirko Stanković, and Lieutenant Colonel Pavel Mešković. The last two officers were with Mihailović from 28 April to 6 May 1941. Although many of the contributors to this volume fought in Chetnik formations during the war and are all blatantly pro-Mihailović, it remains the best source for tracing the first stages of the movement immediately after the capitulation.

[3] Knezević, in *ibid.*, pp. 8–9.

[4] The details of these incidents are, to say the least, somewhat vague. While Knezević claims that Mihailović, on 25 April, beat back an attack by a group of Muslims armed by the Germans near the village of Olovo, Stanković asserts that the clash took place on 26 April at Zepo. *Ibid.*, pp. 9, 25. At any rate, in view of Mihailović's later directives to his subordinates in Bosnia and Montenegro and the whole Chetnik treatment of the Yugoslav Muslims during the war, the incident was one of the first and typical examples of the officers' military strategy and was part of a major pattern of the civil war in wartime Yugoslavia.

Kopaonik area in southwest Serbia, and that General Ljuba Novaković had refused to surrender and was gathering troops.[5]

As it turned out, these reports were wildly exaggerated. Moreover, Mihailović's group was almost completely destroyed when it was surrounded by the Germans in the Užice area on 6 May. Several officers despaired and deserted the colonel, and, by the time Mihailović reached his future headquarters at Ravna Gora in western Serbia sometime in the middle of May, only seven officers and twenty-seven lower officers and troops accompanied him.[6]

Before they could engage in any feasible resistance strategy, the small officers' band had to gain time to recover, attract new recruits, and establish contacts with other still uncaptured officers. The task of organizing also meant that they needed a relatively safe regional "sphere" in which to operate; this in turn required the establishment of friendly relations with the local civilian population and administration. First they developed ties with some peasants in nearby villages, but even more important was their rapid success in winning over the gendarme and police forces of the area. In a short time the officers' ranks were swelled by gendarmes from nearby Brajica, Mijonica, Gornji Milanovac, and Valjevo, and, according to Chetnik sources, Mihailović encouraged this alliance by capturing some runaway convicts who were plundering the countryside and turning them over to the local police forces.[7] Aided by the active support, or at least toleration, of these police officials, Mihailović was able to expand activities. Gendarmes loyal to Mihailović rather than to the puppet Serbian civil administration in Belgrade enabled his group to set up a system of communications through couriers, to collect lists of military personnel who had escaped German captivity, and to provide them with some badly needed financial support.[8]

During this initial phase, the officers desperately needed money to obtain food and supplies and to support anything larger than a small band. Financial resources for the movement, however, were uncertain and inadequate. On the day after they arrived at Ravna Gora, all the officers pooled what money they had in a common treasury[9] and received contributions from sympathizers in the local villages in the form of food, clothing, and money. These measures were barely sufficient, though, and

[5] Stanković, in *ibid.*, p. 26.

[6] Knezević, in *ibid.*, pp. 10–11; Stanković, in *ibid.*, p. 26.

[7] Pavel Mešković, in *ibid.*, pp. 52, 54. Present-day Yugoslav historians, not surprisingly, claim just the opposite. Marjanović (*Ustanak i Narodnooslobodilački Pokret*, p. 78) asserts that the Chetniks began to attract several marauding bands in western Serbia.

[8] Meškovic relates, for example, that the gendarme commander of Vinkovica, Captain Milojko Uzelac, gave Mihailović 300,000 dinars. *Ibid.*, p. 58n.

[9] *Ibid.*, p. 58.

Mihailović was quickly forced to ask one of his female relatives for help; she collected about 50,000 dinars from friends.

The question of material support was crucial because, without adequate money and supplies, Mihailović's group either had to resort to plunder and rupture their emerging alliance with the nearby police officials and civilian population or restrict their activities. Moreover, the pressure to expand the scope of the movement was mounting rapidly as other officers got word of Mihailović and aligned their followings with Ravna Gora. A typical example was Major Vojislav Lukačević, who fled to the woods after the capitulation, returned to Belgrade, where he heard about Mihailović, and then left the capital with a small number of officers and soldiers to organize a Chetnik detachment in the countryside.[10] Others traveled directly to the Ravna Gora headquarters. Major Boško Todorović, for instance, knew about the Mihailović group by the end of May and soon after left Belgrade to join him.[11] Belgrade, in fact, appears to have been the principal place of recruitment for many of the officers who originally joined the Chetniks in western Serbia. This was possible mainly because the Germans apparently made no effort, at least before the outbreak of the Partisan revolt, to track down uncaptured Yugoslav military personnel in the Serbian capital.[12]

A rapid influx of troops and officers into the Ravna Gora area was a mixed blessing at first because they strained the already meager supplies and would ultimately attract the attention of the German occupation authorities. Mihailović rightly feared that too large a collection of recalcitrant troops in western Serbia would result in a reprisal raid which he was not prepared to resist. During the summer months, military considerations dictated a strategy of breaking the organization into small groups rather than trying to create large armed detachments. The immediate objective of organizing over a wide area rather than preparing for imminent military operations also reflected Mihailović's long-range political goals and his perception of the necessary outcome of the war.

The strategy of asserting control over as many "illegal bands" as possible and expanding the movement at least throughout Serbia and prob-

---

[10] Lukačević's testimony is found in Državni Sud, *Sudjenje članovima Političkog i Vojnog Rukovodstva Organizacije Draže Mihailovića* (The sentence against the members of the political and military organization of Draza Mihailović) (Belgrade: Prosveta, 1945), pp. 137–38.

[11] Vojislav Pantelić, in *Knjiga o Draži*, 1: 156–57.

[12] The German authorities did not concern themselves seriously with the presence or number of former Serbian officers in Belgrade until the second half of September. At that time they believed there were about twelve hundred, while Serbian Minister-President Nedić preferred the figure seven hundred. General Bader, the commander of the German forces in Serbia, immediately ordered a new count. Gen. Kdo. XVIII A..K/Ic, "Tätigkeitsbericht für die Zeit vom 14.4–6.12.41," 22 September 1941 (Anlage 14), *T-314*, roll 1457, frame 317.

ably in several other parts of Yugoslavia was designed to build an organization capable of seizing effective political power when the Germans withdrew or were defeated, rather than focusing on fighting them during the occupation. Mihailović revealed these aims to several individuals at Ravna Gora. Either at the end of May or beginning of June, for example, Radivoje Jovanović traveled to Chetnik headquarters to confer with their leader and was told that the strategy was to "organize, not to fight, and when the Germans begin to withdraw, then to move in and seize power."[13] Two future Partisan leaders, a Dr. Jovanović and Dragoilo Dudić, received the same advice from Mihailović at the end of June.[14] In addition, Vojislav Pantelić, when he arrived at Ravna Gora in early July with a band of twenty-seven men, mostly gendarmes, was informed by the colonel that the Chetniks planned to organize the entire country militarily before awaiting the opportune moment for a general uprising.[15]

In order to win time during which they could develop their organization and expand contacts with other armed groups, Mihailović permitted the establishment of indirect links with the puppet Serbian administration in Belgrade. The purpose of these maneuvers was essentially to encourage an attitude of "salutary neglect" on the part of the Serbian civilian and—more important—German military authorities. In late May he sent Second Lieutenant Vladimir Lenac to Belgrade to ask the collaborationist and Serb nationalist Dimitrji Ljotić for the names of Belgrade civilians who could offer the Chetniks financial assistance.[16] Shortly thereafter a Lieutenant Pipan came to the capital to inform Ljotić of the progress of the Ravna Gora movement and to point out that Mihailović had no plans for attacking Germans.[17] Similarly, another Ravna Gora emissary, Lieutenant Neško Nedić, met a special envoy of Belgrade's Ministry for Internal Affairs in mid-July and emphasized that the Chetnik strategy had absolutely nothing to do with "communist terror."[18]

Mihailović's efforts to avoid a confrontation with the occupation administration were temporarily successful. The Germans, in fact, in July even encouraged Aćimović to make an arrangement with the officers.[19]

---

[13] From an interview with Radivoje Jovanović-Bradonija, cited in Marjanović, *Ustanak i Narodnooslobodilački Pokret*, p. 76.

[14] Mešković, in *Knjiga o Draži*, 1: 61.

[15] Pantelić, in *ibid.*, p. 158.

[16] Before the war Lenac was the head of the right-wing Ljotić "Zbor" youth movement at Zagreb University. Bosko Kostić, *Za Istoriju Naših Dana* (Toward a history of our times) (Lille: Jean Lausier, 1949), pp. 32–34. Kostić served as intermediary between Ljotić and the Germans.

[17] *Ibid.*, p. 34.

[18] Marjanović, *Ustanak i Narodnooslobodilački Pokret*, pp. 127–28.

[19] This is described briefly in Bevoll. Kdr. Gen. in Serbien/Verwaltungsstab (Turner), "N. 65/41 vom 3.12.1941," 3 December 1941, *T-175*, roll 126, frame 2651861.

Mihailović refused to go this far, yet there is no evidence that either the Quisling government or the German occupation forces took any effective measures during the summer to hinder the development of the Ravna Gora movement.[20]

The Chetnik officers pursued a basically wait-and-see strategy, not only because they thought it was the only realistic one but also because, as loyal officers who considered their activities to be a continuation of the royal Yugoslav army struggle of April, they believed it had the approval of the émigré High Command. As long as they were convinced that success depended heavily on political and military support from the British, they must have felt it was absolutely necessary to coordinate their actions with the orders of the London government. The émigré officers' authority flowed from the fact that virtually all the still uncaptured Serb generals were among their number, whereas the Chetnik officers in Yugoslavia were for the most part captains, majors, and colonels.

In September, when a Chetnik agent, Miloš Sekulić, succeeded in making his way from Belgrade to Constantinople in order to receive instructions from the Simović government, he finally got directives which explained that the aim of Mihailović's "Yugoslav Army" would be the seizure of power "when the interregnum comes, i.e., after the defeat of the German army." [21] In the meantime, its main tasks were to "preserve order in the country and to permit no brutal measures or robbery." Similarly, General Simović himself, in a radio broadcast of mid-August, advised his compatriots in the occupied homeland to avoid provocations because they would only lead to cruel reprisals.[22]

In order to make these strategic guidelines effective, Mihailović had to undertake the difficult task of imposing some sort of control over the illegal bands of stragglers and fugitives outside his own stronghold in the Ravna Gora area. This meant winning the loyalty of several other officers to his own command and establishing a civilian political arm to complement military activities.

Before leaving for Turkey Miloš Sekulić had met with Mihailović at the village of Ba, where they agreed to set up a Chetnik political committee at Belgrade. Shortly before, some pro-Chetnik political figures in Belgrade began to work out a program which served as the basis for the

[20] A Chetnik document, dated 1 October 1941, which was essentially a situation report by a certain Gradimir Bajloni, pointed out that "up to now, the Germans have not weeded out the supporters of the Mihailović movement (except for one light bombing attack on his Ravna Gora staff) because [the Chetniks] have taken absolutely no measures against the Germans, figuring that it is still too early." Marjanović, *Ustanak i Narodnooslobodilački Pokret*, p. 185.

[21] *Ibid.*, p. 185, n. 97.

[22] Simović broadcast of 12 August 1941 and official communiqué of exiled London government of 20 September 1941, cited in *ibid.*, pp. 195–96.

creation of the "Central National Committee" (Centralni Nacionalni Komitet).[23] Most of the early membership appears to have come from the prewar Serb Agrarian and Republican parties. Dragisa Vasić, a leading Republican and also former vice-president of the Serbian nationalist Srpski Kulturni Klub, became Mihailović's "deputy" at Ravna Gora.[24]

Standing behind this rudimentary and secret political arm was a military organization which by early fall numbered probably no more than three thousand or four thousand officers and men.[25] Despite the steady growth of the main group near Ravna Gora and the fact that it soon commanded significant support from some of the major Serb political figures who had not fled the country, Mihailović was constantly faced with the extremely difficult task of reinforcing his position as the leader of the uncaptured officers and their armed followings. Without any official recognition of the émigré government until the very end of 1941, the Ravna Gora group had to parley and maneuver with a number of officers, some of whom were openly collaborationist, others of whom outranked Mihailović or disagreed with him on fundamental strategy. Before the Germans resorted to a full-scale anti-rebel action in November, the situation in Serbia outside Belgrade and the larger cities was totally anarchic, and several leaders of armed detachments were free to act as virtual warlords within their regions. Mihailović tried to deal with this problem by co-opting and, in some cases, even ostracizing his competitors but never succeeded completely. Although the often very personal disputes between the officers now appear far less significant than the ensuing military struggle between the Chetniks and Partisans, Mihailović's inability to impose his authority over many of the other officers' bands was a tremendous failure for the Chetnik movement and one which he never really overcame at any point during the war.

The Ravna Gora movement was, in fact, one of several "illegal" Chetnik groups. The leader of the "official" Chetnik organization was an aging World War I veteran, Kosta Pećanac. During Serbia's struggle for independence against the Turks in the nineteenth century the Chetniks were small guerrilla detachments which fought in the enemy's rear and

[23] Dušan Plenča, *Medjunarodni Odnosi Jugoslavije u Toku Drugog Svjetskog Rata* (Yugoslavia's international relations during World War II) (Belgrade: Institut Društvenih Nauka, 1962), p. 61.

[24] *Ibid.,* p. 187.

[25] It is impossible to give any precise figures on the strength of the Mihailović movement at this time. Historians like Marjanović (*Ustanak i Narodnooslobodilački Pokret,* p. 184) tend to downgrade his numerical strength, giving figures like three thousand for the early fall. German intelligence reports were extremely vague on this question. One analysis of the Chetnik organization, prepared by the S.D. (Sicherheitsdienst) at Belgrade, estimated its strength at between one thousand and four thousand. Befehlshaber Serbien/Ia, "Aufstellung über die wichtigsten Cetnik-Gruppen," 20 September 1941, *T-314,* roll 1457, frames 640–42.

represented the whole tradition of grass-roots resistance to foreign domination. Pećanac was an organizer of the Serb uprising of 1917 and after the war became head of the Chetnik Union, a strongly nationalist and conservative veterans' association. By the early 1920s, shortly after the assassination of the minister of the interior, Milorad Drašković, Pećanac became a key figure in the rightist agitation to suppress the Yugoslav Communist party and was lionized by Serb conservatives. In the summer of 1941 Pećanac was in at least nominal command of a number of armed bands, mainly in southern Serbia, but immediately after the German invasion of the Soviet Union he publicly renounced any intention of resisting the occupation forces and issued an order in late June forbidding his subordinates from attacking German and Italian troops who "behave politely" toward the Serbs.[26]

Mihailović knew that Pećanac still possessed some potential military significance in the southern parts of Serbia. In mid-August he tried to form an alliance with the old Chetnik head on the basis of a division of Serbia into spheres of influence whereby Pećanac would confine his activities to southern Serbia, the Sandzak, and parts of Albania.[27] In a letter to Pećanac of 15 August, Mihailović made clear that he opposed immediate action against the Axis occupation because "the time . . . is not yet ripe," but he demonstrated that his long-range plans were anti-German, for Pećanac's work in the south was explicitly designed to prevent the enemy from sending reinforcements into Serbia from Greece and Bulgaria.

Already committed to a collaborationist line, Pećanac ignored this attempt to subordinate his units to the Ravna Gora leadership; a week later, he ordered a meeting of his detachment leaders to make plans for operations against the recently launched Communist uprising. By the end of August, he had issued an appeal to civilians to return to order and cooperation with the Axis authorities. Shortly thereafter, he moved to Belgrade, where he set up a so-called Staff of All the Chetnik Units in the Homeland,[28] which had the support of about three thousand armed followers, about the same number as those under Mihailović's direct command.[29] Ultimately—and this was typical of several of the non-Communist guerrilla detachments in wartime Yugoslavia—the Pećanac movement was of little use to either Mihailović or the Germans, and it appears that his bands made their major effort in skirmishes with Albanian Muslim armed groups near the Sandzak and Kosovo-Metohija.

Pećanac's refusal to join the Ravna Gora organization showed the

---

[26] Marjanović, *Ustanak i Narodnooslobodilački Pokret*, p. 75.
[27] Mihailović to Pećanac, 15 August 1941, cited in *ibid.*, pp. 189–90.
[28] *Ibid.*, pp. 174–75.
[29] Gen. Kdo. XVIII A.K./Ic, "Pecanac," 6 October 1941, *T-314*, roll 1457, frame 356.

lengths to which some unit leaders would go in order to retain at least nominally exclusive authority over their own detachments and probably reflected the growing tensions between the older World War I officers and the younger leaders of the Ravna Gora Chetniks. The immediate and decisive issue, as indicated by Pećanac's behavior in August, was the Partisan uprising which broke out in Serbia in early July. The revolt meant that German countermeasures were inevitable and forced each officer with a real or potential guerrilla following to take sides, either joining the Communist operations or giving tactical support to the occupation order. Mihailović tried to restrain the Communists through negotiations rather than compromise his movement and sacrifice the Chetniks' independence by collaborating with Belgrade. This middle course, however, failed, and the Chetniks did not succeed in taming the Communists' zeal for open revolt, in maintaining discipline over all the leading officers, or in dissuading the Germans from turning to a policy of mass reprisals.

The Yugoslav Communist party never recovered fully from the official repression of 1920–21 and, at the beginning of 1940, still numbered only eight thousand members.[30] Between April and June 1941 the party grew to about twelve thousand, but it is debatable what portion of these new adherents were attracted by its anti-German activities.[31] By early July there were apparently only about two thousand Communists in rump Serbia, with about six hundred concentrated in the Belgrade area.[32] After the German invasion of the Soviet Union, they set up a "Supreme Staff of the National Liberation Partisan Units of Yugoslavia" (Glavni Štab Narodnooslobodilačkih Partizanskih Odreda Jugoslavije), headed by Tito, Kardelj, Milutinović, Ranković, and Vukmanović-Tempo, and on 4 July the order for an immediate revolt was issued.[33]

Tito began with a small popular base, and his basic strategy was to

[30] For the interwar communist movement in Yugoslavia, see Vladimir Dedijer, *Tito* (New York: Simon and Schuster, 1953); Branko Lazić, *Tito et la Révolution Yougoslave* (Paris: Fasquelle Editeurs, 1957), pp. 1–50; and Paul Shoup, *Communism and the Yugoslav National Question* (New York: Columbia University Press, 1968).

[31] Naturally, writers sympathetic to the Partisans go to great lengths to show that even before 22 June Tito and the party leadership were planning armed resistance. Ivo Ribar, *Uspomene iz Narodno-Oslobodilačke Borbe* (Memoirs from the national liberation struggle) (Belgrade: Vojnoizdavački Zavod "Vojno Delo," 1961), argues (pp. 21–22) that, immediately after the Yugoslav capitulation, Tito was already thinking seriously of a "peasant-worker" national front against the German occupation.

[32] Marjanović, *Ustanak i Narodnooslobodilački Pokret*, p. 97.

[33] Lazić claims that on 22 June the party leaders had no idea what position to take until late in the evening at which point a telegram arrived from Moscow ordering full-scale armed resisance. *Tito*, p. 57. For the early organization of the revolt, see Jovan Marjanović and Pero Morača, *Naš Oslobodilački Rat i Narodna Revolucija, 1941–1945* (Our war of liberation and the national revolution) (Belgrade: Izdavačko Preduzeće Rad, 1958), pp. 1–46.

remove the party underground from the cities to the poorly supervised rural areas, seek support in the villages and among the roving groups of refugee Serbs, and create enough disorder to stimulate German reprisal actions, which would further radicalize the civilians and create more recruits for the Partisans. The initial armed encounters in early July were directed more against the local native administration, especially gendarme stations, and the communications network than against the small but well-armed German garrisons. In addition, village heads who cooperated too readily with the occupation regime were special targets of the Partisan revolt.[34] By August rebel activities had spread all over western Serbia, and the Communist leaders were soon in a position to rival the Chetnik officers for predominant influence in the Chetniks' own sphere. Moreover, the Communists' early success was due in large part to their raids against the local police and administrative authorities, who were the very groups the officers depended on for support and toleration.

Neither the Acimović gendarmerie nor the weak German occupation divisions were able to cope with the growing chaos in the western parts of rump Serbia. By early September, when Tito moved to Partisan head-quarters, normally at Užice, to begin planning a political program to accompany the armed revolt, the Communist-led resistance was rapidly taking over the anti-German cause. Also, the Partisans' strategy of aggressive and immediate action naturally attracted the "activist" wing of the officers and worked to undermine Mihailović's authority over the non-Communist armed bands.

Some leaders of Chetnik groups began to break with Ravna Gora and to collaborate with the Partisans in joint operations. In the Valjevo area, Chetnik formations led by a local priest, Pop Vlada Sečević, and by Lieutenant Ratko Martinović agreed to work with the Communists and launched a joint attack in early September.[35] Even more significant was the collaboration between the Partisans and the Cer Chetniks, commanded by Captain Dragoslav Račić. In this instance, a detachment leader, nominally under the authority of Mihailović, made a sharp break with the officers' strategy.

Račić was something of a model Balkan revolutionary. Wearing a large beard and the local peasant dress, this former artillery captain represented the aggressively anti-German wing of the Chetnik officers.[36] According to German information, he was also the son of the Montenegrin Serb fanatic who shot the Croat leader Radić in the Belgrade Skup-ština in 1928. In late August he signed an agreement with a Partisan

[34] Marjanović, *Ustanak i Narodnooslobodilački Pokret*, pp. 101–3.

[35] *Ibid.*, p. 140.

[36] 342. Inf. Div./Ic, "Gliederung und Führer der Aufständischen," 8 October 1941, *T-314*, roll 1457, frame 808.

detachment and wrote Mihailović to praise the Communist rebels as "sons of our people who are filled with hatred of the enemy" and to warn that "it is the clear duty of your Chetnik organization to hold a meeting between the Chetnik command and the reresentatives of the Partisan units to approve joint actions for success in defeating the enemy." The Partisans, he stressed, were "irrevocably committed to a struggle to the end, whether the Chetniks participate or not." [37]

Račić's Chetniks and the nearby Partisans carried out combined operations through September and most of October. They even succeeded in capturing a number of German troops and planned a full-scale assault on Šabać for 22 September.[38] When the Germans decided to launch a cleaning-up action in the Cer region, however, Račić, with about fifteen hundred Chetniks and a few thousand Partisans, drew back quickly to avoid a risky confrontation.[39]

Račić was not the only officer whose aggressive patriotism seemed to be pulling the Chetnik movement toward increasingly open collaboration with the Partisans. Artillery General Ljubo Novaković, who had been smuggled out of a hospital by Chetnik sympathizers in May, not only advocated the same course of action as Račić, although inconsistently, but also, as the only officer with the rank of general, posed a very serious threat to Mihailović's leadership.[40]

When he arrived at Ravna Gora, Novaković was at first received rather coldly. When he proposed to the officers that they establish three Chetnik commands, in Montenegro, eastern Serbia, and near Skopje, for the purpose of waging immediate anti-Axis resistance, he was excluded altogether. Novaković stole away from Ravna Gora, began to disarm some of Mihailović's nearby followers, and, in mid-June, moved to the Šumadija in northern Serbia.[41] There, like Mihailović, he tried to make an alliance with the collaborationist Chetnik Kosta Pećanac.[42] By the end of August, after a fruitless meeting with Pećanac, he returned to the Šumadija, where he resumed his original strategy, beginning negotiations with the local Partisans. Although these talks failed, probably because of Novaković's demand that he assume complete command of joint opera-

[37] Račić to Mihailović, 25 August 1941, in Yugoslavia, Belgrade, Vojnoistorijski Institut, *Zbornik Dokumenata i Podataka o Narodnooslobodilačkom Ratu Jugoslovenskih Naroda* (Collection of documents and materials on the national liberation war of the Yugoslav peoples) (Belgrade: Izdanije Vojno-Istorijski Institut Jugoslavenske Armije, 1946) (hereafter cited as *Zbornik*), vol. 1, bk. 1, no. 19.

[38] Hptm. Drf. Ratschitsch, "Vertrauliche Anordnung Nr. 1 für den 10 Sept. 1941" (German translation of captured document), *T-314*, roll 1457, frame 571; Hptm. Drf. Ratschitsch, "Operationsplan für den 21.9.1941," *T-314*, roll 1457, frame 573.

[39] 342, Inf. Div./Ic, "Feindnachrichten," 8 October 1941, *T-314*, roll 1457, frame 808.

[40] Mešković, in *Knjiga o Draži*, 1: 18–19.

[41] Marjanović, *Ustanak i Narodnooslobodilački Pokret*, p. 77.

[42] Aleksander Vitorović, *Centralna Srbija* (Central Serbia) (Belgrade: Prosveta, 1967), p. 115.

tions, he obviously did not abandon the idea of military collaboration with the Communists. In mid-September he issued an appeal for a general uprising in the Arandjelovac area and called for the "brotherly . . . collaboration with all other armed groups who are willing to work with the Chetniks for the national liberation of our Fatherland."[43]

After trying to make an alliance with the Chetnik Mihailović, the collaborationist Pećanac, and the Communist-dominated Partisans, Novaković launched a premature action in the Arandjelovac area in late September with a motley assortment of about three thousand followers, several of whom were armed only with picks and scythes. A good number deserted during the march, and the rest scattered and fled when a small German garrison opened fire. Totally discredited, General Novaković lost practically his entire following and was never again a threat to Mihailović or the Partisans.[44]

The actions of officers like Račić and Novaković, even if short-lived and at time abortive, were typical of the chaotic situation in Serbia before the various armed resistance groups finally coalesced in late 1941 into distinct and mutually hostile Chetnik and Partisan movements. Before the end of the year, Mihailović, although rapidly emerging as the leading Chetnik officer, found himself parleying with a number of other leaders of non-Communist armed detachments who favored everything from open collaboration with the occupation order against the Communists to immediate general uprisings in league with the Partisans.

In Belgrade, the Germans naturally approved only the behavior of Pećanac, were confused and misled by the activities of Račić and Novaković, and suspected that Mihailović was ready to make a military alliance with Tito. Before the end of the summer they had already concluded that the small police force of the Aćimović administration was not reliable and began to worry about Chetnik-Partisan combined actions.[45]

Without a strong occupation contingent, though, the Germans still had to rely on native support. On 29 August, when they replaced Aćimović with a "government of national salvation" (vlada narodnoga spasa), headed by the former minister of war, Milan Nedić, they hoped that, with a collaborationist general in charge of the administration, they could strengthen the "legal" Chetniks of Pećanac, restrain the drift of the other officers into the pro-Partisan camp, and restore order without having to call for a massive German military intervention.[46]

[43] General Ljuba Novaković, "Befehl streng vertraulich N. 20," 18 September 1941 (German translation of captured document), T-314, roll 1457, frame 611.

[44] Bezirksamt Orosac (Stellvertreter Cujetar Djordjević) to Innenministerium, 23 September 1941 (German translation), T-314, roll 1457, frames 575–76.

[45] Benzler to Aus. Amt, "Telegramm N. 493 vom 12.8.1941," 12 August 1941, T-120, roll 200, frame 230/153316.

[46] Benzler to Aus. Amt, 29 August 1941, cited in Marjanović, Ustanak i Narod-

In a short time, however, as the revolt in western Serbia grew more serious, the Germans gave up the Nedić strategy. New gendarme units proved untrustworthy, and different Chetnik groups, although seldom fighting openly against the occupation troops, had apparently made pacts with the Communists for common actions in the future.[47] Already burned by the events of 27 March, the Germans lost all confidence in the prudence of the Chetnik leaders and quickly convinced themselves that the rebellion was now "clearly in the hands of the nationalist Serb officers." [48]

Despite the appraisal of the military authorities in Belgrade, the Chetnik officers were losing control of the national movement. At Ravna Gora Mihailović continued to advocate the postponement of armed clashes with the Germans and finally compromised temporarily with the Partisans' strategy only after he felt he had no other alternative. All evidence indicates that he remained convinced that extravagant actions would only compound the suffering of civilians, force the Germans to strengthen their occupation contingent, and reduce his chances of ultimate success. The overall plan was still to organize the entire resistance under Chetnik command, avoid needless provocations against the Germans in order to avoid costly reprisals, and, finally, link up with an Allied landing in the Balkan peninsula.

To a large degree, the officers must have felt that this course of action would preserve at least one sanctuary in rump Serbia for the Yugoslav Serbs. They also thought that immediate action was safer and more justified in those parts of Yugoslavia under the control of the Croatian Ustaši. The anti-Serb massacres in the western parts of Yugoslavia were part of an open policy and took place for the most part in the villages rather than in concentration camps. The Serb officers knew about them in the summer of 1941 and were determined to prevent the policy of mass reprisals from being employed in Serbia. Moreover, the Chetnik officers must have perceived the situation in this way to some extent as a result of their experience in World War I, when Serbia lost about 20 percent of its population, many in a typhus epidemic in 1915, suffered terribly at the hands of the Austrian and especially the Bulgarian occupations, and was finally liberated by an Allied breakthrough at the Saloniki front.

---

nooslobodilački Pokret, pp. 177–78. Not only did the Germans have to overcome their own reservations about the wisdom of establishing the Nedić government, but they also had to cope with the wrath of the Ustaši leaders, who denounced the move as an act of cooperation with Serb nationalism. Kasche to Aus. Amt, "Telegramm N. 1096 vom 1.9.1941," 1 September 1941, *T-120,* roll 1127, frame 2120H/462026.

[47] Benzler to Aus. Amt, "Telegramm N. 633 vom 12.9.1941," 12 September 1941, *T-120,* roll 200, frame 230/153419.

[48] Bevoll. Kdr. Gen. in Serbien to Wehrmachtbefehlshaber Südost, "N. 3641 vom 21.9.1941," *T-312,* roll 460, frame 8046695.

Throughout September and most of October the tactics of the Ravna Gora group were essentially defensive. In this period the Chetnik leadership first tried to dissuade the Partisans from their aggressive designs and finally decided to make certain tactical changes, basically in order to maintain themselves on an equal footing with the Communist bands. In mid-August and early September Mihailović, his chief political aide, Dragisa Vasić, and officers in Belgrade had meetings with Partisan representatives in which they all argued that the uprising was premature and that the resistance movements had to postpone rebel activities at least until the Germans were defeated on the eastern front.[49] When these efforts failed, Mihailović agreed to meet Tito personally.

Their first encounter took place on 19 September, only a day after Tito had left Belgrade, at a village in western Serbia, Struganik.[50] According to Tito's account, Mihailović stubbornly refused to take part in immediate action against the Germans but did promise that his followers would not attack Partisan units.[51] Other Partisan sources indicate that the Chetnik leader apparently mistook Tito for a Russian and proceeded to harangue him on the treason of the Croats and the reproachable behavior of some of the Serb Partisans.[52] Thus, this first meeting produced no collaboration but little more than a temporary truce. Neither believed in the possibility of real cooperation, but both thought they could derive some benefit from a show of compromise.

The Communist leaders probably recognized that the Chetniks had a good deal of support among the peasants and Serb politicians and that some active cooperation from the officers would be necessary to train and command the Partisan detachments, at least in the first part of the war.[53] Tito also certainly knew that at least some of the officers were ready to break with Mihailović because of his attitude toward the revolt, and he must have hoped that when he offered to collaborate with the Chetniks, Mihailović would refuse and therefore isolate himself from the more aggressive elements in the non-Communist rebel camp.[54] The

[49] For the first encounter, see Marjanović, *Ustanak i Narodnooslobodilački Pokret*, pp. 201–2; the second meeting, which took place in Belgrade on 8 September between the Serb Communist Alexander Ranković and the officers, Colonel Branislav Pantić and Major Velimir Piletić, can be followed in Ranković to Tito, 11 September 1941, *Zbornik*, vol. 1, bk. 1, no. 34.

[50] The best account of the Chetnik-Partisan negotiations of 1941 is Kruno M. Dinčić, "Tito et Mihailovitch," *Revue d'histoire de la deuxième guerre mondiale* 29 (1958): 3–31.

[51] *Ibid.*, pp. 9–10.

[52] Rodoljub Čolaković, *Winning Freedom*, trans. Alec Brown (London: Lincolns-Prager, 1962), p. 147.

[53] For the role of former Yugoslav officers in the Partisan movement seen through the eyes of the British S.O.E., see F. W. D. Deakin, *The Embattled Mountain* (New York: Oxford University Press, 1971), p. 105.

[54] Čolaković, *Winning Freedom*, p. 148.

Partisans had no illusions about the intentions of the Chetnik leadership. Tito was convinced immediately after the talks at Struganik that Mihailović was trying to play a double game and was in fact maintaining contacts with the Germans through Nedić.[55] At the end of September he sent Ranković to the Chetnik headquarters. Little was accomplished, but another meeting was arranged between the two heads to be held on 16 October.[56]

While Tito's immediate aim was to prevent a Chetnik assault from the rear, Mihailović was trying to make sure that the Partisans did not gain the complete upper hand in the anti-German cause. Therefore, although he refused to commit his own followers against the Axis at Struganik,[57] in mid-September he did permit some of his subordinate commanders to take part in joint operations with the Partisans. Chetnik sources indicate that the officers were alarmed at the rapid progress of the Communist bands, especially their seizure of a number of small towns and considerable amounts of rifles and munitions. Mihailović allowed a few of his detachment leaders to collaborate with the Partisans so that the Chetniks could claim a voice in the political affairs of the liberated towns and, more important, share in the captured spoils.[58] By collaborating on this limited basis with Tito, Mihailović was seeking a "guarantee" against

[55] Titoist historians attempt to add credibility to the Partisans' fear of deals between Mihailović and Nedić by pointing out that in early September a Chetnik officer and a Nedić gendarme commander were captured near Belanovica carrying a plan for coordinated Chetnik-gendarme operations against the Partisans hidden inside a spare auto tire. See Marjanović, *Ustanak i Narodnooslobodilački Pokret*, pp. 192–93. Although there is little doubt that Mihailović's agents were in contact with Nedić, there is no proof that any concrete agreements were made. Chetnik sources, obviously, deny the whole thing. Pantelić, for example, writes (*Knjiga o Draži*, 1: 160–61) that on 5 September he met Reserve Major Alexander Mišić, who, having just conferred with Nedić at Belgrade, attacked the minister-president violently. Moreover, if Nedić made any sort of an arrangement with Mihailović in September, he certainly did not so inform the Germans. Sometime in the middle of the month, one of Pećanac's liaison men visited Ravna Gora at Nedić's request and returned with the report that Mihailović could not be trusted to carry out anti-Partisan operations in conjunction with the Serb police. German sources indicate that Nedić's effort to come to terms with the Chetniks was initiated with the approval of the German commanding general in Serbia. Gen. Kdo. XVIII A.K./Ic, "Tätigkeitsbericht für die Zeit vom 19.9.–6.12.41," 25 September 1941 (Anlage 19), *T-314*, roll 1457, frame 329; Bevall. Kdr. Gen. in Serbien/Verwaltungsstab, "N. 65/41 vom 3.12.41," 3 December 1941, *T-175*, roll 126, frame 2651861.

[56] Marjanović, *Ustanak i Narodnooslobodilački Pokret*, p. 276.

[57] According to one German source, Mihailović had only a little over a thousand armed followers under his direct command around Ravna Gora. Gen. Kdo. XVIII A.K./Ic, "Tätigkeitsbericht für die Zeit vom 19.9–6.12.41," 25 September 1941 (Anlage 19), *T-314*, roll 1457, frame 329.

[58] Both Zvonimir Vučković and Pavel Mešković grant that these were Mihailović's basic motives in agreeing to partial collaboration with the Partisans. *Knjiga o Draži*, 1: 63, 135.

the Communists and trying to reassert his own authority over a badly split officers' movement.

In no way, however, did these tactical shifts represent a major change in the Chetniks' long-term strategy and political goals. Only a few days before the Struganik meeting, in fact, Mihailović had conferred with a Serb employee of the Belgrade Bankverein; he explained that he planned no operations against the German occupation troops and that he was opposed to the Communists, but he also implied that he would not attack the Partisans because he wanted to avoid a civil war. His long-range goal was "to be ready, when the German occupation troops are weakened or withdrawn, to maintain and restore order in the land with his own forces." [59]

The exact nature and extent of Chetnik-Partisan armed collaboration is extremely difficult to determine. Some unit leaders like Račić, who had begun working with the Communists on his own initiative, may have been completely out of Mihailović's control.[60] However, by early October, it is clear that he did issue instructions to some of his subordinates to work with Partisan detachments.[61] The most important joint operations took place near Krupanj, Valjevo, and Kraljevo, and, in at least one instance Chetnik units reinforced the Partisans as a result of Tito's personal request to the Ravna Gora headquarters.[62]

From the very beginning, though, the alliance of arms was severely strained. When, for instance, the Germans pulled out of Užice and Požega on 21 September, the nearby Chetnik unit leaders who moved in were immediately surrounded by local Partisans and were expelled from Užice on 24 September.[63] The incident proved to be very significant

[59] George Saal (Direktor der Bankverein), "Aktennotiz: Nikolaević," 7 November 1941, in Yugoslavia, Državna Komisija za Utvrdivanje Zločina Okupatora i njihovih Pomagaća, *Dokumenti o Izdajstvu Draže Mihailovića* (Documents on the treason of Draža Mihailović), vol. 1 (Belgrade: Štampa Državne Štamparije, 1945) (hereafter cited as *Dokumenti o Izdajstvu Draže Mihailovića*), no. 730. Internal evidence places the date of the Mihailović-Nikolaević meeting shortly after 15 September.

[60] A report from the Belgrade S.D. guessed that Račić had severed ties with Mihailović sometime in September. Befehlshaber Serbien/Ia, "Aufstellung über die wichtigsten Cetnik-Gruppen," 20 September 1941, *T-314,* roll 1457, frame 643.

[61] Pantelić received the order from Mihailović to join the Partisans on 10 October. *Knjiga o Draži,* 1: 163.

[62] See Marjanović, *Ustanak i Narodnooslobodilački Pokret,* pp. 248, 260. The operations around Kraljevo provide an excellent example of how difficult it is to reconstruct with any accuracy the facts behind the Chetnik-Partisan military collaboration. Defending the Chetnik point of view, Zvonimir Vučković (*Knjiga o Draži,* 1: 136–37) claims that over 3,000 Chetniks and about 1,000 Partisans fought at Kraljevo, where several Chetnik unit leaders were lost. Marjanović, on the other hand, asserts (pp. 264–66) that only "about 800" Chetniks fought alongside 2,600 Partisans. He goes on to blame the failure of the operation on the "lack of preparation . . . and hard drinking in the villages" on the part of the Chetnik allies.

[63] Marjanović, *Ustanak i Narodnooslobodilački Pokret,* p. 243.

because Užice had an arms and munitions factory which the Partisans could later use as a bargaining tool with the Chetniks. In other liberated areas, friction developed when the Partisans and officers tried to mobilize among the same civilians. There is evidence, too, that Mihailović was preparing all along for a possible future change of allies by treating German prisoners with unusual generosity.[64]

In spite of this, the German occupation authorities took Mihailović's collaboration with the Communists very seriously, and, when Nedić's "armed force" of about twenty thousand men proved incapable of suppressing the revolt, they decided to bring more German troops into Serbia. In early September an infantry regiment arrived from Greece, and soon thereafter O.K.W. agreed to move an entire division from France to Serbia.[65] When General Böhme came to Belgrade to assume command of all German occupation forces in Serbia, he had four entire divisions (the 704th, 714th, 717th, and 342d) plus parts of the 718th division and the 125th infantry regiment.[66]

The Germans were not only better prepared to deal with the situation in western Serbia, but for a variety of reasons they attributed the success of the revolt largely to the Serb officers rather than the Communist leaders. Their mistrust of all Serb military formations, whether formally collaborationist or not, was bolstered throughout September by information that the subordinates of both Pećanac and Mihailović were breaking ranks to take part in the anti-Axis struggle. By the middle of the month General Novaković's transmitter in the Šumadija was broadcasting violently anti-German appeals,[67] while, in the whole area where the Drina and Sava rivers join, Captain Račić was operating against the Germans in conjunction with Partisan bands.[68] Pećanac, whose personal loyalty

---

[64] While the Chetnik Zvonimir Vučković reports (*Knjiga o Draži*, p. 135) that their units "captured" Gornji Milanovac on 2 September, taking over a hundred German prisoners, he goes on to admit that they were treated "most correctly" at Ravna Gora. German intelligence at Belgrade received a report that the small garrison had in fact been surrounded by larger Partisan forces and had sent a message to Mihailović for help. The colonel, according to the report, immediately sent a detachment to Gornji Milanovac and "escorted" about eighty Germans to Ravna Gora. Furthermore, a Chetnik captured in early October near Gornji Milanovac said that Mihailović had given orders not to kill captured German soldiers. Abwehrstelle Belgrad to Bevoll. Kdr. Gen. in Serbien, "Verbleib der aus Gornji Milanovac . . . Kompanie," 30 October 1941, *T-501*, roll 250, frame 976; Gen. Kdo. XVIII A.K./Ic "Mihailovic," 8 October 1941, *T-314*, roll 1457, frame 353.

[65] Franz Halder, *Kriegstagebuch*, arranged by Hans-Adolf Jakobsen, vol. 3 (Stuttgart: W. Kohlhammer Verlag, 1964), entry for 12 September 1941.

[66] Marjanović, *Ustanak i Narodnooslobodilački Pokret*, p. 218.

[67] Gen. Kdo. XVIII A.K./Ic to AOK 12, "Aktenvermerk: Geheim Sender Sumadija," 21 September 1941, *T-314*, roll 1457, frame 659.

[68] Bevoll. Kdr. Gen. in Serbien/Ic, "Lage in Raume Sabac," 24 September 1941, *T-314*, roll 1457, frame 616.

to the occupation regime was beyond doubt, seemed to be losing all control of his formations. In the Kopaonik region, for example, a previous follower of Pećanac, Lieutenant Colonel Masan Djurović, broke off all ties with the legal Chetniks, began seizing gendarme stations, and clashed repeatedly with nearby armed bands of Albanian Muslims.[69] These and similar incidents compelled the Germans to conclude that Pećanac had outlived his usefulness. Pećanac himself wrote to Nedić in early October that the winter months would probably see more defections to the anti-Axis camp and expressed deep regret that Mihailović had been foolish enough to "ally himself" with the Communists.[70] A short while later, the Germans decided to attach the still reliable Chetniks of Pećanac to Nedić's gendarme forces and to stop supplying the rest with weapons.[71]

As far as Belgrade was concerned, it made little difference whether Mihailović's subordinates were collaborating with the Partisans against or in compliance with directives from Ravna Gora. In a thoroughly chaotic situation, in which some officers seemed to be switching sides quickly and attempting various deals with other armed bands, the Germans, who never had much reason to place confidence in the Serb military in the first place, simply resolved the whole problem by assuming the worst regarding the aims of the Ravna Gora Chetniks. As October wore on, instead of thinking that the Chetnik officers had joined the revolt only partially and rather reluctantly, they began to assume that the Ravna Gora headquarters had engineered the alliance and that Mihailović was actually the leading figure behind the whole rebellion.

In short time, the gap between what the Germans in Belgrade discerned to be the size, scope, and strategy of the officers' movement and the actual confused and disorganized state of the Chetnik organization had widened. Intelligence reports began claiming that Mihailović's bands included Communists [72] and that they were growing rapidly as a result of an influx of officers and men formerly allied to Pećanac.[73] Open Com-

[69] Gen. Kdo. XVIII A.K./Ic, "Tätigkeitsbericht für die Zeit vom 19.9–6.12.41," 15 September 1941 (Anlage 22), T-314, roll 1457, frame 333; Wehrmachtverbindungsstelle Belgrad to Bevoll. Kdr. Gen. in Serbien, "Bericht über innere Organisation, befehlsmässige u. räumliche Gliederung, Aktionsaufgabe der Cetnice in Kopaonik—und Rogosna Bereich," 29 September 1941, T-314, roll 1457, frames 577–609.

[70] Gen. Kdo. XVIII A.K./Ic, "Tätigkeitsbericht für die Zeit vom 19.9–6.12.41," 7 October 1941 (Anlage 54), T-314, roll 1457, frames 365–66.

[71] Gen. Kdo. XVIII A.K./Ic, "Tätigkeitsbericht für die Zeit vom 19.9–6.12.41," 10 October 1941 (Anlage 52), T-314, roll 1457, frame 362; Gen. Kdo. XVIII. A.K. to Wehrmachtbefehlshaber Südost, "Nr. 4141 vom 19.10.41," 19 October 1941, T-312, roll 460, frame 8046614.

[72] Wehrmachtverbindungsstelle Belgrad IH, "Bericht über die Widerstandsbewegungen in Gebiet des ehem. Jugoslawien, Stand der Entwicklung in der Zeit vom 19.–26.9.41," 26 September 1941, T-314, roll 1457, frame 773.

[73] Gen. Kdo. XVIII A.K./Ic, "Mihailović," 8 October 1941, T-314, roll 1457, frames 351–52.

munist appeals for collaboration with the Chetniks only served to confirm the reports of captured rebels that Mihailović had formed an alliance with the Partisans and was definitely hostile to the Germans, although, for the time being, he had ordered his followers to attack only weak occupation units. After the first week of October, reports and orders from the highest German authorities in Belgrade stressed that the Chetnik organization was expanding "in all directions" and that, even if they at times behaved cautiously, their ultimate aim was to liberate the land from the occupation order.[74]

Because of the contacts between Ravna Gora and the agents of Nedić and Pećanac, the occupation administration had far more information on the Chetniks than on the Partisans, though it was not always accurate. This, combined with the fact that the Germans were as yet unfamiliar with Communist-led guerrilla movements, led them to underestimate the strength, autonomy, and relative significance of the Partisan movement and to concentrate on Mihailović, overestimating his influence over the whole anti-Axis front and the numerical and organizational strength of the officers' bands. By the end of October reports were stressing that the Chetniks had made common cause with the Communists and were identifying armed detachments loyal to Mihailović throughout former Yugoslavia, as well as in western Serbia.[75]

Just as the Germans were convincing themselves that Mihailović was firmly committed to an aggressive alliance with the Communists against the occupation order, the ever-strained collaboration between Chetniks and Partisans finally broke down. Evidence of conflicts between the two groups, of a number of which even the Germans were aware, had appeared throughout October. Disputes had broken out over the selection of political leaders in the liberated villages, and at Požega there was shooting between Chetniks and Partisans.[76]

These, however, were merely symptoms of broader divisions over strategy and postwar goals. Mihailović's meeting with Tito at Struganik had produced only a very cautious and partial sort of military cooperation on the part of the officers. Moreover, Mihailović and his closest

[74] Gen. Kdo. XVIII. A.K./Ic, "Bericht über die Aufstandsbewegung in Serbien in die Zeit vom 1.–10.10.41," 9 October 1941, *T-314*, roll 1457, frame 825; Bevoll. Kdr. Gen. in Serbien/Ic, "Verhalten gegen Cetniks," 10 October 1941, *T-314*, roll 1457, frame 832.

[75] Abwehrstelle Belgrad, "Bericht über die Widerstandsbewegungen in Gebiet des ehem. Jugoslawien, Stand der Entwicklung in der Zeit vom 10.10–17.10.41," 17 October 1941, *T-314*, roll 1457, frame 990; Abwehrstelle Belgrad, "Bericht über die Widerstandsbewegungen in Gebiet des ehem. Jugoslawien, Stand der Entwicklung in der Zeit vom 10.10–24.10.41," 24 October 1941, *T-314*, roll 1457, frame 1051; Abwehrstelle Belgrad to Bevoll. Kdr. Gen. in Serbien, "Cetnik-Organisation," 28 October 1941, *T-314*, roll 1457, frames 1088–1902.

[76] 342. Inf. Div./Ic, "Feindnachrichten," 17 October 1941, *T-314*, roll 1457, frame 918.

advisers had agreed to join the revolt, albeit halfheartedly, mainly to preserve the position of their own movement in the rebel camp, not because they were willing to risk everything on an immediate struggle with the German occupation.

In a broader sense, the more the revolt in Serbia succeeded, the more the Mihailović group had to lose. Continued rebel activity forced the Germans to stiffen their policies toward the puppet civil administration and the various gendarme and "legalized" armed formations upon whom the Chetniks depended at least partially for information, protection, and future allies. Even more important, the victims of the Serb revolt in the fall of 1941 were for the most part the gendarmes of the Nedić administration, many of whom were sympathetic to the Ravna Gora officers, rather than the small German garrisons.[77]

German troop reinforcements and adoption of a policy of mass reprisals only confirmed Mihailović's belief that the Partisans' excessive zeal would ruin the whole national movement and bring additional suffering to the civilian population. In early October, for instance, perhaps as many as seven thousand civilians were shot at Kragujevac, where there had been no armed attacks on German personnel; at nearby Kraljevo the number of victims was about seventeen hundred, and, in other villages the shootings followed mass burnings of the peasants' homes.[78] These actions created more recruits for the most extreme elements within the resistance, usually the Partisans. Finally, the stronger the Partisans became, the better able they were to deal with the officers on an equal footing, to reject the Ravna Gora strategy, and to gain recognition in the Allied camp as the leaders of Yugoslav resistance.

By October of 1941 the Serb officers at Ravna Gora were confronted with a dilemma. On the one hand, they wanted to preserve their organization as an independent resistance group with Allied backing, ready to act effectively upon an amphibious operation in the Balkans or a German withdrawal. On the other hand, they found themselves firmly opposed to a resistance movement which was rapidly passing out of their control, which favored immediate action, which tended to benefit from the enemy's recourse to mass reprisals and the ensuing radicalization of the masses, and which preferred outside support from the Soviet Union rather than the western Allies.[79]

[77] See, for example, Pantelić, in *Knjiga o Draži*, 1: 162.

[78] Jozo Tomasevich, "Yugoslavia during the Second World War," in *Contemporary Yugoslavia*, ed. Wayne Vucinich (Berkeley, Calif.: University of California Press, 1969), p. 90; Benzler to Aus. Amt/Abt. Ha Pol., "N. 841 vom 29.10.41," 29 October 1941, *T-120*, roll 1178, frame 470307.

[79] This last point has been obscured by the British recognition of the Partisans in 1943 and the difficult relations between Tito and the Russians during the war. It is certainly worth mentioning, though, that even so pro-Partisan a writer as F. W. D.

The Partisans were also aware that the officers had reached an impasse.[80] Tito decided to force Mihailović's hand and on 20 October sent him a letter which called for continued joint operations against Nedić and the Germans.[81] This proposal led to a second and final meeting between the Chetnik and Partisan heads at the village of Brajići on 26 October. The talks produced little more than an exchange of mutual recriminations, as each demanded that his movement assume a dominating position in the resistance.[82]

Tito insisted on close collaboration against the Germans and proposed a comprehensive ten-point program, which included (1) joint operations against Nedić and the Germans; (2) common provisioning of Chetniks and Partisans; (3) the equal division of captured equipment; (4) joint commands in liberated areas; (5) organization of provisional administrations in the liberated areas, popularly elected by all who supported the national liberation struggle; (6) creation of Chetnik-Partisan commissions to settle all disputes; (7) renunciation of forced mobilization; (8) an all-out struggle against traitors and spies with the aid of joint military tribunals; (9) common action against "collaborationist" Chetnik groups; and (10) a mutual commitment not to give identification papers to potential enemies.[83]

Mihailović immediately rejected points 1, 2, 5, and 7, making evident his firm opposition to the whole Partisan military strategy and political reorganization. Although further negotiations did produce a limited agreement (regarding the establishment of united commands in the liberated areas and the sharing of arms produced in the Partisan-held Užice arms factory), Tito's demands at Brajići forced a total break between the two resistance movements. Mihailović, who had demanded that he be recognized as the sole leader of all the rebel forces, decided suddenly to eliminate the Communists.

The Chetnik officers, who would accept nothing less than complete domination of the Yugoslav anti-Axis front, had to regard Tito's program as an unacceptable ultimatum. Also, they recognized that the continued success of the revolt would strengthen the Partisan movement enormously and that if the Communists were to be stopped they had to

---

Deakin points out (*Embattled Mountain*, p. 135) that when the first British intelligence mission passed through Partisan headquarters at Užice on or about 25 October 1941 they got the impression "that Tito was hoping, and would prefer, that any Allied support to his movement would be coming from the Russians."

[80] For a Partisan assessment of the Chetniks' plans, see the letter of 16 October 1941 from the Provincial Committee of the Y.C.P. in Serbia to the Kragujevac District Committee, in *Zbornik*, vol. 1, bk. 2, no. 49.

[81] Marjanović, *Ustanak i Narodnooslobodilački Pokret*, p. 315.

[82] Dinčić, "Tito et Mihailovitch," p. 12.

[83] *Ibid.*

be stopped quickly. Furthermore, there is good reason to believe that Mihailović was encouraged to act decisively by the Yugoslav émigré government and by his understanding of Allied policies regarding the resistance.

Shortly before the meeting at Brajići, the British established their first direct contact with the Ravna Gora movement. Captain William Hudson and two Yugoslav officers arrived at Chetnik headquarters [84] and, after landing on the Montenegrin coast on 20 September, made their way slowly through the revolt-torn area. They arrived first at Partisan-held Užice and reached Mihailović's headquarters in western Serbia the day before the Brajići talks. According to Deakin's recent account, the two Yugoslav officers, Majors Zaharije Ostojić and Mirko Lalatović, had instructions from War Minister General Bogoljub Ilić, which Hudson knew nothing about, to confine their contacts and reports to armed groups loyal to the exiled royal government and led by officers of the dissolved Yugoslav army.[85]

Hudson's directives from Special Operations Executive (S.O.E.) headquarters in Cairo were apparently rather vague, but clearly the purpose of the Ostojić-Lalatović mission was to do everything they could to restrain the revolt, to keep the resistance in the hands of the monarchist officers, and to create the impression in London that rebel activities were the exclusive work of the Mihailović Chetniks. On 13 October the two officers sent a message to Malta, probably over Hudson's wireless set from Montenegro, reporting that "instructions have been delivered to our group which is operating in Montenegro not to cooperate with those leaders of Chetnik *odreds* who do not recognize the Yugoslav government . . . [and that] it has equally been so settled that Colonel Mihailović is receiving orders to refrain from sabotage except against railway tracks, locomotives, etc., where explosives are not needed, so that the population will not be too exposed to reprisals." [86]

When Hudson arrived at Mihailović's headquarters on 25 October after passing briefly through Užice, the colonel quickly criticized him for "having been with the Communist rabble" and threatened to break off relations if he visited Tito's headquarters again.[87] The significance of the arrival of the joint British-Yugoslav mission, though, lies in the fact that it gave the officers confidence that they had the backing of the émigré Yugoslav and perhaps even the British government, and that they could force their resistance plans on the Communist leaders. Mihailović was given a message from the Yugoslav High Command which stated that

[84] Konstantine Fotić, *The War We Lost* (New York: Viking Press, 1948), p. 155.
[85] Deakin, *Embattled Mountain*, pp. 126–30.
[86] *Ibid.*, pp. 131–32.
[87] *Ibid.*, pp. 136–37.

"a rebellion would not be tolerated, that the struggle should be waged for Yugoslavia, and not become a struggle of the Communists for the Soviet Union." [88] At the same time, he received assurance from Ostojić and Lalatović that the Chetniks had the official support of the royal Yugoslav government.[89]

Given England's sponsorship of the royal government of King Peter II, Mihailović was justified in thinking that, at least for the time being, he had the virtual support of the British. According to Hudson's own report: "The British promise of support had the effect of worsening Chetnik-Partisan relations. When I first arrived at Ravna Gora and Užice at the end of October, 1941, Mihailović already knew by telegram that he would get British support. He felt rightly that no one outside the country knew about the Partisans or that he alone was not responsible for the revolt." [90] Although the evidence does not show that Hudson's mission alone created the split between the Chetniks and the Partisans,[91] it does appear probable that the mission encouraged Mihailović to think that the time was ripe for drastic action against the Communists.

Mihailović certainly had reason to believe that his resistance strategy was more in line with the British S.O.E.'s overall guidelines for underground activity in occupied Europe than was the Communist plan. British intelligence agents had been active in Yugoslavia since mid-1940, certainly had something to do with the Simović putsch of 27 March 1941,[92] and, more important, had developed links with Yugoslav figures who were "exclusively Serb, nationalist and conservative in politics." [93]

---

[88] Yugoslavia, Supreme Court, Military Council (Belgrade), *The Trial of Dragoljub-Draža Mihailović: Stenographic Record and Documents from the Trial of D.D.M.* (Belgrade: States Publishing House, 1941), p. 124.

[89] Deakin, *Embattled Mountain,* p. 137.

[90] *The Cetniks* (A.F.H.Q. Handbook, 1944), p. 11, cited in Fitzroy Maclean, *Disputed Barricade* (London: Jonathan Cape, 1957), p. 152.

[91] The whole question is still a matter of historical dispute. Marjanović implies that the chronological proximity of Hudson's arrival at Ravna Gora and the subsequent Chetnik attack on Užice could not have been a mere coincidence but admits that the answer must be sought in the documents of the British Special Operations Executive. "Velika Britanija i Narodnooslobodilački Pokret u Jugoslaviji, 1941–1945" (Great Britain and the national liberation movement in Yugoslavia, 1941–1945), *Jugoslovenski Istorijski Časopis* 2 (1963): 37–38. Deakin, on the other hand, wrote in the same journal that Hudson's mission probably had no effect on the break between Mihailović and Tito. "Britanija i Jugoslavija, 1941–1945" (Britain and Yugoslavia, 1941–1945). *Ibid.*, p. 46. More recently, though, he seems to suggest in *The Embattled Mountain* that the joint British-Yugoslav mission did have something to do with the outbreak of Chetnik-Partisan hostilities, but that the instigators were the émigré Yugoslav generals and majors Ostojić and Lalatović rather than Hudson or the S.O.E. headquarters.

[92] Hugh Dalton, *The Fateful Years: Memoirs, 1931–1945* (London: Frederick Muller Ltd., 1957), p. 375.

[93] Deakin, *Embattled Mountain,* p. 124.

Moreover, at least as late as the close of the summer, S.O.E. headquarters with the British Middle East Command favored a resistance action which paralleled Mihailović's own thinking. S.O.E. director Hugh Dalton had directed in a report of August that "the guerrilla and sabotage bands now active in Yugoslavia should show sufficient active resistance to cause constant embarrassment to the occupying forces . . . but they should keep their main organization underground and avoid any attempt at large-scale risings or ambitious military operations which could only result at present in severe repression." [94]

In October 1941 the British military and government knew practically nothing about the Partisan movement, but from mid-August on they had information on Mihailović.[95] Their intelligence missions were staffed with royalist officers, and Churchill took a sudden interest in the Yugoslav resistance as a result of information passed on by General Simović. At this stage in the war, the British saw resistance and underground movements as sources of information, possible instruments of sabotage, and potential auxiliary forces to harrass the enemy's rear in the event of an Allied landing. The émigré governments in London preferred that the resistance remain underground and prepare for the rapid and efficient seizure of power at the end of the occupation. In any event, all the objectives of the British and the exiled governments demanded that the resistance organizations be controlled from outside.[96] At Brajići, then, where Mihailović rejected flatly the entire Communist program of immediate revolt and political reconstruction, he did not act alone.

Immediately after his meeting with Tito on 26 October Mihailović decided to attack the Partisan headquarters at Užice. According to statements made by Chetnik officers who were captured in early November, preparations for the assault began on 27 October.[97] German sources also demonstrate clearly that he made the decision no later than the day after the Brajići meeting and delayed action only because he lacked sufficient guns and munitions,[98] for which he turned to the Germans.

On the morning of 28 October, two Chetnik liaison officers in Bel-

---

[94] John Ehrman, *Grand Strategy* (London: Her Majesty's Stationery Office, 1956), 5: 77.

[95] Deakin, *Embattled Mountain,* p. 125.

[96] On 28 August, Churchill sent a minute to Hugh Dalton: "I understand from General Simović that there is widespread guerrilla activity in Yugoslavia. It needs cohesion, support and direction from outside." *Ibid.,* p. 126.

[97] Marjanović, *Ustanak i Narodnooslobodilački Pokret,* p. 336.

[98] This explains, no doubt, the Chetniks' willingness to make a partial agreement with Tito at Brajići providing for the equal division of the guns and munitions produced at the Užice arms factory. Almost needless to say, Chetnik sources deny that the Partisans kept their side of the bargain and claim that Mihailović received only six hundred rifles and ten boxes of munitions. Mešković, in *Knjiga o Draži,* 1: 174.

grade, Colonel Pantić and Captain Mitrović, presented themselves to Minister-President Nedić and declared that Mihailović was prepared to offer his services in the anti-Partisan struggle.[99] That afternoon, the two officers, both dressed in civilian clothes, visited the home of Captain Josef Matl of the Armed Forces Liaison Office, where Pantić stated again that he had been empowered by Mihailović to offer his Chetnik troops to the Germans and Nedić "to purge the Serbian area once and for all of the Communist bands." Mihailović, said Pantić, was willing to carry out the action in conjunction with armed bands loyal to Nedić; the Chetniks "recognized that the country was defeated and that the Germans possess the rights of occupation." Alluding to the Partisans' "relative superiority in arms," Pantić asked that the Germans place at Mihailović's disposal "about 5,000 rifles and 375 machine-guns."

Matl relayed the Chetnik offer at once to the German commanding general in Serbia and met with the two Chetnik officers again the next day. He transmitted General Böhme's reply that the Germans would continue negotiations only if Mihailović came to Belgrade, and he offered the colonel complete security for the trip to and from the capital. Both sides then agreed that he would meet Mihailović at Lajkovac for the trip to Belgrade on the afternoon of 3 November.[100]

When Matl came to Lajkovac on the appointed day, Mihailović failed to appear; Pantić and Mitrović arrived from Chetnik headquarters the next morning and informed Matl that Mihailović was not able to come because his units were presently engaged in a bitter struggle with the Partisans in the area around Užice. In view of recent events, Pantić reported, Mihailović could not come to Belgrade before 9 November. In order to convince Matl of the good faith of these proposals, Pantić brought a personal letter from Mihailović to General Böhme, dated 3 November, which explained his reasons for postponing the meeting and asked that the German authorities not order any military operations in the rebel "sphere" in western Serbia during the course of the Chetnik-Partisan fighting.[101]

[99] Wehrmachtverbindungsstelle Belgrad/Ih (Captain Josef Matl), "Zurverfügungstellung der Gruppe des Obersten Draža Mihailović zur Bekämpfung der Kommunisten in Zusammenarbeit mit der Deutschen Wehrmacht," 28 October 1941, T-314, roll 1457, frames 1086–87.

[100] Wehrmachtverbindungstelle Belgrad/Ih, "Zurverfügungstellung der Cetnik-Verbände des jugoslawischen Heeres unter dem Kommando des oberst. Draža Mihailović gegen Kommunisten in Zusammenarbeit mit dem Deutsches Wehrmacht," 30 October 1941, T-314, roll 1457, frames 1110–12,

[101] Wehrmachtverbindungstelle Belgrad/Ih, "Aktenvermerk: Zurverfügungstellung des Oberst Draža Mihailović zur Bekämpfung Kommunistischen Aktion," 4 November 1941, T-314, roll 1457, frames 1336–37; Kommandant Generalstabsoberst D. Mihailović to Militärkommandanten Serbiens in Belgrad (German translation by Matl), 3 November 1941, T-314, roll 1457, frame 1338.

Mihailović, in fact, overestimated both his own military strength and his ability to make deals with the Germans.[102] Events later showed that the officers, feeling that the moment was opportune, had elected an aggressive strategy without the means to carry it out and without seriously considering the Partisans' capacity for resisting it. On 1 and 2 November Partisan units in the Užice area attacked the Chetniks around Požega and seized the city.[103] When Tito rejected an ultimatum that he withdraw from the city,[104] the officers decided to attack the Partisans in nearby Čačak. Chetnik operations against Čačak and Užice on 7 and 8 November failed, and Mihailović lost about a thousand men and considerable amounts of equipment.[105]

By the second week of November the officers' bands were in a desperate situation. Chetnik agents were even spreading reports that the main units were out of munitions and were fleeing south of Valjevo.[106] On 9 November Mihailović ordered his representatives in eastern Bosnia to bring their detachments to Serbia.[107] More important, he turned again to the Germans, but this time as a suppliant rather than a negotiator. He told the Germans that he did not have time to come to Belgrade but preferred a place closer to the front in western Serbia. The Germans agreed, and created a special task force, composed of Matl, Lieutenant-Colonel Kogard, and Dr. Kiessel of the Serbian commander's Administrative Staff, to carry out the negotiations.[108] The meeting between the Germans and Mihailović took place on the evening of 11 November at a hotel opposite the railroad station at Divci (east of Valjero) and lasted about an hour and a half.[109]

The Chetnik-German negotiations proved fruitless. General Böhme had no intention of arriving at any sort of an accommodation with the

[102] See, for example, 342. Inf. Div./Ic, "Übersetzung einer Erklärung des Generalstabsoberst Drag. Mihailović, ohne Datum, in Original übergeben . . . an 342. Inf. Div., Ic um 1.11.41," 1 November 1941, *T-314*, roll 1457, frame 1348.

[103] Abwehrstelle Belgrad, "Bericht über die Widerstandsbewegung in Gebiet des ehem. Jugoslawien, Stand der Entwicklung in der Zeit vom 9.11–16.11.41," 18 November 1941, *T-314*, roll 1457, frames 1411–12.

[104] Marjanović, *Ustanak i Narodnooslobodilački Pokret*, p. 343.

[105] *Borba*, 8 November 1941, cited in *Zbornik*, vol. 1, bk. 1, no. 73; Abwehrstelle Belgrad, "Kämpfe bei Cacak," 14 November 1941, *T-314*, roll 1457, frame 1397.

[106] 342. Inf. Div./Ic, "Feindnachrichten," 16 November 1941, *T-314*, roll 1457, frame 1405.

[107] Marjanović, *Ustanak i Narodnooslobodilački Pokret*, p. 352.

[108] Bevoll. Kdr. Gen. in Serbien, "N. 3621/41 vom 11.11.41," 11 November 1941, *T-314*, roll 1457, frame 1257.

[109] Befehlshaber Serbien, Chef des Verwaltungstabes (Dr. Kiessel) to Bevoll. Kdr. Gen. in Serbien, "Niederschrift über das Treffen mit den serb. Generalstabsoberst Draža Mihailović am 11. November 1941," 11 November 1941, *T-314*, roll 1457, frames 1314–22. Unfortunately, the final two frames (1321–22) of this very important document are barely legible.

officers; he permitted the meeting only in order to deliver an ultimatum to Mihailović. Speaking for the German side, Kogard read a statement which flatly rejected the Chetnik offer of late October, denied that Mihailović could be trusted "as an ally," and accused the officers of having consistently refused to cooperate with Nedić and of having made an "intimate military alliance" with the Partisans in September. Concluding the German argument, Kogard stated that Böhme would discuss with Mihailović only the officers' immediate and unconditional capitulation.

Mihailović had already tried unsuccessfully to negotiate with the Germans for guns through his agent at Belgrade; he had also attempted to obtain from General Böhme a free hand in western Serbia against the Partisans. Now he came to Divci for the sole purpose of obtaining munitions for his battered units as soon as possible. Using every argument imaginable to allay German mistrust, he insisted that he was "neither the representative of London nor of any other government," explained his actions as efforts to "reduce and thwart [the Communist] terror," and denied that he had ever made "a serious agreement" with the Partisan leaders. According to Kiessel's account of the meeting, Mihailović repeated his request for immediate supply of munitions at least five times. The session consisted exclusively of an exchange of accusations and demands.

The German command in Serbia had, in fact, already made a firm decision on how to handle the Chetniks, and, on 11 November the day of Mihailović's meeting at Divci, instructions were issued to all units to carry on "no negotiations with the Chetniks . . . especially the Mihailović people," but to demand only "unconditional surrender, i.e., that they turn over their arms and enter German custody." [110]

Efforts to overcome German mistrust on the part of Mihailović and his liaison officers had no success. Their contacts with Nedić from late October on only bolstered German suspicions that they were trying to play off the Serbian minister-president against the occupation authorities. Also, Mihailović's appeals for guns and munitions and Pantić's claim that Mihailović had no intention of using arms against the Germans and that he would be willing to make an armistice as soon as the Communists were defeated seemed like desperate pleas rather than serious offers and only served to expose the hopelessness of the Chetniks' situation.[111] By mid-November the German command in Serbia was well

[110] Bevoll. Kdr. Gen. in Serbien/Ic to Höheres Kommando LXV, [no file no.], 11 November 1941, *T-314*, roll 1457, frame 1258.

[111] Bevoll. Kdr. Gen. in Serbien/Ic (Kogard), "Oberst Mihailović," 12 November 1941, *T-314*, roll 1457, frames 1334–35; Bevoll Kdr. Gen. in Serbien/Ic to Wehrmachtbefehlshaber Südost, "Bericht über Oberst Mihailović," 13 November 1941, *T-314*, roll 1457, frames 1309–12.

aware that the Chetniks were getting the worst of the fight with the Partisans. The officers, in their view, could not be trusted, had little to offer, and were willing to bargain only when forced by military necessity.

Since the arrival of the British mission in late October, the Chetnik officers had in fact been playing a double game with London and the Germans in their unsuccessful efforts to seize control of the Yugoslav resistance quickly. After two weeks of civil war in western Serbia, the Germans refused to provide Mihailović with help, and Hudson even sent a message to Cairo suggesting that Mihailović be told that "full British help will not be forthcoming unless an attempt is made to incorporate all anti-fascist elements under his command." This union, of course, was to be brought about by negotiation, in which Hudson would play a personal role, rather than by force of arms.

For understandable reasons the officers preferred dealing with the Partisans without British aid or political intervention, and they therefore sought military support from Belgrade. To the Germans they proposed a preventive war against the Communists and a true with the occupation order. To the British they explained, through a telegram from Mihailović to Simović, that the "Communists have attacked us and forced us at the same time to be obliged to fight against the Germans, Communists, Ustaši, and other factions." Appealing now for British support, Mihailović pointed out that "many fighters who are now with the Communists will soon come over to the Chetniks as soon as the latter receive the promised aid from the British." If supplies did not come immediately, "civil war would last long and in the meantime nothing would be undertaken against the Germans." [112]

A combination of German military operations in western Serbia and British diplomacy probably saved the Chetniks from disaster. In mid-November German raids on rebel strongholds compelled Tito to postpone action against the officers. Also, on 16 November London informed Hudson that because "His Majesty's government now consider fight should be Yugoslavs for Yugoslavia, and not revolt led by Communists for Russia," they would ask the "Soviet government to urge Communist elements to rally Mihailović, collaborating with him against Germans, putting themselves necessarily at disposal of Mihailović as national leader." [113] Two days later a Chetnik delegation entered Čačak to begin negotiations with the Partisans, and on 20 November an agreement was signed which called for an end to the civil war.[114]

[112] Simović to Eden, 13 November 1941, cited in Deakin, *Embattled Mountain,* p. 140.
[113] *Ibid.*
[114] Marjanović, *Ustanak i Narodnooslobodilački Pokret,* p. 370. The text of the armistice may be found in *Zbornik,* vol. 1, bk. 1, no. 85.

This was only a truce, however, and not a serious pledge to cooperate. When the officers' delegates failed to get the Communists to agree that all armed formations be placed under Mihailović's command, Hudson reported to Cairo on 21 November that "Mihailović . . . has all qualifications except strength" because "the Partisans are stronger and he must first liquidate them with British arms before turning seriously to the Germans." [115] In the meantime, as Simović radioed to Mihailović on the same day, the Chetnik leaders "must endeavor to smooth over disagreements [with the Partisans] and avoid any kind of retaliation." [116]

Without any substantial aid from the British, beaten badly by the Partisans, and exposed to raids by German troops now in Čačak and Užice, Mihailović had to concentrate on preserving what he could of his organization rather than settling accounts with Tito. At a meeting with the remaining unit leaders at Ravna Gora on 30 November the officers decided to go underground by attaching their troops to Nedić's legalized formations in order to carry on the war against the Serbian Partisans under official protection. [117] They could thus avoid being captured by the Germans [118] and continue fighting the Communist resistance without directly compromising Mihailović's position with the Allies.

What is more significant is that this transformation took place upon the initiative of the unit leaders: although Mihailović sanctioned it, he probably did not control it. [119] This decision was only the beginning of a process whereby the Chetniks in Serbia ceased to be a fairly compact and autonomous resistance group and gradually became attached to collaborationist, "legalized" leaders, where they functioned as police detachments with at least some loyalty to the puppet regime in Belgrade as well as to Mihailović. Mihailović was losing control of some of his officers and had

---

[115] Deakin, *Embattled Mountain,* p. 141.

[116] *Ibid.,* p. 142.

[117] Marjanović, *Ustanak i Narodnooslobodilački Pokret,* p. 388.

[118] The Germans were well aware of the strong sympathy several of Nedić's gendarme and "loyal" Chetnik units had for the Chetniks but, for the time being, took only formal measures to prevent their merger. They had warned Nedić in late November that, in the coming winter months, there was a great danger that hard-pressed rebel groups would try to dissolve themselves by joining the Nedić gendarme or Pećanac Chetnik formations. Militärbefehlshaber Serbien/Verwaltungsstab to Nedić, "Bekämpfung der Kommunistischen Banden," 26 November 1941, *T-314,* roll 1457, frames 1065–66.

[119] A good deal of evidence suggests that a number of officers sought the protection of Pećanac's collaborationist bands and Nedić's officials from early November, after the initial Chetnik defeats at the hands of the Partisans. Some Chetniks, like Major Kalabić, even joined German operations against the Partisans. Bevoll. Kdr. Gen. in Serbien/Ia to Wehrmachtbefehlshaber Südost [no file no.], 7 November 1941, *T-501,* roll 250, frame 1144; Abwehrstelle Belgrad to Bevoll. Kdr. Gen. in Serbien/Ic, "N. 8143 vom 22.11.41," 22 November 1941, *T-314,* roll 1457, frame 146; Bevoll. Kdr. Gen. in Serbien/Ia, "Gespräche," 29 November 1941, *T-501,* roll 250, frame 461.

virtually no effective fighting force left under his immediate command. Toward the end of 1941 his remaining bands were repeatedly forced to give up operations against the Partisans because they lacked munitions,[120] and, in several instances, they dispersed into the hills.[121] On 7 and 8 December units of the German 342d division attacked Ravna Gora, captured about four hundred Chetniks, and drove the remainder of the Mihailović movement underground for most of the winter.[122]

The Chetnik officers, having failed to remove the Partisans quickly in November, were now almost necessarily committed to a long struggle against Tito before they could resume their own resistance plans. Their military reverses, though, become more understandable when one recognizes that, unlike the Partisans, their primary and original objectives included just about everything but fighting. The Communist leaders, although they suffered even more serious defeats in Serbia, did succeed in compelling the British to demand open resistance on the part of all rebel groups if they were to qualify for material support. Without the efforts of the Partisans, London probably would have asked for no more resistance than it did of any other underground organization in occupied Europe. As a result of the revolt in Serbia, Captain Hudson found himself telling Mihailović in November that "if both sides turned against the Germans . . . immediate aid would be at his disposal, and we could help to establish him as unconditional commander-in-chief." [123]

At this point, the demands of the British government and the image created by the Yugoslav émigré government propaganda had little relationship to what the officers would or could attempt. With virtually no effective fighting units or equipment, with his organization in Serbia dispersed and routed, and with only rudimentary contacts with non-Communist resistance groups in other parts of former Yugoslavia, Mihailović was expected to turn against the Germans. Accordingly, he was promoted to the rank of brigadier general and proclaimed commander of the "Yugoslav Army in the Homeland" on 7 December 1941 by King Peter II.[124]

[120] Abwehrstelle Belgrad, "N. 8160/11.41," 26 November 1941, *T-314*, roll 1457, frames 1555–57.
[121] Bevoll. Kdr. Gen. in Serbien/Ia, "N. 1130/41-10, Tagesmeldung," 29 November 1941, *T-314*, roll 1457, frame 1549; Benzler to Aus. Amt, "Telegramm N. 1069 vom 17.12.41," 17 December 1941, *T-120*, roll 200, frame 230/153456; Kostić, *Za Istoriju Naših Dana*, p. 67.
[122] Marjanović, *Ustanak i Narodnooslobodilački Pokret*, p. 389.
[123] Hudson cable of 21 November 1941, cited in Deakin, *Embattled Mountain*, p. 142.
[124] Plenča, *Medjunarodni Odnosi Jugoslavije u Toku Drugog Svjetskog Rata*, p. 85.

III

THE SERB NATIONALIST MOVEMENT IN THE ITALIAN OCCUPATION ZONE

:

In contrast to Serbia, where Mihailović and a small group of officers dominated and directed the non-Communist armed formations from the summer of 1941 on, the Chetniks in the western half of Yugoslavia emerged somewhat later, in most instances during the winter of 1941–42. After the stunning reverses suffered by Mihailović's organization in November 1941, though, the focus of the officers' activities, and indeed of the whole ·Yugoslav resistance, shifted to the west. There, in parts of Italian-annexed Yugoslavia, especially Montenegro, and in areas subject to competing Italian and Croatian Ustaši claims such as Herzegovina and the western parts of Bosnia, the Chetniks had their most striking, although temporary, successes. Probably the most important fact about the Chetniks in western Yugoslavia is that the pro-Mihailović officers, instead of creating the organization, only partially succeeded in taking over an already existing Serb nationalist armed movement. What became the Chetnik movement in the Italian-annexed areas and parts of the Independent Croatian State in 1942 was originally a confusing assortment of Serb armed bands, usually formed spontaneously and under the direction of local leaders, civilian as well as military. The most important catalysts which led to the creation of these groups were the failures and excesses of the occupation system rather than the initiative of the officers.

MONTENEGRO

Italian policies in Montenegro were characterized by a dilemma: the Italians were determined to seal the area off from the rest of Yugoslavia by establishing a protectorate but were unable to find sufficiently strong native separatist support for the civilian administration. As events in the summer of 1941 proved, Rome overestimated the appeal and the scope of the opposition to the prewar centralizing policies of Belgrade; conversely, the small separatist or Zelenasi ("green") movement overestimated what the Italians were willing to offer in exchange for alliance and collaboration. Expecting the revival of the monarchy, Italy's supporters in Montenegro quickly attempted to set up village committees throughout Montenegro and the Sandžak and, in early July, sent delegates to the National Assembly (Narodna Skupština) at Cetinje.[1] When they realized, however, that the Italians had no intention of granting even nominal independence but instead planned a personal union between the House of Savoy and Montenegro, almost all of the delegates went home. On 13 July revolt broke out throughout Montenegro.

The Montenegrin uprising, a spontaneous alliance of several groups, ranging from former officers to Communist party agitators,[2] caught the occupation authorities totally unprepared. Within a matter of days, in fact, the Italians at Cetinje were completely cut off from the rest of the country, and Commando Supremo had to call for immediate reinforcements from Ninth Army units in Albania.[3] Ciano, shocked by the obviously widespread support enjoyed by the insurgent leaders, described the events as a "war between Montenegro and Italy" and had doubts concerning the troops' ability to repress it effectively.[4]

Subsequent developments showed that the first wave of revolt was a grossly premature undertaking[5] but they also showed that the Italians,

---

[1] Milan Bandović, in *Knjiga o Draži,* vol. 1, p. 77.

[2] Communist historians, of course, claim that the revolt was led principally by the Partisans. See, for example, Marjanović and Morača, *Naš Oslobodilački Rat i Narodna Revolucija,* p. 50. Axis intelligence reports credit a handful of Montenegrin officers with leading the uprising. Deutsche Konsul in Sarajevo to Deutsche General in Agram, 3 July 1941, *T-501,* roll 267, frame 901; Wehrmachtverbindungsstelle Belgrad, "N. 6485/41 vom 11.9.41," 11 September 1941, *T-314,* roll 1457, frame 676; WFSt/Abt. Ausland to Aktensammelstelle Süd, "Italienisches Beutegut," 25 April 1944, *T-821,* roll 347, frame 581. This last document is a report from Montenegrin Governor Pirzio-Biroli to Mussolini, dated 26 June 1943, dealing with his occupation policies since 1941.

[3] Ciano, *Diario II,* entry for 15 July 1941.

[4] *Ibid.,* entry for 17 July 1941.

[5] It is interesting to note that even Communist historians harshly judge the actions

like the Germans in Serbia, were never able to assert their authority effectively outside of the larger cities. With the addition of five divisions from Albania, the Ninth Army was able, by late August, to break the rebel ring around Cetinje and seize control of the heavily populated areas, but, lacking any meaningful native support except in the coastal area along the Adriatic, they settled for an unstable truce in most of the central and eastern parts of Montenegro.[6]

The Montenegrin separatists, now discredited by the revelation of the Italians' desire to establish a personal union with Rome, were not capable of providing the administrative and political collaboration which Governor Pirzio-Biroli needed so badly. For want of an alternative, however, the Italians were committed to them, and, by early October, the separatist-federalist leader Sekula Drljević was active in Cetinje promoting their cause.[7] The occupation authorities had few illusions about the sympathies of the mass of Montenegrins; although rebel activity subsided, it did not disappear altogether. By the end of 1941 the Italians were expecting another revolt to break out any time, especially in the central and eastern parts of the province adjacent to the former Serb Partisan and Chetnik strongholds in western Serbia.[8]

Although they recognized the precariousness of the military situation, the Italians refused to make any basic changes in their occupation policies. Cavallero thought as late as the end of October that the Montenegrin rebel movement was led mainly by former Yugoslav officers[9] whose loyalties were with Yugoslavia or Greater Serbia. He therefore refused to sanction Italian cooperation with native armed bands, no matter how anti-Partisan.[10] At the end of the year, Pirzio-Biroli was worried about an influx of Chetniks from Serbia into the Sandzak[11] and

of the Montenegrin Partisans in 1941. For example, Marjanović and Morača (Naš Oslobodilački Rat, p. 120) criticize them for proclaiming the creation of local soviets and the collectivization of agriculture.

[6] Vojmir Kljaković, "Osvobodilački Rat Naroda Jugoslavije i Učešće Talijanu u Rata protiv Sovjetskog Savez" (The Yugoslav people's war of liberation and Italy's participation in the war against the Soviet Union), Jugoslavenski Istorijski Časopis 4 (1964):76; Comando Supremo (Cavallero) to Ministro Affari Esteri, 8 August 1941, Zbornik, vol. 3, 4, no. 167. Several volumes of the official Yugoslav Zbornik collection include, as well as Partisan materials, some very useful captured Italian, German, Ustasi, and Chetnik documents.

[7] Narodna Borba (the journal of the Montenegrin Communists), 1 October 1941, in Zbornik, vol. 3, 1, no. 18.

[8] Comando Supremo/SIM to Comando Supremo/Ufficio Operazioni, "N. 7345 del 25.10.41," 25 October 1941, T-821, roll 356, frame 910; Cavallero, Comando Supremo, entry for 29 October 1941.

[9] Ibid.

[10] Cavallero to Pirzio-Biroli, 3 December 1941, T-821, roll 356, frame 754.

[11] Governatorato del Montenegro/Ufficio Militari to Comando Supremo, "Relazione sulla situazione del Montenegro," 2 December 1941, T-821, roll 356, frames 821–22.

refused a request made by agents of the pro-German Serb Chetnik Kosta Pećanac for permission to send their units into eastern Montenegro.[12]

The Italians persisted in cooperating with only the small pro-separatist collaborationist bands until early 1942. They overestimated the cohesion among the constituent members of the rebel front and the role of the officers in its leadership. In Montenegro, as in several other parts of Yugoslavia, the armed rebel bands, united originally by little more than a common opposition to the occupation order, tended to gravitate in the second half of 1941 either into a Partisan-dominated intransigent resistance movement or into a nationalist camp whose tactics were far more cautious. Until the early part of 1942, then, the officers in Montenegro, whom the Italians persisted in viewing as inveterate rebels or allies of some Belgrade-based Yugoslav or Greater Serbian movement, had no central direction, were not well organized by Mihailović's delegates, and often wavered between resistance and collaboration.

The leaders of the armed detachments which did become the hard core of the Montenegrin Chetniks in 1942 came from several "movements," including collaborationist federalists like Krsto Popović and the revolutionary officers like Bajo Stanišić, and from a group of officers who apparently played no significant role on either side in 1941, like General Djukanović. Although the Chetniks later drew their support from all sorts of non-Communist military leaders, the movement reflected both long-developing strains within the anti-Axis camp and the effect of the organizational efforts of Mihailović's delegate officers.

As early as the late summer of 1941, for example, local insurgent leaders in south Montenegro broke with the Partisans by making regional armistice arrangements with the Italians.[13] Although the evidence is very thin, it appears almost certain that those non-Communist armed formations who made accommodations with the Italians did so on their own initiative and in response to local situations. A number of these groups, especially along the southern and eastern frontiers of Montenegro, made these arrangements initially not so much for anti-Partisan ends but rather to oppose the activities of armed bands of Sandžak and Albanian Muslims. The nationalist formations which retained their arms, either by making a deal with the Italians or by fleeing to the hills, were pursuing non-Partisan rather than openly anti-Partisan tactics. Their aggressive Serb Montenegrin national sentiment perceived neighboring

[12] Comando Supremo Forze Armata Albana to Comando Supremo, "Proposte inoltrate da un fiduciario di Pecanac," 23 November 1941, *T-821*, roll 356, frame 881; Ministero Affari Esteri to Comando Supremo/SIM, "N. 46772 del 29.11.41," 29 November 1941, *T-821*, roll 356, frame 873; Comando Supremo/Ufficio Operazioni/Scacchiere Orientale to Pirzio-Biroli, "N, 22668 del 30.11.41," 30 November 1941, *T-821*, roll 356, frame 879.

[13] Milan Bandović, in *Knjiga o Draži*, vol. 1, pp. 84–85.

ethnic minorities, mainly the Muslims of Albanian background, as the principal enemy. Most non-Communist armed leaders, however, took neither side in the intermittent struggle between the Italian occupation units and the increasingly Partisan-dominated resistance. When Captain Hudson passed through Montenegro in mid-October on his way to western Serbia, he reported that "the communists who are well organized are now leading an action in Montenegro" while "numerous national elements are standing on one side and are waiting."[14]

While Hudson was reporting the waiting tactics of the national leaders, Mihailović was making his first effort to establish influence over the Montenegrin guerrilla movement. He appointed Captain Pavel Djurišić as commander of all "regular and reserve troops" in central and eastern Montenegro and parts of the Sandžak,[15] and some time in the fall Major Djordjia Lašić made his way to Ravna Gora to make direct contact with Mihailović.[16] It was not until the end of the year, however, on 20 December, that Mihailović issued a comprehensive directive on the Chetnik organization in Montenegro.[17] Djurišić was placed in charge of the area around the Lim River (adjacent to the Sandžak), and Lašić was made commander for the rest of Montenegro, or "Commander of the Chetnik Units of the Yugoslav Army, Mountain Staff No. 15." The instructions directed Lašić to avoid collaboration with the Communists "because they are fighting against the dynasty and for a social revolution" but did not urge him to carry out operations against the Partisans. Even more interesting is the fact that Mihailović's orders called on the Montenegrin Chetniks to concentrate their efforts near the Sandžak, Kosovo-Metohija, and Albania to fight the Muslims and Albanians.[18]

The effect of Mihailović's initial instructions must have been to rein-

---

[14] Deakin, *Embattled Mountain*, p. 131.

[15] Mihailović to Djurišić, [?] October 1941, *Dokumenti o Izdajstvu Draže Mihailovića*, no. 1.

[16] Dedijer, *Dnevnik*, vol. 2, entry for 23 June 1942.

[17] Mihailović to Lašić and Djurišić, 20 December 1941, *Dokumenti o Izdajstvu Draže Mihailovića*, no. 185. This important document not only was published by the Yugoslav government, as indicated above, but also showed up in the hands of the Comando Supremo, who received it from the Croatian High Command. The Mihailović directive, found on a dead Chetnik officer, appears in this instance in Italian translation. The published Serbo-Croatian version and the Italian copy are identical in every detail. R. Missione Militare Italiana in Croazia to Comando Supremo, "Disposizione emanate dal Capo Cetnico, Generale Draza Mihailovic," 16 July 1942, *T-821*, roll 347, frames 820-24.

[18] R. Missione Militare Italiana in Croazia to Comando Supremo, "Disposizione emanate dal Capo Cetnico, Generale Draza Mihailovic," 16 July 1942, *T-821*, roll 347, frames 822–23. Djurišić was to move his men into the Bijelo Polje-Sjenica area and "remove" the Muslim and Arnaut (Albanian Muslim) population from Pestar; another group was to push in the direction of Metohija "to clear out the Arnauts"; still another detachment was to seize Scutari and protect southern Montenegro against "Arnaut attacks from Albania."

force the existing hostility between the nationalist bands and the non-Serb ethnic groups to the south and east of Montenegro. In order to put these broad guidelines into effect, however, the officer-delegates needed time, for the varied assortment of non-Communist armed formations were still without any central control. Although the formation of Chetnik groups in Montenegro had begun in November, Mihailović's plans for the officers were somewhat premature, and neither Djurišić nor Lašić seem to have accomplished much during the first few months.

While there is some evidence that the officers were urging on the civilian population a "passive" attitude toward the Italians,[19] there is no indication that they were ready to collaborate with Governor Pirzio-Biroli. Moreover, although the Partisans were in full retreat in Montenegro from early December 1941 to the late spring of 1942, the Chetniks' contribution to the early stages of their demise is extremely obscure.[20] Partisan documents from the middle of December show, for example, that in the Nikšić area they were still negotiating with Chetnik bands, while other reports accuse them of occupying certain villages at the request of the Italians.[21]

At this time, then, despite Mihailović's directives, Lašić and Djurišić had very little influence on most of the non-Communist bands and were unable to develop an effective strategy toward the Italian occupation forces or the Partisan resistance. Even by the end of January 1942, when some of Lašić's troops began to report the capture of Partisan prisoners, the officers decided not to turn them over to the occupation authorities for fear of compromising their popular support.[22] Some officers who became leading Chetniks later in 1942, like Bajo Stanišić, were at this time still at least formally aligned with the Partisans.

Other evidence indicates that in December and January the officers were stepping up activities, especially in eastern Montenegro and the Sandžak. In these areas, as in nearby southwestern Serbia, the first to feel the effects of the Chetniks' growing influence were the local Muslims. As the officers' bands became more aggressive, large numbers of Muslims began to flee their villages and, in some instances, joined Partisan units.[23] By January Chetnik activity in the Sandžak was significant enough for a Communist party Central Committee directive to instruct the Parti-

[19] See *Zbornik*, vol. 3, 4, p. 456n.
[20] Marjanović and Morača, *Nas Oslobodilački Rat*, pp. 97–98.
[21] Report of the staff of the Nikšić National Liberation Partisan Detachment, 17 December 1941, *Zbornik*, vol. 3, 1, no. 144.
[22] Lijeva Rijeka Chetnik battalion to Lašić, 27 January 1942, *ibid.*, 4, no. 191.
[23] Report of the staff of the Montenegrin National Liberation Partisan Detachments, 15 December 1941, *ibid.*, no. 13.

sans there to mobilize Muslim anti-Serb resentment to replenish their dwindling ranks.[24]

Chetnik tactics, especially at this early stage, varied widely according to local circumstances. In the Nikšić sector, where there were few ethnic minorities, local nationalist leaders began in early 1942 to emphasize anti-Communism in their political propaganda and even formed a municipal police force outfitted in Yugoslav army uniforms.[25] The nationalist armed groups probably lacked a coherent political and military strategy and acted as autonomous bands because the officers appointed as yet possessed little effective authority. Partisan documents make no mention of the Lašić-Djurišić Chetniks until the end of January 1942,[26] and even then their activities were confined to eastern Montenegro and the Sandžak, where the Italians had neither the will nor the means to intervene on a large scale.

HERZEGOVINA AND BOSNIA

In these Ustaši-annexed provinces widespread revolt also broke out in the summer of 1941, but, unlike the case of Serbia and Montenegro, the rebel movement at first had almost no political direction. The uprising was, in most instances, a spontaneous and desperate one: entire Serb villages suddenly became guerrilla bands and the entire non-Serb element, whether Ustaši troops or Croatian or Muslim civilians, became the main enemy. Before the summer was over, the popular reaction against the Ustaši policies of massive anti-Serb terror had become violent; total chaos prevailed throughout much of the ethnically mixed territory annexed to Croatia in May 1941, ano the Italians were compelled to assume increasingly large responsibilities and influence in the area. Even before the Italians had extended their occupation zone they found themselves deeply involved in the civil war in Bosnia and Herzegovina, and, basically in order to further their own Balkan ambitions, they tended to align themselves with the Serbs. Neither the drastic shifts in occupation spheres nor the several arrangements between the Italians and the Serb rebel groups succeeded in pacifying these areas. The Italians were still formally tied by an alliance with Zagreb, were progressively less enthusiastic about patrolling half of Croatia, and were unable to control the Serb leaders. The Ustaši for their part never really

[24] C.P.Y. Central Committee to Sandzak Central Committee, [?] January 1942, *ibid.*, vol. 2, 2, no. 82.

[25] Report of Spiro Stajanović (Chetnik battalion commander) to command of the Zeta Chetnik detachment, 12 December 1942, *ibid.*, vol. 3, 4, no. 232.

[26] Head Staff of National Liberation Partisan Detachments of Montenegro and Boka to the Nikšić detachment, 30 January 1942, *ibid.*, 2, no. 48.

reconciled themselves to a restoration of the Serbs' civil rights and resisted the intrusions of the Italians into their own territory. Long before the efforts of the delegate-officers of Mihailović to organize the non-
Communist armed movements had begun to succeed, several local leaders
had elected to work with the Italians, but this collaboration was basically
tactical, was uncoordinated, and served to fragment rather than consolidate the Serb nationalist movement.

Immediately after the April capitulation and before the final treaties
settling the Dalmatian boundaries dispute (17 May 1941), Italian command posts received word of the explosive national tensions within
Croatia. By early May deputations of Muslims from western Bosnia were
already asking the Italians to extend their occupation into Croatian
territory, and representatives of the Serb community made similar
entreaties to the "Sassari" division.[27] To the south, in eastern Herzegovina, the Ustaši took over the civil administration in late May but failed
to recruit enough personnel for police duties from the Croatian minority. They were compelled to ask the Italian "Marche" division to provide
small contingents for occupation duties.[28] Under any circumstances the
Ustaši leaders would have found it extremely difficult to set up an administration and maintain order in the annexed provinces, but when
they embarked immediately upon a totalitarian solution of the "Serb
problem," the result was civil war.

During June the Ustaši massacres in Bosnia and Herzegovina began
in earnest. As the waves of arrests, murders, and forced mass conversions
to Catholicism spread all over the ethnically mixed parts of Independent
Croatia, the Serbs fled their villages, moved into the surrounding hills
and countryside, and organized armed četa ("self-defense bands") on a
spontaneous and local basis. In parts of Herzegovina village heads
journeyed to the nearest Italian garrisons to ask for food and protection;[29] whole communities deserted their villages at night to escape
Ustaši surprise raids.[30]

[27] Comando VI. Corpo d'Armata to Comando 2. Armata, "N. 541 del 10 maggio 1941,"
10 May 1941, *T-821*, roll 232, frame 6; Comando VI. Corpo d'Armata to Comando 2.
Armata, "N. 562 del 11 maggio 1941," 11 May 1941, *T-821*, roll 232, frames 8–9;
Comando VI. Corpo d'Armata to Comando 2. Armata, "N. 680 del 17 maggio 1941,"
17 May 1941, *T-821*, roll 232, frame 27.

[28] Branko Kovačević and Savo Skoko, "Junski Ustanak u Hercegovini 1941" (The
June 1941 uprising in Herzegovina), *Istorija Radničkog Pokreta* 1 (1965):97–99.

[29] Comando VI. Corpo d'Armata to Comando 2. Armata, "N. 926 del 31 maggio 1941,"
31 May 1941, *T-821*, roll 232, frame 78; Comando VI. Corpo d'Armata to Comando 2.
Armata, "N. 1121 del 9 giugno 1941," 9 June 1941, *T-821*, roll 232, frame 116; Comando
VI. Corpo d'Armata to Comando 2. Armata, "N. 1137 del 11 giugno 1941," 11 June 1941,
T-821, roll 232, frame 120.

[30] Comando VI. Corpo d'Armata to Comando 2. Armata, "N. 1209 del 14 giugno
1941," 14 June 1941, *T-821*, roll 232, frame 136.

In early June a small band of armed Serbs attacked about two hundred Ustaši near Dubrovnik, seized a village, and lost it on the next day.[31] This apparently insignificant clash marked the beginning of the collapse of Ustaši rule, first in Herzegovina and soon after in several parts of Bosnia. The revolt of June 1941 centered around Nevesinje and Gacko in eastern Herzegovina, a mountainous region where the Serbs, according to the 1931 census, counted for over 67 percent of the population, the Muslims for 28 percent, and the Croats for almost 4 percent.[32] Not only did the rebels have the natural advantages of geography and superior numbers, but a few Yugoslav army units, composed largely of Herzegovinians, which had fought on the Albanian front against the Italians in April and had never surrendered returned home with large amounts of small arms and munitions. Clashes occurred throughout June, usually rebel raids against the weak and dispersed Ustaši gendarme stations, and at the end of the month a general uprising broke out in the Nevesinje area. The insurgent forces failed twice to take Nevesinje, but, with perhaps as many as fifteen hundred armed men, they posed a serious threat to the whole area well into the month of July.[33]

Among the immediate consequences of the revolt was the progressive extension of the Italian occupation into the threatened area, mainly to secure the lines of communication between nearby Dubrovnik and the Herzegovinian hinterland. In early July small units of the "Marche" division entered Gacko, Bileća, Avtovac, and Trebinje and, significantly enough, encountered almost no rebel opposition.[34] The Serb leaders, rather than resisting the intrusions of Ambrosio's Second Army, were clearly trying to use the Italians to dislodge the Ustaši from the predominantly Serb areas. This tactic proved successful because, when the Serb armed bands sent delegations to the Italians asking for protection against imminent Ustaši counteroffensives,[35] Dalmazzo's Sixth Army Corps took the first steps toward a policy of restoring the Serbs' rights in the rebel-torn areas, obstructing Ustaši efforts at pacification, and dividing the insurgent forces by offering their moderate wing a return to normal life.

General Dalmazzo's reports to Second Army headquarters blamed the

---

[31] Comando VI. Corpo d'Armata to Comando 2. Armata, "N. 1139 del 11 giugno 1941," 11 June 1941, *T-821*, roll 232, frame 122.

[32] Kovačević and Skoko, "Junski Ustanak," pp. 88–92.

[33] Comando VI. Corpo d'Armata to Comando 2. Armata, "N. 1550 del 2 luglio 1941," 2 July 1941, *T-821*, roll 232, frame 240; Comando VI. Corpo d'Armata to Comando 2. Armata, "N. 1580 del 4 luglio 1941," 4 July 1941, *T-821*, roll 232, frame 250.

[34] Comando VI. Corpo d'Armata to Comando 2. Armata, "N. 1565 del 3 luglio 1941," 3 July 1941, *T-821*, roll 245; Kovačević and Skoko, "Junski Ustanak," p. 147.

[35] Comando VI. Corpo d'Armata to Comando 2. Armata, "N. 1665 del 10 luglio 1941," 10 July 1941, *T-821*, roll 232, frame 277.

revolt on both the Ustaši and Muslims, and he was never very happy about the Italians' official hands-off policy regarding the internal affairs of Independent Croatia.[36] He took matters into his own hands by working for an alliance with the Serb rebels. Using the area around Tenin as a test case, he reported confidently that a nearby rebel group of over a thousand men had "no intention of undertaking anything which would call for an [Italian] reaction." [37] The Italian garrison at Tenin quickly disarmed sixty Ustaši troops; [38] the Serb rebels entered the city on 1 August without incident and shortly thereafter promised the Italians not to attack troop movements along the railway lines provided that the trains carried no Croats.[39] In return, the Italians at Tenin cemented their accord with the Serbs by authorizing the renewal of Serbian Orthodox religious services.[40]

These events at Tenin were not isolated but part of a larger pattern. The Italians were attempting to expand their influence at the expense of Zagreb by aligning their occupation policies with the demands of the Serbs and dealing with the resistance by bringing the rebels back to their villages rather than fighting them. In many cases occupation troops were moved into besieged areas without being utilized against the Serb armed bands, thus forcing the rebel leaders to choose between full-scale anti-Axis revolt and accommodation. By early August, for example, Serb groups in the Lika sector of western Bosnia, after seizing Drvar and Knin from the Ustaši,[41] contacted the Italians and promised them that they were rebelling only against Ustaši outrages, had no ties with Communists, and would not invade the nearby Italian occupied zone.[42] Officers of the Sixth Army Corps carried out regular negotiations with the leader of the Lika guerrilla movement, the former Skupština deputy Stevo Radjeno-

[36] Comando VI. Corpo d'Armata to Comando 2. Armata," Notziario N. 48," 19 June 1941, *T-821*, roll 232, frame 163; Comando VI. Corpo d'Armata to Comando 2. Armata, "N. 1665 del 10 luglio 1941," 10 July 1941, *T-821*, roll 232, frame 279.

[37] Comando VI. Corpo d'Armata to Comando 2. Armata, "N. 1950 del 29 luglio 1941," 29 July 1941, *T-821*, roll 232, frames 395–96.

[38] Comando VI. Corpo d'Armata to Comando 2. Armata, "N. 1960 del 30 luglio 1941," 30 July 1941, *T-821*, roll 232, frame 389; Comando VI. Corpo d'Armata to Comando 2. Armata, "N. 1970 del 31 luglio 1941," 31 July 1941, *T-821*, roll 232, frame 384.

[39] Comando VI. Corpo d'Armata to Comando 2. Armata, "2010 del 3 agosto 1941," 3 August 1941, *T-821*, roll 232, frame 414; Comando VI. Corpo d'Armata to Comando 2. Armata, "N. 2114 del 10 agosto 1941," 10 August 1941, *T-821*, roll 232, frame 454; Comando VI. Corpo d'Armata to Comando 2. Armata, "N. 2233 del 8 agosto 1941," 18 August 1941, *T-821*, roll 232, frame 502.

[40] Comando VI. Corpo d'Armata to Comando 2. Armata, "N. 2457 del 30 agosto 1941," 30 August 1941, *T-821*, roll 232, frame 590.

[41] Comando VI. Corpo d'Armata to Comando 2. Armata, "N. 1820 del 20 luglio 1941," 20 July 1941, *T-821*, roll 232, frame 332; Comando Supremo/SIM, 5 August 1941, *Zbornik*, vol. 13, 1, no. 103.

[42] Comando VI. Corpo d'Armata to Comando 2. Armata, "Contatti con elementi ribelli," 4 August 1941, *T-821*, roll 232, frames 417–19.

vić,[43] who asked the Italians to extend their occupation to Knin and promised that "the Serb nation will receive all officers and soldiers of the Italian army as friends and guarantee them full security." [44]

Despite the successful arrangements made by the rebel spokesmen with the Italians in parts of Herzegovina and western Bosnia, the majority of Serbs still lived in constant fear of Ustaši terror and probably remained in the hills or even swung over to the intransigent, mainly Partisan, camp. Serb leaders who offered on occasion to place their units at the disposal of the Second Army for joint anti-Partisan operations [45] or even, as in the case of the Bos Grahovo Serbs, to attach special formations to the Italian army to fight in the Soviet Union [46] were probably attempting to come to advantageous terms with the Italians without disarming themselves.

At the end of the summer there was very little reason to believe that the few pro-Serb gestures made by the Italian occupation authorities were leading to a normalization of affairs in western Bosnia and Herzegovina. Although the Serbs in the Tenin district were able, largely due to Italian connivance, to regain their civil rights by August, this was the exception rather than the rule, and in most other parts of Bosnia and Herzegovina Ustaši terror continued virtually unchecked. In Glamoč, for example, where the Serbs had numbered seven thousand of a population of almost twelve thousand, only fourteen hundred remained in the city by early October. During the same period the Serb population of Mostar dropped from approximately seven thousand to about eight hundred.[47] After months of almost continuous massacres, pillage, and civil war, several parts of eastern Herzegovina faced a serious threat of famine in the approaching winter.

In such conditions what remained of several Serb communities must have been a cross between small guerrilla armies and roving, homeless bands. Often with poor communications with one another, they were likely to behave according to strictly local circumstances. Although some detachment leaders were eager to make deals with the Italians, virtually none were willing, as the Italians had originally hoped, to lay down their

[43] Comando VI. Corpo d'Armata to Comando 2. Armata, "Contatti con i capi di formazioni cetniche," 17 January 1942, *T-821*, roll 53, frame 697.

[44] Comando VI. Corpo d'Armata to Comando 2. Armata, "N. 2292 del 21 agosto 1941," 21 August 1941, *T-821*, roll 232, frame 532.

[45] Comando VI. Corpo d'Armata to Comando 2. Armata, "N. 2645 del 11 settembre 1941," 11 September 1941, *T-821*, roll 232, frame 655.

[46] Comando VI. Corpo d'Armata to Comando 2. Armata, "N. 2470 del 31 agosto 1941," 31 August 1941, *T-821*, roll 232, frame 597; Comando VI. Corpo d'Armata to Comando 2. Armata, "N. 3502 del 2 settembre 1941," 2 September 1941, *T-821*, roll 232, frame 615.

[47] Comando VI. Corpo d'Armata to Comando 2. Armata, "N. 2888 del 20 settembre 1941," 20 September 1941, *T-821*, roll 232, frame 722; Comando VI. Corpo d'Armata to Comando 2. Armata, "N. 3207 del 2 ottobre 1941," 2 October 1941, *T-821*, roll 232, frame 830.

arms. In Herzegovina, for instance, where the events beginning in April had created a permanent gulf between the three national-religious groups, the Serb revolt reinforced a tradition of class antagonism between the Orthodox peasantry and the large landholding Muslim *begs*, and a state of virtual civil war developed between Serbs and Muslims. An Italian summary pointed out that the Montenegrins and the Serbs around Bileća, Herzegovina, were far more harsh toward the Muslims than toward the small Croatian community.[48]

Serb bands, regardless of whether they maintained contacts with the Italians, showed little inclination to surrender the struggle against their real or imaginary national enemies. In western Bosnia Italian efforts to pacify the area by negotiating with the rebels served to divide the latter, and the intransigent wing quickly fell under the predominant influence of the Partisan organizer Ljubo Babić.[49] While Babić's group was able to hold the key city of Drvar until well into September, other "collaborationist" Serb formations asked Italian command posts for approval before launching raids on nearby Ustaši strongholds.[50] Nothing less than a determined effort by the Italians to reduce Ustaši influence drastically throughout the area and a concomitant willingness to expand the Second Army's occupation zone and crush the growing Partisan movement offered any hope of pacifying the Serb rebel movement.

The Italians recognized that their overall goals of restoring order, protecting their position along the Adriatic, and extending their sphere in former Yugoslavia at the expense of the Ustaši state demanded strong action. By now the eruptions of July and August in eastern Herzegovina and much of western Bosnia, especially in the Lika and Bosanska Krajina, had made clear to all the limits of Croatian military capabilities; moreover, contacts between officers of the Italian Sixth Army Corps and Maček's Peasant party strengthened the conviction at Ambrosio's headquarters that moderate Croats had lost all hope in Pavelić and would welcome a temporary occupation of Croatia by Italian troops.[51] In order to emphasize the scope of the Ustaši state's internal disintegration, General Dalmazzo repeatedly emphasized the wish of the vast majority in all predominantly Serb areas for an extension of the Italian occupation.[52]

[48] Comando VI. Corpo d'Armata to Comando 2. Armata, "N. 1497 del 29 giugno 1941," 29 June 1941, *T-821*, roll 232, frame 220.

[49] Communication of commander of Drvar brigade (Babić) to C.P.Y. Provincial Committee in Bosanska Krajina, 2 September 1941, *Zbornik*, vol. 4, 1, no. 77.

[50] Comando VI. Corpo d'Armata to Comando 2. Armata, "N. 2343 del 24 agosto 1941," 24 August 1941, *T-821*, roll 232, frame 596.

[51] Comando VI. Corpo d'Armata to Comando 2. Armata, "N. 2087 del 8 agosto 1941," 8 August 1941, *T-821*, roll 232, frame 444; Comando VI. Corpo d'Armata to Comando 2. Armata, "N. 2170 del 14 agosto 1941," 14 August 1941, *T-821*, roll 232, frame 479.

[52] For example, Comando VI. Corpo d'Armata, "N. 2807 del 6 agosto 1941," 16 August

By the middle of August, Mussolini began to share the points of view of his commanders in Yugoslavia and decided to remove the Ustaši, politically and militarily, from the entire demilitarized zone in Croatia. When the Italian decision to assume control of the entire civil administration in the zone was delivered to Zagreb on 16 August, Pavelić rejected the note and tried, through the German minister, Kasche, to use the Germans to soften Rome's demands.[53] Shortly thereafter the *poglavnik*, trying to salvage whatever he could, sent a telegram to Mussolini which stressed that Ambrosio should not assume full civil authority in the demilitarized zone and proposed the creation of a Croatian General Administrative Office to "coordinate" the activities of the Ustaši functionaries with the Italians and to plan joint Italo-Croatian military operations against the rebels.[54]

Comando Supremo supported the extreme anti-Ustaši course elected by Mussolini, and Cavallero refused to consider Pavelić's proposal for combined operations against the rebel bands in the demilitarized zone.[55] Kasche and the Ustaši received no support from Berlin and were totally isolated in the face of these Italian policies. The whole affair demonstrated that an occupation system based on dismemberment and division into spheres of influence was not capable of producing coherent action against the Serb rebel movements. In the fall of 1941 the Germans were not ready to violate Italy's predominance in western Yugoslavia, and whatever German concern for Balkan affairs existed was confined to efforts to patch up the weak Commissar Administration in Serbia by suppressing both the Partisan and the Chetnik resistance organizations. For the time being the Germans, while bent on crushing the revolt in Serbia, lacked the means to prevent the Italians from handling the Serb rebels very differently. This was the immediate sense of Ribbentrop's reminder to Kasche of 21 August that "the alpha and omega of our foreign policy in the Mediterranean area is the preservation of our cordial alliance with Italy." [56]

The thrust of General Ambrosio's plan for the occupation of the demilitarized zone was that, by removing the whole area from Ustaši influence and restoring Serb administrative control where the latter con-

1941, *T-821,* roll 232, frame 490, which claimed confidently that "no less than 80 percent of the population of Imotski would welcome enthusiastically an Italian occupation."

[53] Deutsche General in Agram to OKW/WFSt/Abt. L, "N. 257/41 vom 18.8.41," 18 August 1941, *T-501,* roll 267, frame 815.

[54] Pavelić to Mussolini, 19 August 1941, *Zbornik,* vol. 3, 1, p. 333 (the entire text is cited in n. 3 to that page); Cavallero, *Comando Supremo,* entry for 20 August 1941, n. 3.

[55] *Ibid.*

[56] Ribbentrop to Kasche, 21 August 1941, *DGFP,* vol. 13, no. 219.

stituted a majority, the Italians could isolate the extremist—mainly Partisan—wing of the rebel movement and eventually suppress it, perhaps with the aid of native anti-Communist formations. Immediately after the Germans made clear that they would not support Pavelić, the Second Army began its fullscale intervention in Croatian affairs. On 22 August Zagreb was compelled to order all the "irregular" Ustaši militia troops to turn over their arms to the nearest Italian garrison; a few days later, a meeting was held to set up a timetable for the Italian assumption of military and civilian authority.[57] Ambrosio's negotiators now demanded that all Ustaši units leave the demilitarized zone by 1 September and informed the Croatian government that the Second Army would take over all administrative responsibilities one week later.[58]

After being assured that the Ustaši would not be able to obstruct their occupation policies, the Italians issued a series of directives regarding administrative changes and economic reparations. Ambrosio insisted that local administrative posts in areas where the Serbs formed a majority be returned to Serbs and that the Croatian government restore all confiscated property to the original owners.[59] Going out of their way to appease the Serbs and win native allies, the Italians also demanded that all the Eastern Orthodox churches be reopened immediately. They followed this with particularly urgent requests for the restoration of the Serbs' property around Tenin and for the immediate removal of an ex-Ustaši Croatian commander at Knin; in both areas Sixth Army Corps officials had established close ties with Serb armed groups.[60]

The Italian efforts to normalize the situation by winning the cooperation of the Serb leaders was only partially successful. In the northern sector of the area now formally occupied by the Sixth Army Corps, for example, the immediate effect of the change in occupation zones was the resurgence of the Partisans. Instead of finding themselves isolated by the Italian pro-Serb policies, they were able to increase their following at the expense of the now-vacillating non-Communist Serb leaders. At Drvar, General Dalmazzo's hopes for an anti-Partisan coup in front of the Italian advance collapsed completely, and the Communists had

---

[57] Comando 2. Armata, "Sintesi degli accordi stabiliti nella conferenza del 26.8.1941 a Zagrabia . . . ," 9 October 1941, *T-821*, roll 398, frame 1013.

[58] Comando 2. Armata/Ufficio Operazioni, "Occupazione zona demilitarizzata," 30 August 1941, *T-821*, roll 474, frame 535.

[59] Comando 2. Armata/Ufficio Affari Civili, "Questioni prospettate dell'Ecc. il Gen. Commandante al Dott. Kardić nel riunione del 6 settembre 1941 a Karlova," 6 September 1941, *T-821*, roll 474, frames 550–51.

[60] Comando 2. Armata/Ufficio Affari Civili, "Questioni trattate nella riunione tenuta il 12 settembre 1941 dall'Ecc. il Gen. Com. ai membri del Commissariato Generale Croato," 12 September 1941, *T-821*, roll 474, frames 419–20.

their most striking, although short-lived, success.[61] By mid-September
the Drvar Partisans, led by Ljubo Babić and strengthened by recently
arrived recruits from Split, Šibenik, and parts of Croatia, were able to
launch a purge of actual or potential collaborationist elements.[62] They
came to exert almost complete influence over the rebel camp in the entire
zone bounded by Petrovac, Jajce, Glamoč, and Livno.[63]

Similarly, in the Gračać-Gospić sector, as soon as the Italians announced the extension of their occupation rights, large numbers of
Croatian civilians, fearing reprisals at the hands of the returning Serbs,
began to flee the towns; a part of the Serb rebel groups, probably because of growing Partisan influence, refused to cooperate with the new
occupation authorities.[64] By the middle of September the Ustaši, revers-
ing the normal pattern, were actually demanding an immediate Italian
military intervention at Gračać to protect the Croats from the Serbs.[65]

The evidence suggests strongly that the Serb armed groups responded
in several different ways to the initial Italian advance into sovereign
Croatian territory. In some areas, like Bosanska Krajina, where Partisan influence was on the rise, the formations avoided any cooperation
with the occupation regime. In other places, where the predominant
mood among the rank and file was for revenge upon the Croats, the guerrilla groups apparently attempted to manipulate the situation to settle
accounts with the local non-Serb population. In several instances the
leaders' attitude was far more defensive, and they sought to facilitate and
even extend further the Italian occupation in order to protect their
civilian following from additional Ustaši reprisals.

At this stage, it was not yet clear exactly how far the Second Army field
commanders would go to prevent a recurrence of Ustaši outrages. In spite
of the formal agreements, Ustaši officials in many parts of the demilitarized zone failed to leave in early September [66] and, in some instances,

[61] Comando VI. Corpo d'Armata to Comando 2. Armata, "N. 2707 del 13 settembre
1941," 13 September 1941, T-821, roll 232, frame 666; Comando VI. Corpo d'Armata to
Comando 2. Armata, "N. 2719 del 14 settembre 1941," 14 September 1941, T-821, roll
232, frame 672.

[62] Comando VI. Corpo d'Armata to Comando 2. Armata, "N. 2775 del 16 settembre
1941," 16 September 1941, T-821, roll 232, frame 691; Comando VI. Corpo d'Armata to
Comando 2. Armata, "N. 2960 del 22 settembre 1941," 22 September 1941, T-821, roll
232, frame 735.

[63] Comando VI. Corpo d'Armata to Comando 2. Armata, "N. 2990 del 23 settembre
1941," 23 September 1941, T-821, roll 232, 735.

[64] Comando VI. Corpo d'Armata to Comando 2. Armata, "N. 2591 del 8 settembre
1941," 8 September 1941, T-821, roll 232, frames 635–39.

[65] Comando 2. Armata/Ufficio Affari Civili, "Questioni trattate nella riunione tenuta
12 settembre dall Ecc. il Gen. Com. ai membri del Commissariato Generale Croato,"
12 September 1941, T-821, roll 474, frame 422.

[66] Comando VI. Corpo d'Armata to Comando 2. Armata, "Licenziamento impiegati
serbi," 17 September 1941, T-821, roll 398, frame 803; Comando 2. Armata/Ufficio
Affari Civili, "Questioni varie," 21 September 1941, T-821, roll 398, frames 797–99.

attempted local intrusions; for example, at Gračać, in the middle of the month they tried to reclose the shops owned by Serbs.[67] Continued Ustaši activities in the zone tended to keep the Serb rebels, who had consistently refused Italian demands to put down their arms, in the hills.[68] In such a situation the Italians still had to convince the Serbs that their occupation would not be temporary, to deal decisively with the remaining Ustaši, and to clear the whole area of Partisan agitation.

In October, when Ambrosio's headquarters decided to expand its occupation sphere even further—now up to the Italo-German demarcation line running down the middle of Croatia—the rebels for the most part continued their habit of cautious, partial, and quid pro quo cooperation. Serb bands agreed to turn over their arms provided that the Italians take measures to disarm the local Muslims.[69] In the Drvar sector, where the Italians had succeeded in overcoming stiff Partisan resistance in late September, a nationalist group refused to lay down their guns until the Italians promised to garrison nearby Petrovac and remove the Croatian civilian population. At Konjica, in the area southwest of Sarajevo, an ex-Yugoslav major demanded similarly that the whole sector be included in an expanded Second Army occupation zone.[70]

By the middle of October 1941, the Italian occupation, extending all the way to the demarcation line, included roughly half of the "Independent" Croatian state. However, General Ambrosio's plan to pacify the Serb rebels mainly by eliminating, or at least reducing radically, Ustaši influence in an area running far behind the Adriatic was not an evident success. An examination of the relevant sources, mainly the operations and intelligence reports of the Second Army field commands, suggests, in fact, that, although Ambrosio's policies gave hope to many Serbs and encouraged the vacillating tendencies of a number of rebel spokesmen, they did not really solve the problem of disorder and revolt.

In a sense this failure was the result of the simple fact that, in an area already overrun by guerrilla and irregular bands, the more the Italians pushed their occupation sphere inland from the Adriatic, the more they were compelled to confine their troops to the populated centers and to neglect the surrounding hills and countryside. This also happened in Montenegro, where the first serious activities of the Chetnik officers took place in the eastern, most remote parts of the protectorate at

---

[67] Comando VI. Corpo d'Armata to Comando 2. Armata, "N. 2757 del 15 settembre 1941," 15 September 1941, *T-821*, roll 232, frame 684.
[68] Comando VI. Corpo d'Armata to Comando 2. Armata, "N. 3057 del 26 settembre 1941," 26 September 1941, *T-821*, roll 232, frame 771.
[69] Comando VI. Corpo d'Armata to Comando 2. Armata, "N. 3035 del 25 settembre 1941," 25 September 1941, *T-821*, roll 232, frame 757.
[70] Comando 2. Armata/Ufficio I, "Notiziario N. 2 del 8 ottobre 1941," 8 October 1941. *T-821*, roll 448, frame 6.

the end of 1941. General Ambrosio's troop strength was at least twice as great as the units then at the disposal of the German general in Belgrade, but the Italians were now widely dispersed over an area extending more than a hundred kilometers into Croatian territory. Moreover, the Italian occupation zone, unlike the greater part of the German sphere in Serbia and eastern Bosnia, was largely mountainous territory and provided a haven for the guerrilla and waiting tactics of the Partisans and several non-Communist armed bands.

The effect of the vast changes in occupation spheres and policies in the western half of former Yugoslavia in 1941 was not sufficient to spell the end of the Serb nationalist movement. With the Ustaši military formations removed from half of their sovereign territory, the Serb population had at least a temporary respite from the persecution and terror of the summer, but the Italians lacked the strength to pacify the areas outside the cities and persisted with a policy of negotiating with all the non-Communist Serb armed formations. One obvious result of the numerous talks, contacts, and exchanges of demands between the Second Army garrisons and the Serbs was that many of the rebel leaders gradually became local spokesmen and intermediaries for the Serb community. This, of course, tended to enhance their importance, and, as the web of arrangements and ties between the Italians and the Serb representatives on the local level became more varied and complex, each group became more nearly autonomous and less capable of cooperating with others.

Regardless of their willingness to make deals with a new occupation order, practically all the rebel leaders seemed determined to preserve an armed following. Also, there is little evidence that negotiations with the Italians went hand in hand with a moderation of the rebels' attitudes toward the Ustaši and the Croatian and Muslim civilians. Some of the formations, for example, in the Konjica-Kalinovik area, pledged their loyalty to the Italians and offered to join operations against the Partisans provided that they be granted a sphere in which they could terrorize the Croats and Muslims.[71] By the end of the year, the group around Kalinovik went as far as to deliver an ultimatum to a nearby Ustaši garrison demanding the immediate delivery of arms and munitions.[72]

A large number of the Serb non-Communist bands demonstrated that they were ready to collaborate, at least partially, but always on their own terms and not in a manner which facilitated the Italian pacification efforts. In a situation characterized by large-scale, but as yet poorly organized, guerrilla activities, the numerous formation leaders shifted

[71] Comando 2. Armata/Ufficio I, "Notiziario N. 13 del 28. dicembre 1941," 28 December 1941, *T-821,* roll 448, frame 68.

[72] Ministarstva Hrvatskog Domobranstva to Comando 2. Armata, "Presidio Croato a Kalinovik," 30 December 1941, *T-821,* roll 54, frame 931.

tactics, disputed among themselves and in general tended to act according to the vicissitudes of occupation spheres and policies. In the Petrova Gora region, for instance, Second Army officials received promises of cooperation from at least two non-Communist groups, but by the middle of November one faction, led by a Professor Stanislao Trkulja, broke off all ties with the Italian garrisons and threatened to sabotage lines of communication throughout the area.[73] In December the Italian command posts found themselves in the frustrating position of making alliances with countless armed detachments in certain key sectors, like Petrova Gora, Glamoc-Livno, and the southern parts of Herzegovina, where the situation either remained out of their control or grew worse.[74]

This state of affairs was to a large degree understandable: neither Mihailović nor any officers acting in his name had made serious efforts by the end of 1941 to impose discipline and a coherent line of action on the wide assortment of Serb nationalist detachments operating in most of Independent Croatia. The formation leaders were often civilian local notables, in many instances Orthodox clergymen, former politicians, civil servants, or village elders, who put regional interests above everything else and were highly influenced by the mood of the rank and file. Despite the terminology employed in the reports of the occupation authorities, these groups were Chetnik only in the negative sense that they were armed guerrilla and self-defense formations acting independent of or even against the Partisan movement. Often the dividing line between Serb nationalist-collaborationist and Partisan-dominated resistance formations was simply not evident. At the end of the year non-Communist Serb leaders around Drvar began to threaten with death anyone who sold food to the Partisans and promised the Italians that they would collaborate in anti-rebel operations,[75] but in the Petrova Gora and Foča-Kalinovik sectors anti-Axis Chetnik groups were at least partly responsible for delicate situations.[76] Moreover, at this point in the war, the Partisan movement, as well as the Chetniks, was almost exclusively Serbian; at Drvar, in spite of all the splits in the rebel camp over the issue of negotiating with the Italians, even the Partisans, according to

[73] Comando 2. Armata/Ufficio I, "Notiziario N. 7 del 10. novembre 1941," 10 November 1941, *T-821,* roll 448, frame 38; Comando 2. Armata/Ufficio I, "Notiziario N. 8 del 19. novembre 1941," 19 November 1941, *T-821,* roll 448, frame 43.

[74] Comando 2. Armata/Ufficio I, "Notiziario N. 12 del 19. dicembre 1941," 19 December 1941, *T-821,* roll 448, frame 61; Comando 2. Armata/Ufficio I, "Notiziario N. 13 del 28. dicembre 1941," 28 December 1941, *T-821,* roll 448, frames 67–68.

[75] Comando 2. Armata/Ufficio I, "Notiziario N. 8 del 12. ottobre 1941," 12 October 1941, *T-821,* roll 448, frame 11.

[76] Comando 2. Armata/Ufficio I to Stato Maggiore Reg. Esercito, "Situazione in Croazia e nelle zone occupate," 2 January 1942, *T-821,* roll 356, frames 540–41.

an Italian source, relied mainly on Serb nationalism for political propaganda.[77]

The Italians were thus led to assume the worst about several of the more intransigent and unpredictable Serb leaders and about prospects in general in dismembered Yugoslavia. Ambrosio began to express doubts regarding the usefulness of the non-Communist Serb bands,[78] Dalmazzo was concerned over recent Chetnik "raids" in southern Herzegovina,[79] and in Rome Ciano foresaw spring revolts in Serbia, Bosnia, and Montenegro.[80] At this point the "Chetniks" had no organization; the Italians barely had a policy. Mussolini had intervened in early November to restrain the Second Army's openly pro-Serb posture, informing Ambrosio that all measures were to be carried out in conjunction with the Croatian civil authorities and that the Italians were at all costs to avoid creating the impression that they favored the Orthodox population.[81] Frustrated by continuing disorders, Cavallero wavered between giving Ambrosio full powers to suppress the revolt militarily by declaring the whole area a zone of war and the far more defensive strategy of pulling the Italian troops back to the cities and along the major lines of communication.[82] Whichever course was chosen, the Italians were hardly prepared, given the course of events in North Africa in late 1941, to send many more troops to the Balkans: in the event of a serious rebel threat in the western half of former Yugoslavia, the Italians would need German, Croat, or Serb collaborationist armed support. The Germans lacked troops to spare and would challenge Italy's Yugoslav sphere; Cavallero had, for similar reasons, rejected an offer from Zagreb to reintroduce Croatian units into the demilitarized zone. The failure of the Italians and their Axis allies to collaborate successfully against the Yugoslav Partisan movement created a "gap" in the occupation system. This fact, combined with the energetic efforts of Mihailović's officers from early 1942 on, led to the organization of a solidly anti-Partisan Serb collaborationist movement.

[77] Comando 2. Armata, "N. 2990 del 23. settembre 1941," 23 September 1941, *T-821*, roll 232, frames 740–41.

[78] Comando 2. Armata/Ufficio I to Stato Maggiore Reg. Esercito, "Situazione in Croazia e nelle zone occupate," 2 January 1942, *T-821*, roll 356, frames 540–41.

[79] Comando VI. Corpo d'Armata to Comando 2. Armata, "Concorso alle operazioni tedesche in Bosnia," 8 January 1942, *T-821*, roll 64, frame 1241.

[80] Ciano, *Diario*, vol. 2, entry for 28 December 1941.

[81] Mussolini to Ambrosio, "N. 05871 del 2. novembre 1941," 2 November 1941, *T-821*, roll 474, frames 413–15.

[82] Cavallero, *Comando Supremo*, entries for 4 and 8 January 1942.

IV
THE FORMATION
OF THE CHETNIK
MOVEMENT

:

During the early part of 1942, while Second Army headquarters and Comando Supremo remained somewhat suspicious of the aims and activities of the Serb armed detachments, General Dalmazzo of the Sixth Army Corps continued to pursue the strategy of negotiating with the non-Communist rebel leaders. By this time, however, both Italians and Chetniks were interested in far more than local truces and pacification. The Italians, although uneasy about the delicate situation in former Yugoslavia, had reason to believe, if only temporarily, that they could expand their occupation sphere over even more of Independent Croatia and that they had discovered officer-allies who would help them in the process. The Serb nationalist forces, on the other hand, appeared to have found a leadership, both military and civilian, which controlled sizeable followings, was willing to work with the Italians, and was seeking an alliance against both the Ustaši and the Partisans. In the first half of 1942 Chetnik leaders emerged, and an officers' organization took form not only in Independent Croatia but also in Montenegro and Serbia. Tactics and degrees of success varied, but everywhere the Chetniks put off anti-Axis resistance, tried to secure their own regional "spheres" within the occupation system, and concentrated their efforts against their domestic opponents.

THE ITALIANS AND THE DANGIĆ AFFAIR
IN EASTERN BOSNIA

Developments in the eastern parts of Bosnia, which now formed a corridor between the German sphere in Serbia and the Italian occupation zone in the western half of Independent Croatia, were decisive in the Second Army's movement toward an openly "pro-Chetnik" course and the officers' concomitant shift towards tactical collaboration. Here, as in other parts of Bosnia and Herzegovina, the Ustaši terrorist policies had plunged the whole area, predominantly Serb and Bosnian Muslim, into a state of total chaos and civil war. The revolt was overwhelmingly Serb, carried out by a multitude of hastily armed bands and usually organized on a local and village basis. Militarily the rebellion took the form of a desperate and popular Serb struggle against the Ustaši and Muslim civilians and thus reflected both the immediate wartime situation and a whole tradition of anti-Muslim nationalism characteristic of the Serbs living west of the Drina River. In eastern Bosnia, though, the officers made their first serious efforts to organize an already existing mass upheaval and to use this leverage both to expand the Chetnik movement in other parts of western Yugoslavia and to make ambitious accommodations with the Axis occupation powers. The officers' activities were largely the work of a former gendarme major, Jezdimir Dangić.

Dangić, forty-five years old, a native Bosnian and long active in the administration of the province, received a law degree, spent some time as a district captain, and finally joined the royal gendarme corps. After the Yugoslav capitulation he was in Belgrade, but, hearing of the Ustaši massacres in Bosnia, he got permission late in the summer to return there to bring his family and relatives back to Serbia. On his way he made contact with Mihailović's group at Ravna Gora, organized a small group of Bosnians to continue to the Drina River, and, after crossing into Bosnia, began to carry out small sorties against Ustaši troops.[1]

Dangić's intentions were clearly to maintain the exclusively Serb character of the revolt and resist cooperation with the Partisans. By early September, after establishing his leadership over the other major Chetnik heads in eastern Bosnia, Aćim Babić and Rade Kosorić, he began issuing public declarations against the Communists and called for the

---

[1] Wehrmachtverbindungsstelle Belgrad to Befehlshaber Serbien/Ia, "Generalmajor Jezdimir Dangić, Führer der in Bosnien operierenden Aufständischen," 29 September 1941, *T-314*, roll 1457, frames 702–3.

creation of a "united national Serb front" against the Partisan bands.[2] Except in rare instances, he pursued a strategy of avoiding armed clashes with the small German occupation force, and by late September he had apparently shot Communist agitators in the rebel ranks, was in some form of contact with Nedić, and enjoyed the full support of the Serb minister-president. When Tito's Partisan organizers in eastern Bosnia, Svetozar Vukmanović-Tempo and Rodoljub Čolaković, tried to negotiate an alliance with Babić on 1 September the Communist agents came away with the impression that Babić "obviously regards himself as the leader of the uprising in the Sarajevo area" and that "his people have bad views regarding the local Muslims." [3]

If Dangić's actions were more openly anti-Partisan than those of the Chetniks in Serbia, it was probably because he had advantages which Mihailović did not. The Bosnian Serb villagers had long engaged in bitter religious and national strife with their Croat and Muslim neighbors and were very susceptible to the nationalist appeals of the Chetniks; more important, the Partisans lacked any organization in eastern Bosnia until well into September.[4] Moreover, the Germans had only one occupation division west of the Drina, the 718th, and there was no immediate common threat to keep officers and Partisans together. As early as the fall, then, the Partisans were already making serious efforts to capitalize on the outrages committed by the Serb rebels by recruiting among the Bosnian Muslims.[5]

Nevertheless, Dangić and his collaborators were certainly in some kind of contact with Ravna Gora and followed Mihailović's lead during his negotiations with Tito. On 1 October, shortly after the first Tito-Mihailović encounter at Struganik, Dangić met with the Bosnian Partisan organizers and agreed to combined operations against the Ustaši; he still refused to include the Muslims in the rebel front and insisted that they add the phrase "Long live the King" to a joint proclamation.[6] Dangić had no intention of engaging in serious anti-Axis activities with the Communists, but as long as the Germans did not increase their occu-

<hr>

[2] *Ibid.*, roll 1457, frame 703.

[3] Report of C.P.Y. Provincial Committee of Bosnia-Herzegovina at Sarajevo, 5 September 1941, *Zbornik*, vol. 4, 1, no. 89.

[4] It should be pointed out that the first Partisan documents in the *Zbornik* volumes dealing with Bosnia-Herzegovina are dated no earlier than August 1941 and consist of broad and general appeals to the civilian population for an anti-Axis revolt.

[5] See, for example, "Proclamation of the Sarajevo Provincial C.P.Y. Staff to the Muslims of the Rogatica and Sarajevo Administrative Districts," 1 September 1941, *ibid.*, no. 74. This appeal included the statement that "some Chetniks from other areas are threatening to burn the Muslims' homes . . . for what the Ustaši are doing to the Serbs in various parts of Bosnia-Herzegovina. The Chetniks who want to attack the Muslims' villages are our enemies."

[6] *Ibid.*, 2, no. 1; Čolaković, *Winning Freedom*, pp. 174–75.

pation contingent in eastern Bosnia he could negotiate with the Partisans, who then had two fairly large formations of about two thousand and twelve hundred men, respectively, without risking armed clashes with German units. His subordinates, especially Babić, continued to plunder Muslim villages and at times used their formal alliance with the Communists to try to entice members of Partisan units into joining the Chetniks.[7]

On November 16, after fighting broke out between Tito and Mihailović, Dangić and the Bosnian Communists held a meeting, in which the Chetniks refused again to admit anti-Axis Croats and Muslims into the rebel ranks and Vukmanović-Tempo accused Dangić of dealing with the Germans and Nedić.[8] The Bosnian Chetniks, though, were finding it difficult to coordinate their own difficult relations with the Partisans with Mihailović's shifting strategy in Serbia. Only a few days later—in fact, at the time when Mihailović made his last temporary truce with Tito—Dangić quickly assembled his subordinates to draw up a program which included the recognition of the Yugoslav émigré government, the military leadership of Colonel Mihailović, and, interestingly enough, an alliance of arms with the Partisan bands.[9] By the end of the year, depending on one's point of view, Dangić was a delegate of Nedić, a rebel officer who followed Mihailović, or a resistance leader ready to make common cause with the Partisans. Mihailović apparently had a good deal of confidence in him, for in his instructions to the Montenegrins Lašić and Djurišić of late December 1941 he ordered their units to work "in cooperation with Dangić's forces." [10]

At the end of 1941, however, when the Germans decided to make their major effort in western Serbia in order to eliminate Mihailović's organization, Dangić still had time to develop plans which were both anti-Ustaši and anti-Partisan and involved some sort of collaboration. If both rebel groups in Serbia were routed by the Germans, in a short time the Axis Powers would take strong action in eastern Bosnia to safeguard the north-south lines of communications in the Balkans.[11] The Dangić Chetniks had to choose between serious anti-Axis resistance and some sort of arrangement with the occupation authorities before the expected anti-

---

[7] Dragon Marković and Slobodan Basiljčić, *Delegat Vrhovnog štaba* (Delegate of the Supreme Staff) (Belgrade: Izdavačko Preduzeće Rad, 1968), p. 57.

[8] *Ibid.*, pp. 63–64.

[9] 342. Inf. Div./Ic, 20 January 1942, *T-501*, roll 250, frame 632. The document, signed by Dangić and Babić, was dated 19 November. Mihailović finally concluded his armistice with Tito on 20 November.

[10] R. Missione Militare Italiana in Croazia to Comando Supremo, "Disposizione emanate dal Capo Cetnico, Generale Draza Mihailovic," 16 July 1942, *T-821*, roll 347, frame 823.

[11] See, for example, KTB/OKW, vol. 1, 8 and 12 December 1941.

rebel operation in early 1942. Dangić chose the latter course, probably without consulting Mihailović,[12] but he did so in a way that would achieve a collaborationist settlement which was anti-Ustaši and played off the Germans and Italians against each other.

At first glance the complicated and apparently contradictory maneuvers of the Dangić Chetniks form no intelligible pattern. In the second half of December, for example, Dangić and his followers were trying to come to terms simultaneously with the Germans, Italians, and perhaps even the Partisans. To a large degree, this was because after the German operations in Serbia and the almost total collapse of Mihailović's organization the Chetniks in eastern Bosnia were confused and uncertain as to what to do next. In another sense, however, the negotiations all paved the way for the emergence of the Chetniks in several parts of western Yugoslavia in 1942.

Convinced that there was no hope in attempting to resist German operations in the area, the immediate aim of the Chetniks in eastern Bosnia was to make an arrangement with the occupying powers which would restore the rights of the Serb civilian population. This was the basic sense of a plan proposed to the Partisans in mid-December by one of Dangić's supporters, Major Boško Todorović. The officers suggested that the best Partisan and Chetnik troops pull back to central and western Bosnia and that Dangić remain in the eastern part with his own forces to parley with the occupation authorities and somehow protect the lives of Serb civilians. The Communists, of course, rejected the idea, for it would have meant sacrificing Partisan-liberated territory to Dangić, who would later appear as a "savior of the people." [13]

Around Christmas time the Chetniks were apparently trying to arrive at an agreement with the Germans through the Serb puppet government. The Partisan negotiator, Čolaković, guessed as much when he met Todorović a second time and the main topic of discussion was the attitude to be taken toward Nedić's aims in eastern Bosnia. The Chetniks, Čolaković reported, were trying to obtain a "mandate" from Nedić and the Germans for eastern Bosnia on the basis of a common anti-Communist and anti-Ustaši strategy; they had no desire to fight but "wanted the capitulation to be concealed by some kind of autonomy for liberated Bosnia." [14] The initial negotiations between the Germans and agents of Dangić took place at Belgrade at the end of the year. Nedić, who later

---

[12] Mihailović spent the early weeks of 1942 with a small group of followers in the Sandžak and Montenegro. Deakin, *Embattled Mountain*, p. 147. Later developments in the Dangić affair suggest that he and his subordinates were acting on their own.

[13] Marković and Basiljčić, *Delegat Vrhovnog štaba*, pp. 75–76.

[14] Rodoljub Čolaković to Supreme Staff of the National Liberation Partisan Detachments of Bosnia-Herzegovina, 31 December 1941, *Zbornik*, vol. 4, 2, no. 94.

claimed he had no "direct and prolonged ties" with Dangić, said that the Chetnik leaders in eastern Bosnia were clearly interested in "arriving at an understanding with the German authorities." [15]

The Chetniks succeeded neither in imposing their plan on the Partisans nor in convincing the Germans to rearrange the occupation system in eastern Bosnia in exchange for an armistice. The Dangić group, however, had made clear to the Partisan leaders and the Germans that they had renounced any effort at full-scale resistance; moreover, during the first Italo-German anti-rebel actions of mid-January, they took no military action against the Germans.[16] Some of their units even circulated reports that Nedić had intervened to prevent hostilities between the two German divisions and the Chetnik rebels.[17] Dangić overestimated, just as Mihailović had, both Nedić's influence with the Germans and the German willingness to negotiate with Serb armed detachments.

The Germans, frustrated by the difficulties encountered in the January operations in eastern Bosnia and pressured by Nedić, who stressed Dangić's willingness to work "in league with and under the protection of Germany," [18] finally consented to send the commanding general in Serbia's chief of staff, Colonel Kewisch, to sound out Dangić personally. In a four-hour conversation with Kewisch on 30 January somewhere south of Zvornik, Dangić went so far as to promise to place his troops under German command, to collaborate against the Partisans, and to recognize the sovereign rights of Zagreb in eastern Bosnia; he even declared himself a loyal follower of Nedić.[19] In return, he demanded that all Ustaši formations be removed from eastern Bosnia and that the administration of the predominantly Serb areas be returned to Serb civil servants. Dangić traveled to Belgrade, made the same appeals to Nedić and General Bader personally, and on 1 February signed a preliminary treaty which placed his entire following under the orders of the German 718th Division headquarters at Sarajevo.[20] The agreement fell apart the next day when the German general in Zagreb, Glaise von Horstenau, the minister to Croatia, Kasche, and the Ustaši state secretary, Vrančić, came to Belgrade and blocked the arrangement on the grounds that it violated Germany's alliance with Independent Croatia.[21]

[15] Colonel Kewisch (chief of staff of the commanding general in Serbia), "Aktenvermerk," 19 January 1942, *T-501*, roll 251, frames 1138–39.

[16] Comando 2. Armata to Comando VI. Corpo d'Armata, "N. 982 del 20. gennaio, 1942," 20 January 1942, *T-821*, roll 64, frame 1148.

[17] Report of the Commander of the Ozren Partisan Detachment First Battalion, 15 January 1942, *Zbornik*, vol. 4, 3, no. 18.

[18] Colonel Kewisch, "Aktenvermerk," 19 January 1942, *T-501*, roll 256, frame 1138.

[19] Bevoll. Kdr. Gen. in Serbien/Ia to Wehrmachtbefehlshaber Südost, "Besprechung mit serbischen Major Dangić," 5 February 1942, *T-501*, roll 256, frames 1089–90.

[20] Bevoll. Kdr. Gen. in Serbien/Ia, "Vereinbarung zwischen Bevoll. Kdr. Gen. in Serbien und Major Dangic," 1 February 1942, *T-501*, roll 256, frame 1123.

[21] Bevoll. Kdr. Gen. in Serbien/Ia to Wehrmachtbefehlshaber Südost, "Die wesentliche

The talks with Belgrade, however, did not exhaust all possibilities because the Italians had equal interests in east Bosnian affairs, thought for a while that their rights there were nearly exclusive, and were far more willing than the Germans to make accommodations with Serb leaders at the expense of the Ustaši. Agents of the Chetnik Major Todorović had been in contact with the Italians since mid-December in the Kalinovik-Goražde sector.[22] Near Višegrad they tried to win the Partisans' agreement to a common strategy of not opposing an Italian expedition into eastern Bosnia.[23] These local gestures at first seem far less significant than the Chetniks' persistent efforts to win the Partisans over to their strategy of tactical accommodation or Dangić's personal negotiations with Belgrade, but they turned out to be the initial steps toward a far-reaching working alliance between the Italian military authorities and the emerging officer leaders of the Serb nationalist movement in Croatia.

In order for these developments to be intelligible, it is necessary to distinguish between the immediate motives and calculations on both sides and the longer-range consequences for Italian occupation policies and the officers' collaboration. The Italians, in fact, out of long-standing hostility to the Ustaši regime and to German Balkan pretensions, led themselves to believe that they could manipulate the Serb nationalists, that Dangić was a reliable collaborator with an impressive following, and that by giving material support to a number of other Chetnik leaders they could stop the rebellion and enhance their own sphere in former Yugoslavia. During the winter of 1941–1942, military developments on other fronts took sharp and drastic turns, the Germans had not yet decided to make a serious commitment to the Balkans, and the Yugoslav resistance was still polarizing into discernible Chetnik and Partisan camps. Italian policies that winter were founded on misinformation and wishful thinking as much as anything else.

As early as mid-November, Dalmazzo's Sixth Army Corps placed Dangić's strength at almost ten thousand armed followers,[24] and soon the Italians were holding talks with Major Todorović's representatives. These contacts suddenly expanded, and ambitious gestures were made by both the officers and the Italians at the end of the year, when military

Punkte der Verhandlung vom 2.2.1942," 4 February 1942, *T-501*, roll 256, frame 1098; Bevoll. Kdr. Gen. in Serbien/Ia to Wehrmachtbefehlshaber Südost, "Besprechung mit serbischen Major Dangic," 5 February 1942, *T-501*, roll 256, frame 1093.

[22] Comando VI. Corpo d'Armata, "Viaggio Maggiore Gallo," 16 January 1942, *T-821*, roll 64, frame 975.

[23] National Liberation Partisan Detachment Staff at Višegrad to Chetnik command at Višegrad, 20 December 1941, *Zbornik*, vol. 4, 2, no. 84.

[24] Comando VI. Corpo d'Armata to Comando 2. Armata, "Notiziario N. 206 del 26. novembre 1941," 26 November 1941, *T-821*, roll 400, frame 511.

events on the eastern front suddenly intervened to upset the whole system of occupation and spheres of influence in former Yugoslavia.

The near collapse of the German Army Group Center in front of Moscow in December induced Hitler to transform hastily the struggle against the Soviet Union from an almost exclusively German affair to a European crusade against bolshevism. Willing to accept help from almost any source, the Führer was now particularly anxious to increase Italian, Rumanian, and Hungarian detachments in the east. Moreover, the reverses suffered at the hands of the Red Army also had the effect of forcing into the background all proposals for large-scale operations against rebel strongholds in the Balkan Peninsula. As for Croatia and Serbia, the shift in Hitler's priorities was so drastic that by the middle of December he told his generals that the entire German occupation force in former Yugoslavia, now almost six divisions, had to be withdrawn as soon as possible. Occupation responsibilities would be passed on to the Italians in Croatia and to the Bulgarians and possibly the Hungarians in rump Serbia.[25]

Soon after, O.K.W. moderated its proposals and decided to reduce the German occupation contingent from six to two divisions, but this still meant that they were in effect giving up almost all their influence in Croatia.[26] What was more significant, though, was that Germany's suddenly announced military withdrawal from Croatia gave new life to Italian designs to push their sphere of influence further into the Balkans. Mussolini accepted the offer immediately, and Army Chief of Staff Roatta the Second Army commander Ambrosio thought that just two additional corps, or about five divisions, would be sufficient to meet the expanded occupation responsibilities.[27]

All Italian plans for the extension of their occupation into Croatian territory, especially Bosnia, had a strong anti-Ustaši thrust. General Dalmazzo recommended "removing the Ustaši immediately and the regular Croatian troops [Domobran] gradually" from Italian-occupied eastern Bosnia, while Ambrosio, now convinced that "the large part of the civilian population in the operation zone, for the most part Serb Orthodox and Muslim, hate the Croats in general and the Ustaši regime in

---

[25] Aufzeichnung des Botschafters Ritter, 16 December 1941, in *Akten zur Deutschen Auswärtigen Politik (1918-1945)* (Götingen: Vandenhoeck u. Rupprecht, 1969) (hereafter cited as *ADAP*), ser. E (hereafter cited as E), vol. 1, no. 14.

[26] For the reaction of the Ustaši government and the German officials in Zagreb, see "Aufzeichnung des wissenschaftlicher Hilfsarbeiters Ruhe über die Unterredung des Herrn Reichsaussenministers mit S. E. dem Kroatischen Gesandten," 16 December 1941, *ibid.*, no. 17; Kasche to Aus. Amt, 16 December 1941, *ibid.*, no. 19.

[27] Unsigned account of meeting held at Rome, entitled "Dal Duce 18/XII/1941—presente: Ciano, Roatta, Ambrosio, Casertano, Magli," 18 December 1941, *T-821*, roll 84, frames 1006-7; unsigned account describing all major Italian discussions in the second half of December to extend the occupation sphere in Croatia, entitled "Riunione giorno 30 dicembre," 30 December 1941, *T-821*, roll 64, frame 993.

particular," proposed similarly that "immediately after the occupation, the regular units of the Croatian Army and the Ustaši formations be removed to another zone."[28]

What the Italians were planning, then, was to extend the basically anti-Ustaši and pro-Serb administrative measures which they had already implemented in the demilitarized zone throughout all of Bosnia. By pursuing a policy supported by the Serb nationalist leaders, they thought they could eliminate the disorders in Bosnia, create an effective barrier against the Croatian Ustaši, and preserve the whole area from German influence. Ambrosio was proposing as the basis for Italian policies (1) pacific occupation of Bosnia, as far as possible, by inducing the rebels to return to their homes; (2) avoidance of provocation of the Chetniks to keep them from joining the Communists; and (3) a struggle to the end against the Communists and their followers.[29]

These Italian hopes lasted only a little over a week. While the Italians were making plans to include all of Bosnia in their Balkan occupation sphere, Hitler was quickly giving way to pressure from Zagreb and Belgrade to maintain a strong German foothold in Croatia. By 23 December O.K.W. had announced that the plan to turn over the Ustaši state to the Italian Second Army had been dropped.[30] As a result of the German about-face and with no prospect now of expanding influence in Croatia, the Italians, especially Mussolini, became more suspicious than ever of Ustaši-German intrigue and refused to cooperate fully in even a small-scale anti-rebel operation in eastern Bosnia.[31] While the Germans, Italians, and Ustaši tried to arrive at a common policy on dealing with the Bosnian revolt, the main Partisan force withdrew to the Foča area and reorganized there from February to May. Dangić, with about four thousand Chetniks,[32] also withdrew to the same general area, avoided clashes with either Italian or German units,[33] and spent the

[28] Dalmazzo to Ambrosio, "Estensione della nostra occupazione," 22 December 1941, *T-821*, roll 64, frames 1305–8; Ambrosio to Stato Maggiore R. Esercito, "Occupazione della Croazia," 22 December 1941, *T-821*, roll 64, frame 1123.

[29] Ambrosio to Dalmazzo, "Estensione della nostra occupazione," *T-821*, roll 64, frame 1304.

[30] Aufzeichnung des Botschafters Ritter, 23 December 1941, *ADAP*, E, vol. 1, no. 54.

[31] Ambrosio to Stato Maggiore R. Esercito, "N. 14359 del 24. dicembre 1941," 24 December 1941, *T-821*, roll 64, frames 1115–16; Comando 2. Armata, "Riunione giorno 30 dicembre," *T-821*, roll 64, frames 994–1001; L'Adetto Militare Italiano a Belgrado to Comando 2. Armata, "N. 78 del 31 dicembre 1941," 31 December 1941, *T-821*, roll 64, frame 1089; Comando 2. Armata to Superesercito Operazioni, "N. 14615 del 31 Dicembre 1941," 31 December 1941, *T-821*, roll 64, frame 1095; Stato Maggiore R. Esercito to Ambrosio, "Operazione in Bosnia," 4 January 1942, *T-821*, roll 64, frames 1062–63.

[32] Comando 2. Armata to Comando VI. Corpo d'Armata, "N. 982 del 20 gennaio 1942," 20 January 1942, *T-821*, roll 64, frame 1148.

[33] AOK 12/Ia, "Tätigkeitsbericht für die Zeit vom 1.1.–31.1.42," 29 January 1942 (Anlage 43), *T-311*, roll 175, frame 190.

remainder of the spring trying to parley with the Axis occupation authorities.

While Major Dangić had no success with the Germans, his agents easily found grounds for bargaining with the Italians. Interestingly enough, the rapprochement was based on the illusion, held in common by both the Bosnian Chetniks and the Italian field commanders, that the Second Army, despite recent German decisions, would occupy all or most of Bosnia. Dalmazzo typically took the initiative when he informed a number of Herzegovinian Serb nationalist leaders in December of the Italians' Bosnian project,[34] and by the second half of January the Bosnian Chetniks themselves were fully involved in the talks. The major impetus came from a number of local arrangements made during the first anti-rebel operation. The Italians refused to undertake military action against the rebel concentration around Foča,[35] and, according to one Partisan source, the Romanija Chetnik group, led by Captain Sergije Mihailović, even entered the area under an agreement reached with the Italians, who left them about two thousand rifles and large amounts of ammunition.[36] In mid-January, according to German information, representatives of the Foča Chetniks met with Italian officers at nearby Višegrad and promised that Dangić would not oppose the units of the Second Army.[37] Meanwhile agents of one of Dangić's chief subordinates, Major Todorović, were opening up negotiations outside of the zone of operations. Todorović's representatives with Dalmazzo's Sixth Army Corps, Mutimir Petković and Milan Šantić, had signed a preliminary treaty on 11 January calling for the mutual renunciation of the use of arms in the event of an Italian expedition in eastern Bosnia.[38]

During the talks between the Italians and the Bosnian Chetniks, a group of Serb nationalist spokesmen in Herzegovina acted as intermediaries, presenting themselves as civilian representatives of the Dangić movement and thereby enhancing their own stature with the Italian command. The chief figures in the group were Dobroslav Jevdjević and Colonel Ilija Trifunović-Birčanin, both of whom had established ties with the Italians during the previous summer. Jevdjević, a native of

---

[34] Dalmazzo to Ambrosio, "Estensione della nostra occupazione," 22 December 1941, *T-821*, roll 64, frames 1305–8.

[35] Comando 2. Armata to Nucleo Collegamento Italiano a Belgrado, "N. 938 del 19. gennaio 1942," 19 January 1942, *T-821*, roll 64, frame 1151.

[36] Čolaković, *Winning Freedom*, pp. 206–7.

[37] Nucleo Collegamento Italiano a Belgrado to Comando 2. Armata, "N. 120 del 18 gennaio 1942," 18 January 1942, *T-821*, roll 64, frame 1152.

[38] Unfinished report of Moše Pijade of early April 1942, entitled "Why and How the Chetnik Leaders Fight," *Zbornik*, vol. 2, 3, pp. 331–32. Pijade wrote this article on the basis of the captured archives of Todorović, whom the Partisans killed on 20 February, and quoted directly from the treaty.

eastern Bosnia, had been elected four times to the Skupština and was an opposition leader during King Alexander's dictatorship of 1929–1934; Trifunović was a former Chetnik *vojvoda* during the Balkan Wars and later became head of the ultra-nationalist Narodna Odbrana,[39] At the end of January 1942 Jevdjević offered to "prepare the ground" with Dangić and the Bosnian Serb heads so that the Chetniks would offer no resistance to an Italian occupation of Bosnia and would collaborate with the Second Army "by organizing armed Chetnik detachments to work alongside [the Italians] . . . against the Communists."[40]

While Dangić was preparing his personal mission to Belgrade and the Germans, the agents of Todorović and Jevdjević were offering the services of the eastern Bosnian bands to the Italians. In mid-February Captain Bogdan Marjanović of the Rogatica Chetnik detachment talked with some Italian officers at Višegrad and reported that he had arrived at "a complete agreement regarding collaboration and further action in Bosnia against the Partisans."[41] At this point Todorović went directly to Nevesinje, Herzegovina, conferred with Jevdjević, and instructed him to negotiate with the Second Army's new commander, General Mario Roatta, for the simultaneous withdrawal of Croatian and German troops from eastern Bosnia and the establishment of an exclusively Italian administration in the area.[42]

Not only did Jevdjević and Todorović appear more than willing to work with the Italians but they also demonstrated to the satisfaction of General Dalmazzo their strong influence on the eastern Bosnian Chetniks. Nationalist Serb bands in the Foča-Goražde sector, for instance, had swung over to a firm anti-Partisan line and suddenly adopted a more cooperative attitude toward the Italians when Dalmazzo's officers informed them of Jevdjević's and Trifunović's ties with Sixth Army Corps headquarters.[43] By the end of January, in fact, Dalmazzo was urging Roatta

---

[39] Comando VI. Corpo d'Armata/Ufficio Informazione to Comando 2. Armata, "Contatti con i capi di formazioni cetniche," 17 January 1942, *T-821*, roll 53, frames 697–98.

[40] Comando 2. Armata/Ufficio I to Capo di S. M. dell' Esercito, "Linea di condotta," 2 February 1942, *T-821*, roll 53, frames 1162–63.

[41] Marjanović's letter to one of his subordinates, dated 16 February, was found among his captured papers and is cited directly in Vladimir Dedijer, *Dnevnik* (Diary), vol. 1 (Belgrade: Državne Izdavački Zavod Jugoslavije, 1945), entry for 14 March 1942.

[42] The contents of the Todorović-Jevdjević plan were revealed through Jevdjević's ensuing conversation with Croatian State Secretary Vrančić and were reported to Berlin and the South-East High Command by Kasche and Glaise. The origin of these reports would seem to cast doubt on their reliability were it not for the fact that Italian sources show that Jevdjević was making similar proposals to Roatta at least as early as the end of January. Kasche to Aus. Amt/B. des U. St. Sek. Pol., "N. 603 vom 6.4.42," 6 April 1942, *T-120*, roll 208, frames 160999–161000; Deutsche General in Agram/Ia to Wehrmachtbefehlshaber Südost, 6 April 1942, *T-501*, roll 266, frames 122–24.

[43] Comando VI. Corpo d'Armata/Ufficio Informazione to Comando 2. Armata, "Con-

to expand the numerous local accords with Serb non-Communist armed groups into a full-fledged alliance with the Chetnik officers.

In the early part of 1942, then, the Italians, mainly because they wanted active armed allies to restore order, fight the Partisans, and support their claims to an enlarged occupation sphere, were developing policies which had as much to do with the development of the Chetnik movement as did the activities of the officers themselves. In order to deal effectively with the Chetniks, the Italians looked for leaders who had influence with both the officers and the rank and file of the various groups. The Serb nationalist spokesmen, both civilian and military, cooperated by pretending that the armed bands were far better organized than they actually were.

Italian policies reached a turning point during the spring of 1942. In early March, while talks of a second cleaning-up action in eastern Bosnia were under way and Italian hopes for expanded occupation rights in Croatia once more revived, General Roatta, impressed by what he thought to be the potential of Dangić's followers, suspected that the Germans were trying to use the major for their own ends and began to advocate the development of closer relations with the Bosnian Chetniks. Because they overestimated the officers' willingness to engage in trustworthy collaboration and because they needed to justify their decisions to Rome, Berlin, and Zagreb, the Italians tended to see the Chetniks as a fairly well-coordinated movement which was ready to join the Axis powers and the Serb Quislings in a struggle aimed exclusively at the Partisan rebellion. Dalmazzo, for example, after negotiating with some of Dangić's followers in January, was convinced that he could easily open relations with Mihailović himself; [44] similarly, Roatta explained to Army Chief of Staff Ambrosio that not only Dangić but now also Mihailović was in touch with Nedić.[45] Moreover, the assortment of Serb nationalist bands in Herzegovina were now, according to Roatta, the "Herzegovinian Chetniks," who were "represented by Jevdjević" and "more or less tied to Dangić."

As regards the Dangić affair in eastern Bosnia, virtually everyone's short-term calculations failed. Nedić and the Germans in Belgrade did not succeed in their efforts to use Dangić for their own ends. Dangić, however, persisted in his efforts, journeyed to Serbia a second time, and was

tatti con i capi di formazioni cetniche," 17 January 1942, *T-821*, roll 53, frame 699; Comando VI. Corpo d'Armata to Comando 2. Armata, "Situazione in Bosnia ed Herzegovina," 26 January 1942, *T-821*, roll 399, frames 212–13.

[44] Comando VI. Corpo d'Armata, "Viaggio Maggiore Gallo," 16 January 1942, *T-821*, roll 64, frame 975.

[45] Comando 2. Armata to Stato Maggiore R. Esercito, "Cetnici," 6 March 1942, *T-821*, roll 53, frames 1062–65.

arrested by the Germans in mid-April.[46] His chief military subordinate, Major Todorović, was killed by the Partisans in Herzegovina in late February.[47] The Italian military authorities, with whom he had begun negotiations, failed to secure German agreement to a military operation in eastern Bosnia which would recognize the Chetniks as tactical allies.[48] In spite of all this, the Italians, largely because they grasped at far more than they could control militarily, maneuvered themselves into a position in which they needed native armed allies. The succession of offers, promises, and negotiations between Italian officers and the Serb nationalists were only ostensibly abortive, for the talks created in the minds of the Italians at Sixth Army Corps and Second Army headquarters a picture of the Chetniks as willing to collaborate, as anti-Partisan far more than anti-Ustaši, and as possessing a reliable leadership.

HERZEGOVINA AND WESTERN BOSNIA

In Herzegovina the civilians Jevdjević and Trifunović took full advantage of the Italians' dilemma by suddenly declaring that they were in effective control of a Chetnik armed movement and ready to collaborate on General Roatta's terms. Taking advantage of Todorović's death to strengthen his ties with the Italians, Jevdjević sent a message to Dalmazzo which explained that the Herzegovinian Chetniks desired revenge for their murdered leader and were gathering around Nevesinje to wait for "an opportunity to demonstrate in a positive way their loyalty to the Second Army." [49]

For the Serb civilian nationalist leaders, negotiations with the Italians proved somewhat difficult because the various armed formations had as yet not demonstrated that they were useful military allies, nor did they all recognize any one leadership. While Jevdjević claimed that he had sent delegates to Herzegovina, eastern Bosnia, Montenegro, and the Sandžak for the purpose of restoring tranquillity, the Italians believed

[46] Benzler to Aus. Amt/Pol. IV, "Telegramm N. vom 10 April 1942," 10 April 1942, *T-120*, roll 200, frame 230/1533585; AOK 12/Ia, "Tätigkeitsbericht für die Zeit vom 1.4.-30.4.1942," 11 April 1942 (Anlage 25), *T-311*, roll 175, frames 250–51; Bevoll. Kdr. Gen. in Serbien, "Aktenvermerk vom 12.4.42," 2 April 1942, *T-50*, roll 250, frame 402.

[47] Communication of Operations Staff of the Herzegovinian National Liberation Partisan Detachments, 23 February 1942, *Zbornik*, vol. 4, 3, no. 79.

[48] For the difficult negotiations leading to the joint operation of April, see Cavallero, *Comando Supremo*, entry for 5 March 1942; Glaise von Horstenau, "Zur Lage in Kroatien," 6 March 1942, *T-501*, roll 266, frame 147; Kvaternik to Roatta, "N. 140/1942 del 31 marzo 1942," 31 March 1942, *T-821*, roll 66, frame 312; Kasche to Aus. Amt/U. St. Sek. Pol., "N. 591 vom 3 April 1942," 3 April 1942, *T-120*, roll 208, frame 245/160991; OKW/WFSt to Aus. Amt/U. St. Sek. Pol., "N. 001165/42 vom 4 April 1942," 4 April 1942, *T-120*, roll 208, frame 245/160997.

[49] Comando 2. Armata to Stato Maggiore R. Esercito/Ufficio Operazione, "Cetnici," 6 March 1942, *T-821*, roll 53, frames 1065–68.

that officers in touch with Mihailović were fomenting not only anti-Croatian but anti-Italian propaganda in parts of Herzegovina.[50] Information continued to arrive at Second Army headquarters that individual Chetnik groups, for example, around Drvar, were being badly mauled by the Partisans, while others, including Todorović's followers near Kalinovik, were being "infiltrated" by Communist agents.[51]

The Italians, however, had little choice but to rely on some sort of native armed backing in order to restore order in their occupation zone. General Dalmazzo thought that an alliance with the Serb nationalists would lessen the Italians' burden of occupation duties [52] and would at the same time open negotiations with the leaders of the Muslim community of Bosnia-Herzegovina.[53] The overriding sense of Italian policies, then, was to use official toleration and arms supplies to curb the anti-Croatian and anti-Muslim excesses of the Serb bands and to transform them into an exclusively anti-Partisan auxiliary force. The Italians, although never altogether free of illusions regarding the reliability of the Chetniks, seized upon intermediaries like Jevdjević and tried to enhance their status with the local detachment leaders and thereby dissipate the influence of more anti-Axis officers like Mihailović.

Roatta agreed to tolerate the officers' formations provided that they fight only the Partisans, avoid all acts hostile to the Croats, and operate in close collaboration with Italian units. In mid-March the Second Army commander presented his pro-Chetnik policies to Rome with the cautious proviso that collaboration with the officers would be confined to Herzegovina. He felt confident enough to Ambrosio's support to inform Glaise on 11 April, while visiting Zagreb, that Comando Supremo had approved talks with the Herzegovinian bands, although he did stress that he would not give them arms for a certain "trial period." [54]

At this time the Italians' cautious confidence in the Serb nationalist leaders proved to be warranted. In Herzegovina, while Jevdjević and Trifunović were acting as intermediaries with the Second Army officers, the Chetniks were actively organizing themselves as a kind of collaborationist police force. After Todorović's death local leadership passed into

[50] Comando 2. Armata/Ufficio I, "Notiziario N. 7 del 9. febbraio 1942," 9 February 1942, T-821, roll 448, frame 94.

[51] Comando 2. Armata/Ufficio I, "Notiziario N. 16 del 31 gennaio 1942," 31 January 1942, T-821, roll 448, frames 88–89; Comando 2. Armata/Ufficio I, "Notiziario N. 15 del 24 gennaio 1942," 24 January 1942, T-821, roll 448, frame 81.

[52] Comando VI. Corpo d'Armata/Ufficio I to Comando 2. Armata, "Situazione in Bosnia ed Herzegovina," 26 January 1942, T-821, roll 399, frames 212–13.

[53] Ibid.

[54] Comando 2. Armata to Superesercito Operazioni, "N. 3693 del 18 marzo 1942," 18 March 1942, T-821, roll 53, frame 1070; Kasche to Aus. Amt/U. St. Sek. Pol., "N. 662 vom 16 April 1942," 16 April 1942, T-120, roll 208, frame 245/161011.

the hands of a civilian, the former Serb Agrarian party politician and rebel leader Petar Samardžić, and Chetnik activities were centered in Nevesinje. As early as April the Nevesinje Chetniks were cooperating in anti-Partisan cleaning-up operations with the Italians; by May Samardžić had begun to exercise considerable influence over several other Serb armed groups throughout Herzegovina.[55] In this as in other cases, the tactic of the civilian regional representatives was to support Italian efforts to eliminate the Partisans and then extend their own control over the pacified areas. As the Partisan threat receded, the wavering leaders of the non-Communist bands tended to move toward a collaborationist line and to fall under the influence of the civilian intermediaries with the Italians. With more followers, Samardžić, Jevdjević, and Trifunović had more bargaining power with the Second Army. Samardžić, therefore, made considerable efforts to prevent the anti-Muslim manifestations of some of his followers. He issued directives, cosigned by Jevdjević, calling on the Chetniks in the Goražde, Kalinovik, and Foča sectors to avoid confrontations with Italian troops and promised that the Second Army would provide reliable protection against Ustaši reprisals.[56] Jevdjević and Trifunović contributed politically by making regular tours through the surrounding villages for the purpose of exhorting the Chetnik rank and file and the Serb civilians to continue the anti-Partisan struggle and to behave loyally toward the Italian troops.[57]

Throughout the spring and summer of 1942, as the hard-pressed Partisan leaders were forced to undertake the "long march" to the mountains of western Bosnia, the Serb collaborationists extended their influence over most of the armed bands and gained de facto political authority in several rural areas, using their position with the Italians to arrange for the protection of Serb communities from Ustaši and Partisan reprisals. In addition to large parts of Herzegovina, this process was most evident in the northern sector of the Italian occupation zone, northern Dalmatia, the Lika, and western Bosnia. In several instances Serb leaders purged the area of anyone associated with the Communists and then sent petitions to a nearby Italian division to protect the area from the Partisans and Ustaši.[58] Throughout April delegations from predominantly Serb rural areas asked the Italians to provide security against local Partisans,

---

[55] Report no. 116 of Croatian Armed Forces Ministry, 26 April 1942, *Zbornik*, vol. 4, 4, no. 133.

[56] Directive of Staff of Military-Chetnik Detachments at Nevesinje and Gačko, [?] May 1942, *ibid.*, 5, no. 141.

[57] Comando 2. Armata/Ufficio I, "Notiziario A. C. del 31 luglio 1942," 31 July 1942, *T-821*, roll 448, frame 254.

[58] Comando v. Corpo d'Armata to Comando 2. Armata, "N. 02/1/1743 del 8. aprile 1942," 8 April 1942, *T-821*, roll 400, frame 1027.

apparently because the latter were forcing the peasants to sacrifice much of their already meager food supplies.[59]

As in Herzegovina, however, the crucial change in Italian policies and Serb tactics was that these alliances, although largely defensive and still directed to some degree against the Ustaši, rapidly assumed an offensive character with the Partisans as principal enemy. During the summer of 1941 the Italians had sought to dissolve the Serb bands by forcing out the Ustaši and inducing the "Chetniks" to return to their homes; now the Second Army command was more interested in maintaining the Chetniks' armed strength for employment against the Partisans.

In the Diraric Alps and Lika sector the Chetnik movement, as it did with Samardžić, Jevdjević, and Trifunović in Herzegovina, gradually formed under the leadership of a Serb civilian notable, the Orthodox cleric Pop Djujić. Djujić was in his late thirties and was a native of the Lika; like Samardzić, he had been a member of the Serb Agrarian party before the war. His emergence was rapid: although Italian reports credited him with a following of only three hundred around Tenin in early April,[60] by the middle of the month his group was launching raids in conjunction with the Italians against several Partisan-controlled villages in the Grahovo-Drvar region.[61] He soon negotiated an official pact of nonaggression and won approval for the constitution of armed detachments with a strength of three thousand men.[62]

In addition to the protection and direct military cooperation provided by the Italians, the Chetniks in the Lika and Bosanska Krajina were apparently helped to a large degree by the simultaneous crisis within the Partisan ranks and the mistakes of the Communist leaders. During April, for example, Partisan units around Drvar, hard-pressed to find food supplies in the area, reported "wavering" tendencies on the part of some of their detachment leaders.[63] According to Italian sources, a significant part of the rapidly growing Chetnik formations was made up of deserters from the Partisans.[64] Moreover, the Partisans at times employed tactics

[59] For example, Comando 2. Armata/Ufficio I, "Notiziario N. 23 del 13 aprile 1942," 13 April 1942, *T-821*, roll 448, frame 138.

[60] *Ibid.*

[61] Report of Staff of Fifth Krajina National Liberation Partisan Detachment, 15 April 1942, *Zbornik,* vol. 4, 4, no. 74.

[62] The Italian documents do not include this agreement, probably because it was made at the division level. It is described, however, by the extremely pro-Chetnik David Martin in *Ally Betrayed—The Uncensored Story of Tito and Mihailovich* (New York: Prentice-Hall, 1946), pp. 141–42.

[63] Report of Staff of Fifth Krajina National Liberation Partisan Detachment, 15 April 1942, *Zbornik,* vol. 4, 4, no. 74.

[64] Comando 2. Armata/Ufficio I, "Notiziario A. C. del 23 aprile 1942," 23 April 1942, *T-821*, roll 448, frame 150; Comando 2. Armata/Ufficio I, "Notiziario A. C. del 11 luglio 1942," 11 July 1942, *T-821*, roll 448, frame 441.

which had the effect of driving several undecided non-Communist Serb leaders into an openly collaborationist position. Just as the murder of Major Todorović pushed many Serb nationalists in Herzegovina into the arms of the Italians, Communist efforts elsewhere to purge actual or potential Chetnik "traitors" frightened local armed chiefs into seeking Italian support. In the Drvar region the Partisans in April announced a manhunt for Uroš Drenović, an anti-Communist but still a non-collaborationist. Drenović instantly pulled back his bands to nearby Varkar Vakuf, asked the Italian garrison there for protection, and soon emerged as one of the major Chetnik organizers in western Bosnia.[65]

By the summer of 1942, by which time considerable parts of the Italian occupation zone had been temporarily "normalized," Chetnik detachment heads like Samardžić, Djujić, and Drenović and their principal political spokesmen with Second Army headquarters Jevdjević and Trifunović had successfully established themselves as recognized auxiliaries to the Italian occupation troops. In the early summer Roatta authorized deliveries of arms, munitions, and supplies; by July Petar Baćović, one of Jevdjević's military organizers, wrote Mihailović that the numerical strength of the Herzegovinian Chetniks stood at about seven thousand, practically all of whom were well-armed with light weapons and "legalized" by the Italians.[66] Together with Djujić's group, the legalized Chetnik detachments in the Italian zone must have numbered at least ten thousand troops.

The Chetnik rank and file consisted of the collaborationist leaders own formations, groups led by wavering, non-Communist commanders who had recently swung over to the collaborationist camp, and a number of former members of Partisan-dominated units who deserted to the Serb nationalists. The Chetniks were expanding not so much by mobilizing new recruits but rather by extending their influence over already-armed bands previously neither pro-Partisan nor collaborationist and by absorbing recently demoralized elements of Partisan formations.[67] In other words, the Chetnik organization emerged most dramatically in a period

[65] Comando 2. Armata/Ufficio I, "Notiziario A. C. del 23 aprile 1942," 23 April 1942, *T-821*, roll 448, frame 153.

[66] Baćović to Mihailović, 16 July 1942, cited by Petar Kačavenda, "Kriza Četničkog Pokreta Draže Mihailovića u Drugoj Polovini 1942 godine" (The crisis of Draža Mihailović's Chetnik movement in the second half of 1942), *Istorija Radničkog Pokreta* 1 (1965): 261. In this highly useful article, Kačavenda cites Chetnik sources currently held in the Archives of the Military Historical Institute in Belgrade which otherwise would have been unavailable to me.

[67] This last fact not only indicates the profound crisis suffered by the Partisan resistance movement during 1942 in several parts of Yugoslavia and the weak hold of the party leaders over several of their rank and file but also bears a striking resemblance to the simultaneous Chetnik tactic in Serbia of joining the legal police formations of the Nedić administration.

of declining anti-Axis rebel activity and of general normalization. The civilian leaders of the collaborationist bands enjoying Italian support now were very successful in expanding their accommodation with the occupation order in return for concessions from Zagreb and the Germans. Jevdjević was the key figure in the efforts of the Serb nationalists to bargain with the Ustaši government and the German military authorities in Croatia. A year of intermittent civil war between the Serbs and the Ustaši military had made nearly impossible any sincere and lasting accord between the Chetnik spokesmen and Zagreb. Nevertheless, Jevdjević and others—in part to convince the Croatian government that the Chetniks were less anti-Ustaši than they really were, in part because real concessions could be extracted from Zagreb on a regional basis, and to some degree to avoid relying exclusively on the Italians—did succeed in carrying out at least temporarily successful negotiations.

Jevdjević himself had discussed the confiscated property of the Serbs and the status of the Orthodox religion in Croatia with an agent of Pavelić at the end of 1941 without arriving at any agreement.[68] In mid-March of 1942 Croatia's recently named "administrative commissar" with the Second Army, Vrančić, announced to Roatta that he was prepared to establish relations with the Serb armed formations operating in the Italian zone.[69] Vrančić soon met with Jevdjević and his close collaborator Radmilo Grdjić at Split and told them that the Croatian government was ready to restore the Serbs' rights, mainly economic and religious, in the Second Army occupation zone.[70] By early April word had spread that Zagreb was giving serious thought to the creation of a national Croatian Orthodox church;[71] toward the end of the month, as noted earlier, Uroš Drenović presented himself to the local Croatian garrison to request an armistice on the basis of a restoration of religious and civil rights for the Serb villages around Varkar Vakuf.[72] Zagreb's apparent willingness to

[68] Comando Supremo/Ufficio Operazione/Scacchieri Orientali to Ministero Affari Esteri, "Colloquio fra il Dr. Jevdjević e l'inviato del Poglavnik Logornik Poljak," 26 January 1942, *T-821,* roll 356, frame 578; Comando 2. Armata/Ufficio Operazione, "Sintesi del colloquio avvenuto il 30. dic. 1941 . . . a Spalato fra . . . Jevdjević ed il Logornik Poljak addetto al G. Q. Ustascia di Zagrabia inviato del Poglavnik," 2 January 1942, *T-821,* roll 356, frames 581-84. Indicative of the Italians' still very cautious attitude toward the Chetniks is the fact that they hid a recorder in Jevdjević's home to intercept this conversation.

[69] Comando 2. Armata to Comando VI. Corpo d'Armata, "N. 5606 del 20 marzo 1942," 20 March 1942, *T-821,* roll 66, frame 587.

[70] Stato Ind. di Croazia/Commissariato Generale Amministrativo, "Relazione," 2 April 1942, *T-821,* roll 400, frames 1010-13.

[71] Comando V. Corpo d'Armata to Comando 2. Armata, "Istituzione di una chiesa nazionale ortodossa in Croazia," 13 April 1942, *T-821,* roll 400, frame 1061.

[72] Croatian Armed Forces Ministry daily report no. 120, 30 April 1942, *Zbornik,* vol. 4, 4, no. 136; Deutsche General in Agram/Ia to OKW/Abt. Ausland, "N. 52/42 vom 1. Mai 1942," 1 May 1942, *T-501,* roll 264, frame 1056.

make concessions to the Serb Orthodox population, coupled with the Partisans' manhunt for Drenović as a national traitor, had the immediate effect of drawing the Croatian authorities and the Chetniks together in this single area. Drenović signed a declaration in which he recognized the sovereignty of the Ustaši state provided that Pavelić return religious freedom to the local Serbs and agreed to join operations against the Partisans.[73]

Shortly after, Pavelić accepted Drenović's conditions as a basis for further negotiations;[74] in mid-May Drenović made a definitive accord in Banja Luka with a Croatian general staff officer on anti-Partisan collaboration.[75] At the urging of Glaise von Horstenau, the Croatian government came to terms with a number of smaller armed groups and in late May even agreed to an armistice with a number of former followers of Major Dangić in eastern Bosnia.[76] The rapprochement between Zagreb and the Bosnian Chetniks, however, was more apparent than real and reached its peak in the summer.

Available evidence indicates that the Croatian government, and especially the Ustaši military authorities, were never enthusiastic about making armistice arrangements with Serb armed formations.[77] The Ustaši and Croatian regular armed forces, however, were unable alone to control the widely dispersed and inaccessible Serb bands even though the Serbs had lost some potential leaders like Dangić and were not actively

[73] Declaration of Uroš Drenović (commander of the Chetnik group "Petar Kočić"). 27 April 1942, *Dokumenti o Izdajstvu Draže Mihailovića*, no. 160; the Chetnik-Croatian accord, also signed on 27 April at Varkar Vakuf, was captured by the Partisans later in the summer and is reproduced in *Zbornik*, vol. 4, 5, no. 55.

[74] Deutsche General in Agram/Ia to OKW/Abt. Ausland, "N. 52/42 vom 1. Mai 1942," 1 May 1942, *T-501*, roll 264, frame 1056.

[75] Communication of Partisan intelligence bureau of Bosanska Krajina Operations Staff, [?] June 1942, *Zbornik*, vol. 4, 5, no. 55. This report, based on a letter of late May 1942 from a Partisan sympathizer in Banja Luka, was published in the *Krajiskih Partisanskih Novina*, 3 June 1942, and agrees with other evidence regarding Drenović's later collaboration with the Ustaši. A Croatian report of early August, for example, singled out Drenović's group as the most loyal Chetnik detachment in the entire Krajina region and added that he was also in good standing with the Germans at Banja Luka. Armed Detachment of the Jajce command to Fifth Armed Regiment, 6 August 1942, *Zbornik*, vol. 4, 6, no. 157.

[76] Nesavizna Država Hrvatska/Ministerstvo Hrvatskog Domobranstva to Comando 2. Armata, "Collaborazione con i cetnici," 6 May 1942, *T-821*, roll 53, frame 1057; Comando 2, Armata to Ecc. Capo di Stato Maggiore dell' Esercito Croato (Kvaternik), "Collaborazione con i cetnici," 11 May 1942, *T-821*, roll 53, frame 152; minutes of the Ustaši-Chetnik negotiations of 28 May 1942 at Lipei (near Prijedor), *Dokumenti o Izdajstvu Draže Mihailovića*, no. 112. Partisan units captured the original draft of the treaty in July 1942. Report of Ivo Lola-Ribar to Serb provincial committee, 1 August 1942, *Zbornik*, vol. 2, 5, no. 63.

[77] For the German assessment of the progress of Ustaši-Chetnik collaboration, see Deutsche General in Agram/Ia to Bevoll. Kdr. Gen. in Serbien/Ic, "N. 142/42 vom 19.6.1942," 19 June 1942, *T-501*, roll 266, frame 46.

involved in anti-Axis resistance. In certain sectors, like the area around Prijedor, recent Partisan intrusions gave Zagreb even more compelling reasons to make its peace with the Serb nationalists. The Croatian government was forced to undertake some rather substantial changes in policy, and the resultant Chetnik treaties were basically the result of military necessity and German prodding.

Developments in Bosnia, too, were related to the recent activities of the Herzegovinian Chetnik leaders. In May talks with German intelligence officers in Dubrovnik, Jevdjević was asked whether he would cooperate with the Axis authorities in their efforts to pacify Bosnia.[78] In spite of Jevdjević's efforts to cast himself as the representative of the Bosnian Serbs, most of the latter groups came to terms with Zagreb for local reasons. They were rewarded in June with the official establishment of a Croatian Orthodox church (Hrvatska Pravoslavna Crkva) and were soon able to conclude a broader agreement with Pavelić's régime which divided large parts of Bosnia into spheres of influence, giving the Chetniks a measure of authority in the predominantly Serb districts and obliging the Croatian armed forces to provide them with supplies.[79]

The Chetnik treaties probably did little more than officially sanction the fluid and chaotic situation that persisted in those parts of Bosnia outside the Italian occupation zone. The Serb armed formations, although several probably considered Jevdjević to be their moral leader, lacked any real leadership, were widely dispersed geographically, and were quite small numerically. Drenović, the first and best known of the Bosnian Chetnik collaborators, was credited with an armed following of about 350 in the spring and only 600 in June.[80] Armed collaboration between the Bosnian Chetniks and the Croatian armed forces was rare,[81] and even the general armistice appeared to many to be temporary at best.[82] Serb political spokesmen and Chetnik officers outside of the

[78] Deutsche Gesandtschaft in Agram to Aus. Amt/Pol. IV, "Telegramm N. 955 vom 13. Mai 1942," 13 May 1942, *T-120*, roll 1141, frame 2027/444153; Nucleo "I" Sarajevo to Comando 2. Armata, 26 May 1942, *T-821*, roll 66, frame 48. Jevdjević described his meeting with the Germans in a letter to Mihailović of 9 May, cited by Petar Kačavenda, "Kriza Četničkog Pokreta Draže Mihailovica u drugoj polovini 1942 godine," *Istorija Radničkog Pokreta* 1 (1965):276.

[79] Broszat and Martin Ladislas Hory, *Der Kroatische Ustascha Staat (1941–1945)* (Stuttgart: Deutsche Verlags-Anstalt, 1964), p. 96; Kačavenda, "Kriza Četničkog Pokreta," p. 274; Stato Independente Croata/Quartiere Generale del Poglavnik (Kvaternik), "Procedimento nei riguardi dei cetnici," 26 June 1942, *T-821*, roll 400, frames 560–63.

[80] Report of Staff of Bosanska Krajina National Liberation Partisan Detachments, 11 June 1942, *Zbornik*, vol. 4, 5, no. 76; Comando 2. Armata/Ufficio I, "Notiziario A. C. del 13 giugno 1942," 13 June 1942, *T-821*, roll 448, frame 213.

[81] One example was the joint action in early June to retake Prijedor from the Partisans.

[82] For an Italian assessment of the situation in Bosnia, see Comando VI. Corpo

Croatian-administered parts of Bosnia who attempted to intervene in any way apparently had little success. Officers near Foča, for example, had several skirmishes with Ustaši units in June,[83] and at Mostar, Herzegovina, Jevdjević had to seek Italian protection when some Croatian military personnel entered the "demilitarized" third zone and threatened his life.[84] By the middle of 1942, when Mihailović and his delegates were making their first serious efforts to assert some sort of influence over the Chetniks in the western half of former Yugoslavia, their greatest difficulties were with the confusing array of local Serb bands in Bosnia.

MONTENEGRO

Along with Herzegovina Montenegro became a major Chetnik stronghold in 1942 and a source of troops for Mihailović in the struggles of 1943. Unlike the Chetnik groups in the Italian-occupied parts of Independent Croatia, however, the Montenegrin organization was always controlled by officers rather than civilian notables, and it emerged as a result of their initiative rather than from widespread popular appeals for protection and pacification. The Italian governor, Pirzio-Biroli, and the commanders of the Ninth Army Corps in Montenegro, always suspicious of native armed movements with any sort of Serb ties, nonetheless arrived at an easy accommodation with the officers, basically because they could not by themselves control the countryside and eastern portions of the protectorate and because they recognized that they could not rely exclusively on the support of the weak separatist movement.

In Montenegro early in 1942 a significant shift in the occupation system took place suddenly, and a collaborationist officers' movement appeared just as quickly. The immediate cause was not the activity of Mihailović's delegates, Lašić and Djurišić, but rather the final collapse of the Partisan-dominated rebel movement and the sudden emergence of the resistance-leader-turned-collaborator Colonel Bajo Stanišić. In early February he withdrew two units from the rebel ring surrounding Danilovgrad, permitting the Italians to break out and overcome the Partisans.[85] Stanišić's detachments not only helped the Italians enter

d'Armata to Comando 2. Armata, "Relazione mensile," 25 May 1942, *T-821*, roll 400, frame 718.

[83] Roatta to R. Missione Militare Italiana a Zagabria, "N. 9733 del 2 giugno 1942," 2 June 1942, *T-821*, roll 66, frame 269; Comando VI. Corpo d'Armata to Comando 2. Armata, "N. 10341 del 23 giugno 1942," 23 June 1942, *T-821*, roll 53, frame 783.

[84] Comando VI. Corpo d'Armata to Comando 2. Armata, "Divieto a reparti ustascie di scendere nella terza zona," 21 May 1942, *T-821*, roll 53, frame 644; Comando VI. Corpo d'Armata to Comando 2. Armata, "Battaglione ustascia a Mostar," 22 May 1942, *T-821*, roll 53, frame 598.

[85] Report of C.P.Y. Provincial Committee of Montenegro, Boka, and the Sandžak, 13 February 1942, *Zbornik*, vol. 3, 2, no. 70.

nearby Nikšić but soon constituted themselves the Montenegrin National Army.[86] Although he behaved at first like a particularly ambitious warlord and even claimed to be the Chetnik commander for Herzegovina, as well as Montenegro, Stanišić's immediate arrangement with the Italians was basically a local accommodation. On 20 February he sent one of his agents to the Italian garrison at Danilovgrad to discuss the terms of the "national organization" in that area [87] and by the end of the month was receiving supplies from General Mentasti's Ninth Army Corps depots.

While he laid the groundwork for his local collaboration with the Italians, Stanišić began to link his activities to those of other officers and soon was acting in some sort of concert with other principal Montenegrin Chetniks. In late February, for example, he met with a delegation from the recently formed Montenegrin National Committee, and when he sent a request to the Italians for supplies he included the suggestion that the Committee be permitted to carry on its activities in specific parts of Montenegro.[88] The officers' committee, recently formed in Podgorica under the leadership of General Blago Djukanović,[89] was maneuvering for an accommodation with the Italians through Stanišić and with Mihailović's personal approval.[90] During the next few months, Stanišić's followers fought beside the Italians around Nikšić; in the Kolašin sector one of Mihailović's first delegate-officers, Captain Djurišić, turned openly against the Partisans and routed their last sizeable unit in Montenegro, the Durmitor detachment, in May.[91]

The Montenegrin officers, then, proved themselves to be useful militarily against the Partisans before they sought a general "political" arrangement with the Italians. Also, in order to swell their own ranks and mask the predominantly pro-Yugoslav and pro-Mihailović orientation of their leaders, they agreed to work with the Montenegrin sepa-

[86] Staff of Nikšić National Liberation Partisan Detachment to Staff of the Grahovo battalion, 18 February 1942, *ibid.*, no. 84; communication of Staff of Nikšić National Liberation Partisan Detachment, 26 February 1942, *ibid.*, no. 100.

[87] Report of Spiro Stojanović to command of Zeta [Chetnik] detachment, 12 December 1942, *ibid.*, 4, no. 232.

[88] Report of delegates of Montenegrin Chetnik Committee to General Luigi Mentasti, commander of occupation troops in Montenegro, 26 February 1942, *ibid.*, no. 54.

[89] Dr. Savo Radović, n.d., *Dokumenti o Izdajstvu Draže Mihailovića*, no. 10.

[90] *Ibid.* Mihailović ordered one of his agents, Rilja Piletić, to join Stanišić, probably in late February or early March.

[91] Boško Agram to Bajo Stanišić, 5 May 1942, *Dokumenti o Izdajstvu Draže Mihailovića*, no. 41; Bajo Sekulić to Durmitor National Liberation Partisan Detachment, 27 February 1942, *Zbornik*, vol. 3, 4, no. 57; report of Bjelopolje National Liberation Partisan Detachment, 9 April 1942, *ibid.*, no. 86; Obrad Cicmil, *Durmitorski NOP Odred i njegova Područije (1941–1945)* (The territory of the Durmitor National Liberation Partisan Detachment [1941–1945]) (Belgrade: Vojnoizdavački Zavod, 1966), pp. 157–64.

ratist Krsto Popović. With the Partisan cause in Montenegro in full retreat, the officers' armed groups filled a void, especially in the central and eastern parts of the province, and their numbers grew rapidly. In the western coastal sector, the "federalist" bands were suddenly allies of the Chetniks. In the east, Djurišić had about fifteen hundred men in February but after overcoming Partisan resistance was in a position to expand his following by mobilizing freely in the towns and countryside. In addition, according to Communist sources, the Chetniks in Montenegro received numerous last-minute deserters from the Partisans.[92]

In midsummer, the principal officers gave formal shape to these developments when they met at Cetinje, recognized General Djukanović as the National Committee's chief intermediary with the Italians, and sorted out spheres of influence among the field commanders. Roughly speaking, Popović was granted supremacy in the west, Stanišić took the central regions, and Djurišić, with the most openly pro-Mihailović background, received the remote eastern part of Montenegro.[93] On 24 July 1942 Djukanović, head of the seventeen-member Montenegrin Nationalist Committee at Cetinje, and Pirzio-Biroli signed a final agreement whereby the Italians sanctioned the formation of the Montenegrin Flying Detachments, to be divided into three groups commanded by Popović, Stanišić and Djurišić and numbering no more than fifteen hundred troops each.[94]

Because the Italians were anxious to keep their troop commitment in the protectorate as low as possible, especially after disorders in Albania began to assume serious dimensions,[95] the Chetniks in Montenegro were able, far more successfully than the officers' movement anywhere else in former Yugoslavia, to develop into something of a parallel occupation and police force. As far as the Italians were concerned, the Chetniks provided a convenient means of supervising the protectorate's more inaccessible rural and mountainous areas and acted as a useful buffer between the Ninth Army and the civilian population by carrying out reprisals against those implicated in the revolt. The officers, on the other

---

[92] Milovan Djilas to Supreme Staff of Yugoslav National Liberation Partisan Detachments, 22 April 1942, *Zbornik*, vol. 3, 4, no. 91; Staff of Montenegrin-Sandžak National Liberation Partisan Detachments, 1 March 1942, *ibid.*, no. 64; Cicmil, *Durmitorski NOP Odred*, pp. 141, 186.

[93] Article in pro-Chetnik *Glas Crnogorca*, 30 May 1942, in *Dokumenti o Izdajstvu Draže Mihailovića*, p. 84.

[94] Treaty between the Chetnik Committee and the governor of Montenegro, 24 July 1942, *Zbornik*, vol. 3, 4, no. 219; the main provisions of this accord are also described in Ministero degli Affari Esteri/Gab. A. P., "Appunto per l'Ecc. il Ministro," 21 January 1943, *T-821*, roll 247, frame 736.

[95] For the development of the Albanian resistance in 1942, see Nina D. Smirnova, *Obrazovanie Narodnoi Respubliki Albanii (1939–1946)* (The formation of the Albanian People's Republic, [1939–1946]) (Moscow: Izdatel'stvo Akademii Nauk, 1960), pp. 77–92.

hand, were often given almost a free hand in village political affairs, had an excuse to enlarge their armed followings, and could engage openly in competition for spheres of influence.

Stanišić, for example, went out of his way to demonstrate the sincerity of his about-face in order to gain more leverage and toleration from the Italians. In May his followers announced a strict policy of punishing everyone who took part in the "bloody" and "a-national" uprising of the previous summer [96] and filled Chetnik detention camps with all sorts of real or supposed Partisan sympathizers.[97] In June, Stanišić gave orders that peasants found guilty of having supplied the Partisans with food were to be shot immediately.[98] At Nikšić they turned over prisoners to the Italians to be shot and had instructions to refrain from making arrests without previously consulting the local Carabinieri.

In return for this sort of cooperation, Stanišić was able to expand his detachments, usually by negotiating with the Italians at the division level for the absorption of gendarme units by his legalized Chetniks.[99] Somewhat less openly, he tried to encroach on the west Montenegrin "sphere" of his supposed ally, General Popović, by sending agents into the Kotor area secretly,[100] and he even laid claim to at least moral leadership over the nationalist formations in Herzegovina, where Jevdjević and Samardžić had already established themselves as the principal Chetnik spokesmen. Colonel Stanišić, therefore, was at the same time an aggressive collaborator, an officer who wholeheartedly supported the anti-Partisan terror in 1942, something of a local warlord, always trying to increase his armed following and sphere of activity, and finally, a former rebel leader with Chetnik ties who could turn against the occupation at an opportune moment under Mihailović's command.

In eastern Montenegro, where the Italians had relatively few occupation units, Djurišić had even more freedom to combine collaboration with actions dictated by the Chetnik officers' most ambitious goals. Djurišić had the final say in the political affairs of the smaller villages, and at the request of the Italians he also appointed "nationalist com-

[96] Boško Agram to Bajo Stanišić, May 22, 1942, *Dokumenti o Izdajstvu Draže Mihailovića*, no. 43.

[97] Jakov Jovović to Bajo Stanišić, 30 May 1942, *ibid.*, no. 88.

[98] Order of commander of Nikšić gendarme units (Captain Petar Drasković), 26 June 1942, *Zbornik*, vol. 3, 4, no. 213; order of Chetnik commander at Nikšić, 26 August 1942, *ibid.*, no. 224.

[99] Command of the division "Ferrara" to the Nationalist command at the Ostrog monastery, 21 August 1942, *Dokumenti o Izdajstvu Draže Mihailovića*, no. 52; Supreme National Command (Djukanović) to commander of the Zeta Flying Detachment (Stanišić), 8 September 1942, *ibid.*, no. 52.

[100] Dušan Živković, *Boka Kotorska i Pastrovici u Narodnooslobodilačkoj Borbi* (Kotor and Pastrovici in the national liberation struggle) (Belgrade: "Vojno Delo," 1964), pp. 162–63.

mittees" in the larger cities, like Kolašin, Berane, Andrijevica, and Prijepolje.[101] This did not mean that his troops were interested mainly in pacification, for, unlike Stanišić, whose main activity was carrying out reprisals against suspect civilians, Djurišić concentrated on an aggressive policy toward the whole neighboring Muslim population, for the most part in the Sandžak. To some degree, the atrocities perpetrated by the pro-Mihailović officers were an extreme reflection of the anti-Muslim component of Serb nationalism represented by the Chetniks. Also, it should be recalled that both the Germans and the Ustaši had made appeals to the Muslims' anti-Serb sentiments in 1941 [102] and that the Italians had employed Albanian Muslim auxiliary formations to aid in the suppression of the Montenegrin revolt. The Muslims of the Sandžak, Kosovo-Metohija, and Albania were the traditional and immediate enemies of the Montenegrin Serb nationalists. Probably even more important, unlike the Chetniks' other domestic opponents, the Croatian Ustaši and the Partisans, these Muslims were vulnerable.

By the fall of 1941, especially after the Germans evacuated Novi Pazar in early October, practically all of the Sandžak fell under the nominal control of the Italians but in fact became easy prey for Serb armed bands operating in southwest Serbia and eastern Montenegro.[103] The Italians steadfastly rejected offers from Nedić to employ collaborationist bands from Serbia in the Sandžak [104] but were apparently willing to tolerate anything carried out by their own "Montenegrin Nationalist" formations. Djurišić, of course, in addition to being aligned with Djukanović's committee in Cetinje, was a Mihailović delegate who was at least as loyal to the Serb Chetniks as he was to the organization of collaborationist Montenegrin officers. From the middle of 1942, the main thrust of his activities consisted of establishing a dominant position in the Sandžak in order to create a link between the Montenegrin and Serb officers' detachments and of carrying out a policy of terror against the Muslim civilian population.[105] Djurišić, then, was probably

[101] Command of the division "Venezia" to Captain Paolo Giurisic, 5 May 1942, *Dokumenti o Izdajstvu Draže Mihailovića*, no. 11.

[102] In April 1941 a German general had promised the Muslims and Albanians that the occupation regime would follow an exclusively pro-Muslim, Shiptar, and Catholic line and recolonize the Sandžak Serbs in Serbia. In May the Ustaši even sent a gendarme batallion from Sarajevo to the Sandžak wearing fezzes. Mirko Čuković, *Sandžak: Srbija u Narodnooslobodilačkoj Borbi* (The Sandžak: Serbia in the national liberation struggle) (Belgrade: Prosveta, 1964), pp. 57–59.

[103] Comando VI. Corpo d'Armata to Comando 2. Armata, "N. 3425 del 12 ottobre 1941," 12 October 1941, *T-821*, roll 232, frame 916.

[104] Nedić's most recent proposal, made in June 1942, was immediately turned down by Cavallero. Comando Supremo to Ministero Affari Esteri, "Proposte da parte serba di collaborazione nella lotta contro il comunismo," 8 June 1942, *T-821*, roll 53, frames 1073–74.

[105] Stato Maggiore R. Esercito/SIE, "N. 0548 del 25 luglio 1942," 25 July 1942, *T-821*,

the most striking example of a military leader who was really a double agent, cooperating with the Italians in order to gain toleration and a sphere of action which he used for ends directed by Mihailović and which had little to do with a policy of normalization.

SERBIA

The emergence of the officer-degelate Djurišić indicates that at least some of the Chetnik leaders in the western half of former Yugoslavia not only made arrangements to suit local needs but tried to link their activities with what remained of Mihailović's parent but now routed Chetnik organization in Serbia. From the end of 1941 until the very end of the war, the striking fact about Serbia, in contrast to the remainder of Yugoslavia, was that there was very little serious resistance activity carried out by either the Chetniks or the Partisans. Nevertheless, although Mihailović and the officers who escaped capture and remained in Serbia had practically no armed following left, the Chetniks in rump Serbia did keep the skeleton of the organization intact and were able, in fact, to bring about a partial recovery in 1942. This was basically the result of a stalemate: the Germans were determined not to compromise with Mihailović's followers,[106] and the Chetniks both renounced open anti-Axis action and "disappeared" by posing as loyal components of the Nedić administration.

During the first third of 1942, the Germans in Belgrade, although excessively suspicious of Mihailović and even Pećanac,[107] lacked sufficient military means to patrol the countryside adequately, were mainly preoccupied with affairs in eastern Bosnia, and therefore could not undertake actions against what remained of Mihailović's organization. Contrary to what the Germans consistently supposed, however, the Chetniks had no intention of resuming an armed rebellion in the spring. They were more concerned with maintaining the organization and surviving the inevitable reprisals by dissolving the independent armed movement and attaching themselves to Nedić's regional administration and police forces. In a real sense, Mihailović probably had little choice in the matter;

---

roll 347, frame 810. A rather dubious short work, written by Serb émigrés who were in some way associated with Nedić's Volunteer Corps, even asserts that Djurišić traveled to Belgrade to discuss anti-Partisan strategy with Nedić and Ljotić and asked them for supplies. "Anon.," *Srpski Dobrovoljci* (The Serb volunteers) (Munich: Iskra, 1966), pp. 41–42.

[106] For General Bader's efforts to dictate a hard anti-Chetnik strategy to the wavering Nedić, see Kdr. Gen. in Serbien, "Zur Besprechung General Bader mit Ministerpräsident Nedic," 16 December 1941, *T-501*, roll 256, frames 1145–46.

[107] For example, see Benzler to Aus. Amt., "N. 114 vom 30.1.1942," 30 January 1942, *ADAP*, E, vol. 1, no. 185; Chef der Militärverwaltung Südost, "Abschlussbericht," [?] 1945, *T-501*, roll 264, frame 230.

several unit leaders had joined the forces of Nedić and Pećanac in late 1941 in order to escape German raids. Viewed from another perspective, however, this transformation of the Chetnik movement in Serbia, which Mihailović probably merely sanctioned rather than initiated, was basically a return to his original plan of building up an organization capable of carrying out limited, mainly sabotage, resistance activities and, more important, ready to seize administrative power quickly at the end of the war.

The revival of the Chetnik organization in Serbia was somewhat similar to the emergence of the officers in Montenegro, based on a small number of key "double agents," but because there were no formal accords between the Chetniks and the Nedić administration, the whole process of infiltration is very difficult to follow precisely.[108] It seems certain that several of the armed detachments operating in the rural areas and along the frontiers of rump Serbia were heavily infiltrated by former Mihailović Chetniks, although these formations were usually "legalized" Chetniks. As in the previous year, the Chetniks were strongest in western Serbia and in the area bordering on the Sandžak, where they maintained contact with the Montenegrins under Djurišić.

It is interesting to note that in Serbia, where German influence was unchallenged, there is evidence that the Italian legation in Belgrade, probably benefiting from Roatta and Pirzio-Biroli's recent policies of accommodation with Serb nationalists, had the best information on the Chetnik organization in Serbia. Sometime in June 1942 it was able to establish ties with an armed group, numbering about fifteen hundred and led by a certain Captain Matić, which "patrolled" an area along the Drina River. Through Matić, the Italians discovered that Nedić's prefect in Pozarevac, former Lieutenant-Colonel Nikola Kalabić, was Mihailović's chief representative in western Serbia.[109] Kalabić probably provided official protection for Matić's group, which avoided provoking the Germans, while another Chetnik, the *vojvoda* Gordić, was well enough supplied to send them food regularly. The Mihailović movement also had allies in the Nedić administration in Belgrade; again through Matić, the

---

[108] Chetnik sources throw no light on this period. The Germans lacked solid information on the Mihailović movement in Serbia until the late summer of 1942, when they succeeded in intercepting and decoding Chetnik radio messages. A number of subsequent developments, though, such as the sabotage work on the rail lines, indicate that Mihailović had been quite successful at penetrating the Nedić administration throughout the first half of 1942.

[109] Ministero degli Affari Esteri/Gabinetto AP (Croazia) to Commando Supremo/SIM, "Azione e organizzazione di Draza Mihailovic nei territori ex-jugoslavi," 20 July 1942, *T-821,* roll 347, frames 814–17; Ministero degli Affari Esteri/Gabinetto AP (Croazia) to Comando Supremo, "Notizie circa la situazione in Serbia, Bosnia e Montenegro," 3 August 1942, *T-821,* roll 347, frame 799.

Italians discovered the names of the Chetnik agents attached to the gendarme forces in Belgrade and organized by Captain Sassa Mihailović, a member of the Serb State Guard intelligence division.

In July, however, the Germans made a major breakthrough: they succeeded in intercepting and decoding Chetnik radio messages. The officers' movement, as it turned out, had recovered slowly and on a makeshift basis and consisted mainly of a group of officers and pro-Mihailović agents, like Kalabić and Sassa Mihailović, who were working from within Nedić's police and military organizations in order to feed information to and offer protection for other officers who remained in remote areas and usually lacked significant armed followings.[110] Matić, for example, remained close to the Drina River, probably so that he could seek safety in eastern Bosnia or the Sandžak in the event of a German raid, while Captain Račić stayed in northwestern Serbia and Major Keserović in the southwest. The officers had no means to fight and obviously felt that the best strategy was to preserve their weak position through infiltration and to wait for Axis reverses on other fronts to force Hitler to relax his grip on Serbia. Mihailović certainly shared this defensive mood and at the end of March 1942 even instructed that a temporary armistice be offered to Nedić.[111] The Germans and Nedić rejected the Chetnik proposal, but by the middle of the year Mihailović's steady refusal to act against the occupation regime induced Belgrade to postpone projects for the disarmament of all suspect armed formations.[112]

By the middle of the year, then, the Chetniks in Serbia had evolved into essentially an underground organization which could be potentially useful to Mihailović and the Allies but which for the time being was paralyzed. The Germans as yet gave no indication, in spite of the growing cooperation between Serb nationalists and the Italians, that they were prepared to come to terms even with individual former Chetniks and that, with a better idea now of the identity of the officer infiltrators, they were preparing to eliminate the organization. Raids into the hilly and remote parts of western Serbia—for example, the 717th division's small cleaning-up action in the Kopaonik Mountains in August—proved fruitless, however, because the weak officer groups fled without attempting to resist.[113] On the other hand, Mihailović by this time had far greater

---

[110] Kdr. Gen. in Serbien/Kommand der Nachrichten Aufklärung 4, "N. 806/42," 11 September 1942, T-312, roll 470, frames 8060380–86.

[111] Benzler to Aus. Amt./Pol. IV, "Telegramm N. 452 vom 31.3.1942," 31 March 1942, T-120, roll 200, frames 230/152576–77.

[112] Local police officials had information that Mihailović had ordered his subordinates in Serbia to avoid clashes with the Germans and Nedić's troops. District Prefecture of Kraljevo to Nedić, "N. 7/42 of 10.6.1942," 10 June 1942, Dokumenti o Izdajstvu Draže Mihailovića, no. 659.

[113] Wehrmachtbefehlshaber Südost/Ia, "Tätigkeitsbericht für die Zeit vom 1.–31.8 1942," 3 August 1942 (Anlage 1), T-311, roll 175, frame 338.

possibilities with the Chetnik formations in the Italian zone; as far as Serbia was concerned, he was in a good position to engage in sabotage against the roads and rail lines running to Greece but would do so at the risk of losing the whole organization to German reprisals. In Serbia, aggressively anti-Axis measures would cost the Chetniks dearly; in the western half of former Yugoslavia, an uncoordinated occupation system, toleration and supplies from the Italians, and competition from the Partisans provided Mihailović and the officers with far more opportunities and more urgent tasks.

V

THE DILEMMA
OF TACTICAL
COLLABORATION

:

By the middle of 1942 the geographical focus of the resistance in Yugoslavia, its political orientation, and the distribution of occupation spheres had changed drastically from the previous summer and fall. Rebel activity had all but ceased in Serbia and Montenegro and now was confined to Independent Croatia, especially western Bosnia; instead of representing a hasty and strained alliance of all anti-Axis elements, the resistance was now predominantly a Partisan effort. The occupation system created by the treaties of May 1941 had broken down due to competition over zones of influence, disputes over policies towards the civilian populations, and some notable failures to deal with the anarchy and civil war in Croatia. In the western half of former Yugoslavia, the Italians had extended their occupation zone dramatically, mainly in opposition to the Croatian Ustaši, and gave several indications of pursuing a basically pro-Serb policy. This had the effect of hastening the falling out between the non-Communist Serb nationalists and the Partisans; the result of such divisions was usually to pit former Yugoslav officers and local Serb notables against the Communist party leaders. As a result of these changes, the parent Chetnik movement, dominated by Mihailović and his fellow officers and based in Serbia, became a weak underground

90

organization; in Independent Croatia and Montenegro, Italian policies and the initiative of officers and civilian intermediaries had conspired to create a whole web of armed movements, which were anti-Partisan collaborationist, usually at odds with the Ustaši government and the non-Serb civilian populations and at least potential allies of a revived Mihailović movement.

After the end of 1941, General Mihailović, unlike Tito, had no sizeable armed following under his immediate command but had to organize somehow the confusing assortment of bands commanded by the Montenegrin officers and the local chiefs in Bosnia and Herzegovina. This involved the difficult tasks of imposing some form of military organization capable of coordinating the activities of the various Serb groups and establishing a common adherence of unit leaders to Mihailović's personal authority and long-range goals. As early as the beginning of 1942, when he made his first efforts to lay the groundwork for the organization of the Montenegrin Chetniks, he stressed his perference for the command of active and reserve officers rather than local civilian notables and prescribed that each detachment (*odred*) consist of three bands or companies (*četa*); mobile fighting units would include only men under the age of thirty; older recruits would train themselves for sabotage warfare and take care of local police functions.[1] These instructions were, almost needless to say, somewhat unrealistic since the Montenegrin officers had not yet put together a well-organized movement and most of the formations in Italian-occupied Croatia were led by civilians.

As regards immediate strategic guidelines, Mihailović's staff was at first hampered by their ignorance of the situation in western Yugoslavia and was thoroughly inconsistent. In his important instructions to the Montenegrins Lašić and Djurišić of December 1941, Mihailović closed with an exhortation to "attack, kill and sabotage the occupation troops with the slogan 'Death to the Occupiers' "[2] but in January urged them to avoid clashes with the Germans, Italians, and Partisans. In February Mihailović supported and sanctioned Stanišić's move toward active anti-Partisan collaboration, but by this time the Partisans were on the verge of complete collapse in Montenegro and Mihailović was almost certainly

---

[1] Command of Chetnik Detachments of Yugoslavian Army/Mountain Staff (Mihailović), "Instructions for Carrying out Mobilization," 7 January 1942, *Dokumenti o Izdajstvu Draže Mihailovića,* no. 9. Another order, dated 5 February 1942, which also deals with measures to be taken for the organization of the Chetnik formations in Montenegro, is cited by Dušan Živković, *Boka Kotorska i Paštrovići u Narodnooslobodilačkoj Borbi* (Belgrade: Vojno Delo, 1964).

[2] As indicated previously, this document can be found in the collection of evidence used during the Chetnik trials after the war (*Dokumenti o Izdajstvu Draže Mihailovića*), in the *Zbornik* series, and in the Italian microfilmed documents. R. Missione Militare Italiana in Croazia to Comando Supremo, "Disposizioni emanate dal capo cetnico, Generale Draza Mihailović," 16 July 1942, *T-821,* roll 347, frame 822.

following events rather than initiating them. According to Chetnik sources, he was not successful in establishing direct ties with Djukanović and Jevdjević until late spring, and when he wrote them in late April, he refused to give precise orders for their next course of action because he lacked contacts with their formations and, therefore, adequate information on the confusing events in the western provinces.[3]

Until the middle of 1942, Mihailović was a general without a fighting organization in Serbia and still lacked control over developments in the rest of Yugoslavia. Nonetheless, the Chetnik staff thought they could rebuild the movement by co-opting the collaborationist formations and, with Allied recognition and support, were certain of Germany's ultimate defeat and the reconstruction of Yugoslavia along Serb nationalist lines. The postwar goals of the Chetniks, as Mihailović saw them in December 1941, bore no relation to what the weak officers' movement could hope to accomplish in the immediate future and went far beyond a restoration of the political *status quo ante bellum*. In his orders to Lašić and Djurišić, he outlined an ambitious set of aims which combined his expected anti-Communist and pro-monarchic orientation with plans for territorial adjustments and domestic reconstruction inspired by both Greater Yugo-slav and the most extreme sort of Greater Serb passions. Reminding the Montenegrins that he was relying for final victory on the aid of "the great democracies, England, America, Russia and China," he estab-lished as the Chetnik long-range program:

1. the struggle for the freedom of all our people under the scepter of his Majesty King Peter II;
2. the creation within a Greater Yugoslavia of a Greater Serbia, ethnically pure, which will include Serbia, Montenegro, Bosnia, Herzegovina, Syrmia, Banat, and Bačka;
3. the struggle for the annexation to our state of all Slavic territories ruled by the Italians and Germans (Trieste, Gorizia, Istria, Carniola);
4. the removal from the state territory of all minorities and a-national elements;
5. the creation of a common frontier between Serbia and Slovenia and Serbia and Montenegro by removing from the Sandžak all the Muslims and from Bosnia-Herzegovina the Muslims and Croats;
6. the punishment of all the Ustaši and those Muslims who have in these tragic days pitilessly destroyed our people;
7. the punishment of everyone guilty for the April catastrophe;
8. the colonization of those areas purged of minorities and a-national elements with Montenegrins.[4]

[3] Radmilo Grdjić, *Knjiga o Draži*, vol. 1 (Windsor, Canada: Srpska Narodna Odbrana, 1956), pp. 115–16.
[4] R. Missione Militare Italiana in Croazia to Comando Supremo, "Disposizioni emanate dal capo cetnico, Gernerale Draza Mihailovic," 16 July 1942, *T-821*, roll 347, frame 822.

Mihailović and his staff assumed that the Axis Powers would lose the war, but, before that happened, the officers had to eliminate or at least reduce drastically the influence of the Partisan resistance and take all measures necessary to protect the Serbs, especially those in Independent Croatia, from the ravages of Axis and Ustaši reprisals. Collaboration with the Italians served both of these ends, yet there was always the danger that the Serb nationalist formations would gradually be reduced to the level of police formations attached to the occupation forces, that the tactic of collaboration would lead to a weakening of the Chetnik political position in London, or even that the Italians would soon drop out of the war, thus isolating the Chetniks. In any event, Mihailović's long-range program, not to mention the events in Serbia of 1941, placed an immediate priority on a Partisan defeat; moreover, the spontaneously formed and often civilian-led Serb nationalist bands in western Yugoslavia were already bound to an anti-Communist line, and even those Chetniks who were enthusiastic about resisting the Ustaši often had to cooperate, at least formally with the occupation powers' anti-Partisan measures.

Mihailović, then, had to establish his own authority over collaborationist bands without frightening the Germans and Italians and, so that their cooperation with the occupation order would be temporary, had to bring about the rapid collapse of Tito's Partisan republic in western Bosnia. The Chetnik officers felt compelled to collaborate, but only selectively and on their own terms, and they were just as determined to prepare to turn against the Axis at the right moment. This effort would perhaps take place in the event of an Italian exit from the war or a Partisan collapse, for the Germans would then be in a position to wage an unobstructed struggle against the officers; it would certainly take place if the Allies launched an amphibious operation in the Balkans. In the meantime, Mihailović and his staff officers had to take drastic measures to coordinate and direct the activities of the several armed formations so that collaboration served their ends and so that they would be in a position to transform the Chetniks suddenly into a resistance force as soon as they felt events justified a general uprising.

These efforts began to show results by midsummer of 1942. In April Radmilo Grdjić, a close collaborator with Jevdjević and intermediary with Roatta, visited Trifunović in Split and General Djukanović in Cetinje and won their agreement to place their formations under Mihailović's control. Chetnik headquarters, however, had practically no ties with the formation leaders themselves, except probably Djurišić, and, a few months later, Mihailović decided to do more than rely on couriers and letters, and prepared for a personal encounter with the Herzegovinian leaders.

The immediate aim of these contacts was to bring about a working alliance between the Herzegovinian civilian spokesmen and the Montenegrin officers. Mihailović, whose ties with the Montenegrins were closer, must have had some role in arranging a meeting between Trifunović and Colonel Stanišić in mid-July at Gačko, Herzegovina; [5] he certainly sent a permanent personal delegate, Petar Baćović, for the purpose of maintaining continuous contact with Jevdjević and Trifunović.[6] About a week after the meeting with Stanišić, Mihailović himself slipped over the Montenegrin border and presided over a two-day conference at Avtovac, Herzegovina, with Jevdjević and Trifunović.[7]

Although the only source for this meeting is an account of what the Herzegovinian leaders told the Italians about it, it is possible by examining this and other evidence to situate Mihailović's actions in an intelligible pattern of Chetnik strategy. His encounter with Jevdjević and Trifunović and his subsequent approval of their collaborationist policies make it clear that he was fully aware of and in agreement with the temporary arrangements with the Italian command in Yugoslavia.[8] There is no reason to believe that Mihailović had altered in any serious way the postwar aims of the Chetnik movement as given to Lašić and Djurišić in December 1941. On 23 July, in fact, the second day of the Mihailović conference, Jevdjević and Trifunović left for nearby Trebinje, conferred with Radmilo Grdjić and another of the Chetnik political agents, Milan Šantić, and established as their ultimate goals and immediate strategy: (1) the creation of Greater Serbia; (2) the destruction of the Partisans; (3) the removal of the Catholics and Muslims; (4) nonrecognition of Croatia; (5) no collaboration with the Germans; and (6) tempo-

---

[5] Stato Maggiore R. Esercito/SIE, "Montenegro-Contatti di capi cetnici," 10 August 1942, *T-821*, roll 347, frames 795–96.

[6] Petar Kačavenda ("Kriza Četničkog Pokreta Draže Mihailovića u drugoj polovini 1942 godine," *Istorija Radničkog Pokreta* 1 [1965]: 260) quotes a letter, taken from *Izdajnik i Ratni Zločinats Draža Mihailović pred Sudom* (Belgrade: n.p., 1946), p. 435, which describes the Baćović mission.

[7] The source for this meeting is a German translation of an Italian intelligence report to the Foreign Office in Rome: Vittorio Castellani (representative of Ministry of Foreign Affairs at Second Army headquarters) to Königliche Ministerium Aus. Angeleg, "Treffen des serbischen Führer mit Draza Mihailovic und seine Erklärung," 23 August 1942, *T-821*, roll 252, frames 297–300.

[8] This, of course, is stoutly denied in all the pro-Chetnik literature, most of it written right after the war and primarily designed to rehabilitate Mihailović after his trial. Often the argument is that Mihailović was vaguely aware of the collaboration of his supporters but was unable to prevent it since he had no control over them. In other instances the denials are even more extreme. For example, John Plamenatz, *The Case of General Mihailović* (Gloucester: John Bellows, 1944), writes that "though Mihailović was in occasional contact with the Serbs in Dalmatia, there is no evidence that he urged them to get arms from the Italians to fight the Partisans," (p. 18) and that "Mihailović, however, never sought Italian help against the Partisans, neither directly nor through subordinates, nor did he advise anyone else to do so" (p. 19).

rary collaboration with the Italians for weapons, munitions, and food.[9]

Mihailović's immediate strategy was based on a selective and tactical sort of collaboration, a refusal to attempt arrangements with the Germans, and, most important, a determination to carry on parallel civil wars against both the Partisans and the Chetniks' national enemies. The officer leadership, as Serb nationalists, not only encouraged the recurrent outrages committed by the armed formations against the Croats and Muslims as a part of general policy and in a spirit of revenge for everything the Serb civilians had suffered but also were convinced in the middle of 1942 that they were about to be faced with a new wave of Ustaši violence. Jevdjević and Trifunović, in a rather startling admission to the Italians, related that Mihailović was considering evacuating the Serb civilians from Herzegovina to Montenegro and moving Montenegrin Chetniks north to meet the Ustaši. The basic reason for this strategy was that the Serb nationalists and Mihailović had by then discovered that the Italian anti-Ustaši policies in Yugoslavia were being revised and that the Second Army had already agreed to restore a large part of occupied Croatia to Zagreb's control.[10] The Italian decision, confirmed by an agreement signed with the Croatian government on 19 June, to withdraw practically all the Second Army occupation troops from the third zone was part of a general retreat from their earlier attempts to establish predominant influence in Independent Croatia and reflected Rome's growing concern over the mounting disorders in Slovenia and Dalmatia.

The meeting between Mihailović and the Herzegovinian Chetnik leaders came shortly after the announcement of the shift in occupation zones, which the officers understandably thought would work to their disadvantage by contracting the area in which they enjoyed Italian toleration. Moreover, underestimating the disintegration of the Croatian armed and police forces,[11] the Chetniks, as indicated by Mihailović's frantic pro-

[9] The source for this meeting is a report by the German consulate in Sarajevo. The program outlined above agrees with Mihailović's earlier instructions and has to be taken seriously because the Germans at Sarajevo had established ties with Jevdjević in May and could have gotten this information through collaborationist Chetniks, like the group led by Savo Derekonja, in the vicinity of the Bosnian capital. Deutsche Konsulat in Sarajevo to Deutsche Gesandtschaft in Zagreb, "Milan Santić vor Cetnici-Führern in Trebinje," 20 August 1942, T-501, roll 265, frame 1026.

[10] For the immediate background of Rome's changes in policy toward Yugoslavia in mid-1942, see Giacomo Zanussi, Guerra e catastrofe d'Italia (Rome: Casa Editrice Libraria Corso, 1945), p. 181; Ciano, Diario, vol. 2, entries for 18 May and 10 June 1942; Ugo Cavallero, Comando Supremo: Diario 1940–1943 del Capo di S.M.G. (Bologna: Capelli, 1948), entries for 17 and 18 May 1942; and Comando Supremo to Ministero degli Affari Esteri, "N. 21707 del 22 maggio 1942," 22 May 1942, T-821, roll 400, frame 224.

[11] A little over a month after the Italian evacuation, Croatian authorities were already asking Roatta to send help to their hard-pressed forces at Livno, which the Partisans

posals at Avtovac, braced themselves for clashes with the returning Ustaši and attempted to shore up their arrangements with the Italians by pressing for a major joint anti-Partisan drive in western Bosnia.

Further events in the summer confirmed the Chetniks' suspicions that Italian cooperation and support against the Ustaši was ending and that it had to be exploited immediately against the Partisans. Mihailović rejected an offer made jointly by Jevdjević and the Italians to arrange a meeting between himself and Second Army officers,[12] permitted one of his closest collaborators, Major Ostojić, to launch a counterattack against Ustaši troops at Foča in August,[13] and instructed his chief agent in Bosnia, a Chetnik from Serbia, Captain Račić, to prepare the Bosnian Chetniks for military operations.[14] In short, while the Italians were trying to mend fences with Zagreb and were even agreeing to rearm Croatian anti-Partisan formations,[15] Mihailović's subordinates, especially Ostojić and Račić, appeared bent on pursuing a basically anti-Ustaši course.[16]

The prospects of a continued Italian withdrawal to the Adriatic and a revival of Ustaši activities in the Serb parts of Bosnia and Herzegovina had the added effect of hastening Mihailović's adoption of a tactically collaborationist line. Faced with a confrontation with both the Partisans and the Ustaši in Independent Croatia and convinced that effective Italian support would not last long, the officers tried to salvage what they could with the Second Army and to fulfill one of their basic aims by proposing a grand joint operation against Tito's Partisan republic in western Bosnia. Mihailović probably conveyed this plan to his associates at the Avtovoc conference; [17] soon after, both Bacović and Trifunović

---

were besieging. Commissariato Generale Militare/Capo di Stato Maggiore to Comando 2. Armata, "N. 76 del 31 luglio 1942," 31 July 1942, T-821, roll 64, frame 221.

[12] Vittorio Castellani to Königliche Ministerium der Aus. Angeleg, "Treffen der Serbischen Führer . . . ," 23 August 1942, T-821, roll 252, frame 299.

[13] Kdr. Gen. in Serbien/Kommand der Nachrichtenaufklärung 4, "Organisation der Draža Mihailovic Bewegung," 11 September 1942, T-312, roll 470, frame 8060384.

[14] Bačović to Chetnik command in eastern Bosnia, 8 August 1942, cited by Kačavenda, "Kriza Četničkog Pokreta," p. 261.

[15] Comando 2. Armata/Ufficio I, "Notiziario N. 37," 20 August 1942, T-821, roll 448, frame 279.

[16] In September Račić was sending instructions to various Chetnik groups in Bosnia with such openly Greater Serb phrases as "Who will rule Bosnia: the Communists or the Serbs?"

[17] Present-day Yugoslav historians like Plenča (Dušan Plenča, Medjunarodni Odnosi Jugoslavije u Toku Drugog Svjetskog Rata [Yugoslavia's international relations during World War II] [Belgrade: Institut Društvenih Nauka, 1962], p. 130) and Kačavenda ("Kriza Četničkog Pokreta," p. 281), employing evidence presented at Mihailović's trial in 1946, assert that the general told Trifunović, Jevdjević, and Bačović at Avtovac to begin negotiations with the Italians immediately for a combined operation, using Chetnik units from Montenegro, Herzegovina, Dalmatia, and the Lika against the Partisans in western Bosnia. The only Italian source on this meeting makes no specific mention of Mihailović's plan for an anti-Partisan operation, although it is

brought up the project at the headquarters of the Italian Sixth and Eighteenth Army Corps.

The Italians, who were trying to patch up relations with Zagreb to ensure adequate Croatian troop strength in the evacuated areas, found themselves in a delicate position and even refused for a while to sanction the proposal.[18] By the end of August, though, Mihailović was issuing directives to his units, many of which were operating in Croatian sovereign territory, to prepare for an anti-Partisan action in Bosanska Krajina in conjunction with Italian and Ustaši troops.[19] Trifunović soon took the Chetnik scheme to Roatta's headquarters at Sussak, where he argued for a large-scale combined anti-Partisan operation in northern Dalmatia and the Lika.[20] On 9 and 10 September Trifunović was continuing to press the matter with the Italians, arguing that the first snowfalls would begin in the mountainous western Bosnian area in the second half of October. According to Chetnik plans, roughly 7,500 "militiamen" would join the Italians in the operation; the largest contingents would be 3,000 troops under the command of the Bosnian Drenović and, most significant, another 3,000 men from Herzegovina.[21]

Roatta evidently appeared receptive to the Chetnik project, for Trifunović wrote to Mihailović on 20 September that "not only our own troops but also Italian units will undertake a single operation of very wide proportions against the Partisans in the Jajce-Glamoc-Livno-Duvno-Gornji Vakuf sector."[22] Roatta, in fact, flew to Rome on 13 September, where Comando Supremo cautiously approved the plan but only on the rather unlikely condition that Zagreb be consulted and that Croatian troops participate in the operation.[23] A week later, when Roatta visited Pavelić, the whole project seemed about to collapse. The *poglavnik* rejected absolutely the use of Chetnik formations in areas populated by Croats

---

quite clear that he encouraged their collaboration with the Italians for anti-Communist ends as a matter of general policy. Vittorio Castellani to Königliche Ministerium der Auswärt. Angeleg., "Treffen der serbischen Führer mit Draga Mihailović und seine Erklärungun," 23 August 1942, *T-821*, roll 252, frames 299–300.

[18] This is clear from letters from Baćović to Trifunović of 6 August and Trifunović to Mihailović, sent some time in August, cited in an excellent article by Miso Leković, "Planovi Draže Mihailovića za Uništenje Partizanske Države u zapadnoi Bosni u drugoi polovini 1942 godine" (Draža Mihailović's plans to destroy the Partisan state in western Bosnia in the second half of 1942), *Jugoslovenski Istorijski Časopis* 1 (1966): 84.

[19] The order went out on 28 August 1942. Plenča, *Medjunarodni Odnosi Jugoslavije*, p. 131.

[20] Leković, "Planovi Draže Mihailovića," p. 86.

[21] Oberkommando der Streitkräfte "Slovenia-Dalmazia," "Auszug aus der Unterredung mit dem Wojwoden Trifunovic am 10,9, 1942," 11 Sept. 1942, *T-821*, roll 252, frames 310–11.

[22] Leković, "Planovi Draže Mihailovića," p. 86.

[23] *Ibid.*, p. 87.

and Muslims.[24] In Zagreb, the Second Army commander not only refused to back the Chetnik strategy strongly but also confided to Croatian officials that he was seriously concerned about the recent behavior of the Serb armed groups.[25]

Mihailović's first major effort to employ a collaborationist strategy with the Italians was a failure almost from the start. Officials at Second Army headquarters were alarmed by their recent discovery of Jevdjević's and Trifunović's ties with Mihailović, tended to assume that all Serb armed bands were being organized by the officers,[26] and had serious reservations regarding the Chetniks' long-haul political program. Mihailović's intermediaries did little to allay these suspicions; Trifunović, in fact, after pledging that the Chetniks would willingly fight alongside both Catholic and Muslim anti-Partisan militia forces, appealed for Italian support for a Chetnik-inspired postwar reconstruction of Yugoslavia in which Serbia would be enlarged to include Bosnia, Herzegovina, and Montenegro.[27]

At this point, Mihailović probably had little if any control over many of the Serb armed formations and was in no position to turn suddenly against the Axis. The occupation authorities, however, were more impressed by his recent contacts with the chief Serb spokesmen and tended to overestimate dramatically his influence with the non-Communist formations. The Chetnik officer-delegates had, in fact, only just begun to put together an organization in western Yugoslavia, were attempting to pursue a strategy which was at the same time anti-Ustaši and anti-Partisan, and proposed to the Italians the use of only about one-third of the Serb nationalist units in the anti-rebel drive.

By the latter part of September, Second Army headquarters, after a month of negotiations with the officers' spokesmen concerning an anti-Partisan action, was basically interested in sounding out Jevdjević and Trifunović for the purpose of ascertaining the exact nature of their relations with Mihailović, the long-range goals of the movement, and the precise strength of their formations. On 21 September, in a conference with two Chetnik deputies, Roatta himself reaffirmed the Italian decision to avoid any kind of support or toleration of the Chetniks' postwar political aims and stressed that the Serb formations were to fight for "exclusively anti-Communist ends" and must shun "any sort of political activity of an anti-Croat nature." Trying to smooth over their tense rela-

---

[24] *Ibid.*, p. 88.

[25] Kasche to Aus. Amt./Pol. IV, "Telegramm N. 2637 vom 19.9. 1942," 19 September 1942, *T-120*, roll 208, frame 245/161299.

[26] See, for example, the Italians' unrealistic estimate of Chetnik strength in eastern Bosnia and the Sandžak in Comando 2. Armata to Comando Supremo, "Milizie cetniche," 26 September 1942, *T-821*, roll 31, frame 364.

[27] Oberkommando der Streitkräfte "Slovenia-Dalmazia," "Auszug aus der Unterredung mit dem Wojwoden Trifunović," 11 September 1942, *T-821*, roll 252, frames 309–10.

tions with the Italians, Jevdjević and Trifunović insisted that Mihailović was "the effective leader only in Serbia and Macedonia" and agreed that their formations be employed only in areas populated predominantly by Serbs.

The Chetnik negotiators refused, however, to back down completely. They promised to cooperate with Croat and Muslim anti-Partisan formations and to submit to the Italians' overall command, but they demanded that Serb units operating outside the Italian zone take orders from Trifunović and their own unit leaders, and, in spite of Roatta's warnings about their Greater Serb political designs, they declared again that "the aim of the Chetnik forces is to save the Serb people and to create the means which, at the end of the war, can materialize the boundaries of the Serbian nation." [28]

The Chetnik leaders, in fact, gave little indication that they were willing to accept the status of auxiliary police formations under Italian command. On 22 September, shortly after Trifunović and Jevdjević had dismissed Mihailović as only a "moral" head of the armed formations in western Yugoslavia, they were forced to admit to the Italians that they had held another meeting with the general on 16 September near Nevesinje.[29] Trifunović suddenly charged the Italians with doubting his loyalty and insisted that cooperation between the Chetniks and the Second Army would be possible only if Roatta tolerated the continuation of propaganda "in the Serb nationalist spirit" and permitted "the greatest possible autonomy of action as far as their internal affairs are concerned."

While Mihailović's negotiators persisted in demanding the freedom to develop a Serb nationalist program, the armed formations continued to terrorize Croat and Muslim civilians. In August and September various Serb bands fanned out from the Nevesinje area throughout Herzegovina and into parts of Dalmatia, where they often wreaked vengeance on Croat peasants.[30] In this area, which included most of Herzegovina and had recently been evacuated by the Italians, none of the contending occupying powers or rebel groups had effective control. The situation was becoming increasingly anarchic, local bands were taking matters

---

[28] Comando 2. Armata, "Sintesi del colloquio tra l'Ecc. Roatta, il Voevoda Ilija Trifunovic e l'On. Dobroslav Jevdjevic," 21 September 1942, *T-821*, roll 31, frame 352.

[29] Comando 2. Armata/Ufficio I, "Appunti sulla seduto . . . fra il Voevoda Trifunović, l'On. Jevdjevic e il giornalisto Grdjic dall'una parte e il Col. Carlà dall'altra," 22 September 1942, *T-821*, roll 31, frames 349–50.

[30] Nezavisna Država Hrvatska/Glavni Stan Poglavnika to Kr. Talijansog Vojnoj Misiji, 24 August 1942, *T-821*, roll 54, frame 5; Kasche to Aus. Amt/Pol. III, "Aufstandslage in Kroatien," 12 September 1942, *T-501*, roll 265, frame 1019; Stato Ind. di Croazia/C.G.M.C. to Comando 2. Armata, "N. 653 del 23. 9. 42," 23 September 1942, *T-821*, roll 53, frame 744.

into their hands, and the Axis occupation authorities, for understandable reasons, tended to suspect the worst of the Chetnik officers. At the end of September Pavelić refused again to sanction a combined anti-Partisan drive in which Chetniks would take part, and Roatta acquiesced. At the same time, Trifunović wrote to Mihailović that the Italians were becoming very suspicious of the ties between the Serb representatives and the officers and that Second Army headquarters was determined to prohibit "anti-Croat manifestations as well as our public propaganda for the creation of a free, national state." Mihailović's organization had to deal now with increasing "meddling of the Italian Army in the Chetniks' internal affairs." [31]

The Germans, whose main concern was the safety of the bauxite mines in Herzegovina, finally intervened to encourage the Italians to launch the action, but the proposed operation, whose goals were the Livno-Prozor area north of Mostar, fell far short of what Mihailović had hoped. In early October final preparations for a combined anti-Partisan operation in western Bosnia called for a two-pronged thrust: the German 714th and 718th divisions and Croat units would operate from the north, and the Italian "Messina" division and about three thousand Herzegovinian Chetniks would drive from the Neretva River toward Prozor.[32] The Germans and, therefore, Pavelić tolerated this limited participation of Serb formations only in order to induce the Italians to make a greater contribution. Almost immediately after the operation began, individual Chetnik bands, acting contrary to Italian directives and perhaps also to Mihailović's orders, used the opportunity to seize Ustaši functionaries, kill over five hundred Croat and Muslim civilians, and launch a campaign of Serb nationalist revenge.[33]

Chetnik officers and civilian unit leaders indulged in a flurry of wildly anti-Croat and anti-Ustaši political activities. In Dubrovnik a group of former Yugoslav officers were reported to have created an underground organization dedicated to the destruction of the Ustaši state.[34] In other instances, the Serb leaders were more open about their long-range goals. Djujić, whose formations in the mountains of western

[31] Trifunović to Mihailović, (?) September 1942, cited in Leković "Planovi Draže Mihailovića," pp. 89–90.

[32] *Ibid.*, p. 91.

[33] Deutsche Gesandtschaft/Deutsche Polizeiattache in Zagreb to Reichsführer SS. u. Chef der deutschen Polizei, "Förderung der Cetniks auf Auslieferung von Ustaschen seitens der ital. Militärbehörden in der Herzegowina," 2 October 1942, *T-120,* roll 1141, frame 2026/444111; Kasche to Ritter, "Telegramm N. 2834 vom 4.10.42," 4 October 1942, *T-120,* roll 395, frame 999/305607.

[34] Deutsche Gesandtschaft/Deutsche Polizeiattache in Zagreb to Reichsführer SS. u. Chef der deutschen Polizei, "Gründung einer gegenkroat. Geheimorganisation in Dubrovnik," 21 October 1942, *T-120,* roll 1141, frame 2026/444115.

Bosnia were operating near Tito's Partisan republic, gave a speech to his followers in which he declared that "we Chetniks have to be in good relations with the Croats for the time being in order to get a large number of arms and munitions, but when the proper time comes we will settle accounts with them." [35] At Mostar, a letter signed by Jevdjević, setting forth a Chetnik program of establishing a postwar Greater Serbia and urging that all Serbs maintain a hostile attitude toward Pavelić's régime, was widely circulated.

By the end of October it became clear that the Chetnik intermediaries were making certain promises to the Italians while encouraging the rank and file of the armed formations to do just the opposite. The evidence suggests strongly that in these parts of Yugoslavia, formally attached to Croatia and occupied successively by Ustaši and Italians, the Chetnik groups were motivated far more by intense hatred for the Croats and Muslims than by anti-Partisan sentiments. Mihailović, although primarily interested in destroying Tito's movement as soon as possible, evidently did little to restrain the prevailing mood of national revenge. His own appointees, like Petar Baćović, a former reserve officer and lawyer and then commander of the Chetniks in Herzegovina and eastern Bosnia, openly announced plans to destroy whole Muslim villages.[36]

Over the short term the officers and the Serb bands succeeded in waging an anarchic civil war and escaping major reprisals. Pavelić and the German representatives in Zagreb, Kasche and Glaise von Horstenau, dispatched a stream of complaints to Rome and Berlin [37] but had to be satisfied with Roatta's vague promises to reduce his support for the Chetnik formations.[38] In actual fact, most of Herzegovina was in a state of total chaos and, until someone with the troops and inclination intervened, was prey to an array of ravaging armed groups. Pavelić spoke of reprisals against the Serb formations but encountered Italian resistance and could not carry them out.[39] Hitler could not afford to shape his Balkan policy according to Kasche's recommendations, and

[35] Comando 2. Armata/Ufficio I, "Notiziario N. 42 del 10 ottobre 1942," 10 October 1942, *T-821*, roll 448, frame 353.

[36] Comando 2. Armata/Ufficio I, "Notiziario N. 43 del 20 ottobre 1942," 20 October 1942, *T-821*, roll 448, frame 369.

[37] Kasche to Aus. Amt/Pol. IV, "Telegramm N. 2857 vom 6.10. 1942," 6 October 1942, *T-120*, roll 212, frame 245/162006; OKW/WFSt to Ritter, "Säuberungsaktion in Raum um Mostar u. Livno," 6 October 1942, *T-120*, roll 395, frame 999/305579; Kasche to Ribbentrop, "Telegramm N. 2891 vom 8.10.1942," 8 October 1942, *T-120*, roll 212, frame 245/162101; Deutsche General in Agram/Ia to OKW/Abt. Ausland, "N. 367/42 vom 13.10.1942," 13 October 1942, *T-501*, roll 264, frames 952–53.

[38] Comando 2. Armata/Ufficio I to Comando V. Corps d'Armata, "Accordi col Poglavnik circa le formazione M.V.A.C. cetniche," 18 October 1942, *T-821*, roll 474, frames 461–62.

[39] Zanussi, *Guerra e catastrofe*, p. 268.

Ribbentrop once more had to point out to the German minister that "now as before the Italo-German alliance is the basis of our foreign policy and that under no circumstances must we let ourselves be dragged into a conflict with the Italians on account of Croatian interests." [40] Roatta, despite all his misgivings regarding the political activities of the Chetnik leaders, favored pulling the Italian units back to the Adriatic and avoiding the drain of major anti-Partisan operations. By the fall of 1942, when the prospects of an Axis victory in North Africa appeared unlikely, Second Army headquarters was thinking more and more in terms of the final defense of the Italian peninsula and was less interested than ever in hunting Communist guerrillas or taking drastic action against Mihailović.[41]

The Chetniks survived the fall basically unmolested not because they were strong and well organized but because their numerous opponents either could not or would not act. Not only were their successes essentially negative, but their overall strategy was a complete failure. Militarily they depended more than ever on the Italians, and the major drive from Herzegovina against Tito's stronghold in western Bosnia never materialized. The "Messina" division, for example, which took Prozor and Livno from the Partisans, was quickly withdrawn to the coast and the Chetniks had to pull back with them.[42] Italian generals began to lose whatever illusions they had about the discipline, organization, and combat-effectiveness of the Serb formations.[43] More important, in the western Bosnian sector, where the Chetnik leaders Djujić and Drenović had hoped to join forces,[44] the Partisans not only were holding on but seemed to be gaining the upper hand.[45]

In short, Mihailović's hurried strategy of stopping Tito and asserting Chetnik strength in the Serb parts of the Ustaši state failed to achieve either objective. By the late fall of 1942, the Chetniks had little military strength outside of Herzegovina and Montenegro, where Italian toleration, more than anything else, accounted for their temporary ascendancy. In Herzegovina, where Mihailović's agents and spokesmen were most active, the Chetniks' savage reprisals against the Croat and Muslim

[40] Ribbentrop to Kasche, "Telegramm N. 1330 vom 17.10.1942," 17 October 1942, *T-120*, roll 395, frames 999/305551–52.

[41] Zanussi, *Guerrae catastrofe*, pp. 264–65.

[42] Jovan Marjanović and Pero Morača, *Naš Oslobodilački Rat i Narodna Revolucija, 1941–1945* (Our war of liberation and the national revolution) (Belgrade: Izdavačko Preduzeće Rad, 1958), p. 157.

[43] Comando XVIII. Corpo d'Armata to Comando 2. Armata, "Bande anticommuniste," 24 October 1942, *T-821*, roll 503, fram 50.

[44] Živko Topalović, *Pokreti Narodnog Otpora u Jugoslaviji, 1941–45* (Paris: n.p., 1958), p. 73.

[45] Tito to staff of First Proletarian Brigade, 30 October 1942, *Zbornik*, Vol. 2, bk. 6, no. 131.

civilian communities forfeited whatever chances they might have had of expanding their popular base [46] and did little to improve their image in the eyes of their Italian sponsors.

To the extent that Mihailović was pursuing any overall strategy in 1942, it was to wage a series of simultaneous parallel wars. In western Yugoslavia, he attempted to capitalize on Italian support by challenging the Ustaši and to knock Tito out—before the expected Allied Balkan landing, he hoped. In order to maintain the confidence of the British, which his tacit cooperation with the Italians was bound to strain, he also decided to employ his underground organization in Serbia in a sabotage campaign against German railway movements. This form of anti-German resistance was the least risky, since the Chetniks no longer had a significant armed movement in Serbia, and it served to demonstrate to the Allies that the Chetniks had the means to create diversions in the German rear in the event of an amphibious operation in the Balkans.

Until well into the summer of 1942 the remainder of the Chetnik organization in Serbia was so weak and inactive that the German authorities even rejected Nedić's requests that the "illegal" formations be disarmed immediately.[47] The Chetniks refrained from armed clashes with either the Germans or Nedić's forces and preferred infiltrating the Quisling administration; the Germans refused to consider any anti-rebel drives before September, had few battle-worthy troops in rump Serbia, and feared that military operations would fail anyway, since Mihailović's agents would surely get advance word of German plans.[48]

In May Mihailović took the first step which finally upset this uneasy truce. He requested from the British Middle East Command heavy explosives for the purpose of destroying the German supply lines running south to the Aegean for Rommel's troops in North Africa.[49] According to

[46] According to Topalović (*Pokreti Narodnog Otpora*, p. 95), who was one of Mihailović's closest collaborators and the chief political organizer of the St. Sava Day Congress at Ba, Serbia, in January 1944, the Chetniks killed perhaps as many as forty thousand Muslims during the war, mainly in Bosnia, Herzegovina, and the Sandžak. Partisan sources suggest that a good deal of their early support in Herzegovina was Muslim. In June 1942 Vlado Šegrt told Dedijer that "about 80 percent of the Mostar Muslims stood with them and that practically all the Partisan terrorist activities were the work of Muslim schoolboys. Vladimir Dedijer, *Dnevnik*, (Belgrade: Državni Izdavački Zavod Jugoslavije, 1945–46), entry for 18 June 1942.

[47] Bevoll. Kdr. Gen. u. Bfh. in Serbien/Ia, "Kriegstagebuch (Juli 1942)," 2 July 1942 (Anlage 7), *T-501*, roll 351, frame 1008; Bevoll. Kdr. Gen. u. Bfh. in Serbien/Ia, "Kriegstagebuch (Juli 1942), 6 July 1942 (Anlage 17), *T-501*, roll 351, frame 111.

[48] Benzler to Bader, "Die politische Lage in Serbien," 30 August 1942, *T-501*, roll 256, fram 1045; Benzler to Aus. Amt/Pol. IV, "Telegramm N. 1347 vom 19.9.1942," 19 September 1942, *T-120*, roll 200, frame 230/153680.

[49] Živan L. Knežević, *Knjiga o Draži*, 1:273.

available evidence, he did not order his subordinates to begin the sabotage campaign until early August, when the directives were issued to small Chetnik bands in southern Serbia.[50] The sabotage campaign was apparently a shortlived gesture, for neither Mihailović nor the exiled Yugoslav government, remembering the events in Serbia of 1941, wanted to expose the civilian population to German reprisals or to jeopardize the tenuously reconstructed Chetnik organization of infiltrators and double agents. Sometime in September Mihailović even turned down a request from General Alexander to expand Chetnik attacks on German rail movements.[51] The head of the émigré government, Slobodan Jovanović, wrote to the British ambassador, Sir George Randall, that "attacks on the lines of communication, if successful, would without doubt elicit an action of the Axis troops against General Mihailović." [52]

Chetnik sabotage actions in Serbia fell short of British expectations, and they also determined the Germans to settle accounts once and for all with Mihailović's organization. In late September they began to round up Chetnik officers, weed out Mihailović's agents in the Nedić administration, and break up the sabotage groups. The first of Mihailović's chief organizers in Serbia to fall into German hands was Major Gordić; at the end of the first week of October the number of arrested Chetnik officers had risen to twenty-one.[53] The Germans soon succeeded in rounding up Mihailović's entire sabotage organization in Belgrade, composed for the most part of civil servants and railroad employees.[54] This reaction caught the Serb Chetniks off guard and showed how vulnerable their slowly rebuilt organization of infiltrators really was. Throughout the rest of the fall the occupation forces arrested stray bands of "unreliable" Chetniks, seized Mihailović's small munitions depots, and proceeded to dissolve most of the "legal" armed formations.[55]

---

[50] *Ibid.*, p. 274. On 4 August 1942 Mihailović informed the Middle East Command, through Captain William Hudson, that he was about to start the railroad sabotage operations. The Germans, who succeeded in intercepting Chetnik radio messages in July, picked up Mihailović's orders for the sabotage compaign in early August. Kdr. Gen. u. Befh. in Serbien/Kommand der Nachrichten Aufklärung 4, "N. 806/42 vom 11.9.1942," 11 September 1942, *T-312,* roll 470, frames 8060425–26.

[51] F. W. Deakin, "Britanija i Jugoslavija, 1941–1945," *Jugoslovenski Istorijski Časopis* 2 (1963):50.

[52] Cited by Vojmir Kljaković, "Promjena Politike Velike Britanije prema Jugoslavije u prvoj polovine 1943 godine" (The shift in Great Britain's policies toward Yugoslavia in the first half of 1943), *Jugoslovenski Istorijski Časopis* 3 (1969):25.

[53] Wehrmachtbefehlshaber Südost/Ia to OKH/Gen. Stab. d. H., "N. 3682/42 vom 24.9.1942," 24 September 1942, *T-78,* roll 329, frame 6285998; Wehrmachtbefehlshaber Südost/Ia to Bevoll. Kdr. Gen. u. Befh. in Serbien, "N. 3822/42 vom 4.10.1942," 4 October 1942, *T-78,* roll 329, frame 6285977.

[54] Kdr. Gen. u. Befh. in Serbien/Ia to Wehrmachtbefehlshaber Südost, "N. 5268/42 vom 7.10.1942," 7 October 1942, *T-501,* roll 352, frames 275–76.

[55] Wehrmachtbefehlshaber Südost/Ia to OKH/Gen. St./Op. Abt., "N. 4290 vom

Toward the end of 1942, the Germans, who were preparing for a major anti-rebel operation in western Yugoslavia in January, became determined to prop up the Nedić régime by crushing the Mihailović movement politically. Their basic strategy was to disarm the armed bands in the rural areas, whether legalized or not, and to eliminate the center of the Chetnik organization in Serbia through a campaign of mass terror against the officer double agents and the pro-Mihailović civil servants in Belgrade. During the month of December from about ten to a few dozen Chetnik officers and agents were arrested daily and, in most instances, executed immediately; at the same time, General Bader's police succeeded in destroying at least temporarily Mihailović's intelligence network within the Nedić administration and broke off his radio ties with Belgrade.[56] The German reprisals, although carried out in a hasty and haphazard manner,[57] did succeed in nullifying most of the Chetniks' reorganization work in Serbia since the end of 1941.

These developments in Serbia were very significant: the officers had counted on preserving a well-developed organization in the capital ready to seize power in the event of a German defeat. In a more immediate sense, though, it marked an important change in the occupation policies of the Axis Powers, not only in rump Serbia, but everywhere in former Yugoslavia. Mihailović's recourse to acts of sabotage in August and September, the expansion of the Partisan movement deep in Croatian territory, and the rapidly deteriorating military situation in North Africa from late October on all led the Germans to favor extraordinary measures for dealing with resistance movements in the Balkans. Fearing that an Allied invasion of southeastern Europe would help Mihailović more than Tito, the Germans tended to overestimate the Chetniks'

31.10.1942," 31 October 1942, *T-78*, roll 239, frame 6285918; Wehrmachtbefehlshaber Südost/Ia to OKH/Gen. St./Op. Abt., "N. 4406/42 vom 6.11.1942," 6 November 1942, *T-78*, roll 329, frame 6286320; Kdr. Gen. u. Befh. in Serbien/Ia, "N. 558/42 vom 18.11. 1942," 18 November 1942, *T-501*, roll 352, frame 572.

[56] Helmut Heiber, ed., *Hitlers Lagebesprechungen. Die Protokollfragmente seiner militärischen Konferenzen (1942–45)* (Stuttgart: Deutsche Verlags-Anstalt, 1962), entry for 12 December 1942 (Mittagslage); Wehrmachtbefehlshaber Sudost to OKH/Gen. Stab. d. H./Op. Abt., "N. 5264/42 vom 29.12.1942," 29 December 1942, *T-78*, roll 329, frame 6286182.

[57] Some of the armed formations were disarmed and dissolved but reappeared again, newly armed, as "village guard units." In Belgrade German countermeasures often took the form of reprisals against innocent hostages. Of the approximately five hundred "Chetniks" executed during December, several had been in no position to carry out services for Mihailović. Bevoll. Kdr. Gen. u. Befh. in Serbien/Ia to Höh. SS. u. Polizeiführer, "N. 530/42 vom 7.11.1942," 7 November 1942, *T-501*, roll 352, frame 486; Generale Pieche to Ministero degli Affari Esteri, "Riassunto della situazione in Serbia agli' inizi del '43," 22 January 1943, *T-821*, roll 247, frame 650; Deutsche Gesandtschaft Belgrad to Aus. Amt/Pol. IV, "N. 135 vom 12.2.1943," 12 February 1943, *T-120*, roll 380, frame 274824.

potential for resistance activity and made no significant distinction between the two movements.[58] Significantly enough, the Armed Forces Command South-East attached a supplement to Hitler's "no prisoners" policy that the policy also applied to "anyone who declares himself for Mihailović or is in his service." [59]

Outside of Serbia, where Italian policies had acted as a protective umbrella for the Chetnik revival, the Germans prepared for a settling of accounts with Tito and Mihailović. In fact, they were filling a vacuum created by the progressive disintegration of the political and military authority of Zagreb and the steady withdrawal of Roatta's Second Army units to the Adriatic coast. By late fall the Ustaši hierarchy was falling apart, armed forces head Slavko Kvaternik launched an abortive coup, and desertion from the regular, or Domobran, army units to the Partisans was assuming serious proportions.[60] General Löhr, the armed forces commander southeast, had recommended that a German officer be attached to every Croat regiment to ensure discipline and, in his conference of 17 September with Hitler, thought it necessary to ask what the Germans should do in the event of the collapse of the Ustaši government.

Immediately after the Allied invasion of northwestern Africa, Roatta ordered a study to determine the minimum number of troops necessary for the Italians to maintain a firm hold on the Adriatic while sending as many units as possible back to Italy.[61] In mid-November, Cavallero gave his approval to a plan for Roatta's army to cede from two to seven divisions for the defense of the mother country; meanwhile, Second Army units were evacuating practically all their garrisons in the second zone. Second Army headquarters had less and less to offer the Chetniks but dared not provoke disturbances in their rear. Roatta therefore met Jevdjević in November and even agreed to authorize and legalize three thousand more Chetniks; moreover, he recognized virtually all of eastern Herzegovina as the Chetnik zone.[62]

In addition, the Italians, in part because they lacked confidence in many of the Chetnik leaders and in part because they opposed German methods of dealing with the officers, made a number of efforts to tighten their control over the Serb anti-Partisan formations. Roatta tried to get Jevdjević to agree to confine the activities of his Herzegovinian detachments to a specific "sphere"; on 12 November the Italian commander told

[58] In April 1942 Roatta had won Bader's agreement to the policy of treating captured Chetniks in the eastern Bosnian operation as prisoners of war rather than as rebels.
[59] Wehrmachtbefehlshaber Südost/Ia, "N. 2868/42 vom 28.10. 1942," 28 October 1942, *T-311*, roll 197, frame 84, which is a supplement to OKW/WFSt., "N. 003830/42 vom 18.10.1942," 18 October 1942, *T-311*, roll 197, frames 81–82.
[60] *KTB/OKW*, vol. 2, entry for 17 September 1942 (Aufzeichnungen Greiners).
[61] Zanussi, *Guerra e catastrofe,* pp. 281–82.
[62] Kačavenda, "Kriza Četničkog Pokreta," pp. 261–63.

a group of Chetnik delegates that they would have to accept the presence of an Italian liaison officer at all their formations of regiment strength or more and that they must agree not to harm Muslim and Croat civilians.[63] On 15 November Jevdjević arrived in Mostar where he had to support formally the Italian decision to begin arming Muslim anti-Partisans.[64]

The immediate result of these changes, especially the further contraction of the Italian occupation sphere, was to enlarge the military vacuum in western Yugoslavia. In some areas, for example, around Bos Grahovo and Višegrad, the Chetniks now had exclusive rights of occupation in sectors they had formerly patrolled along with the Italians.[65] In reality, though, the officers had little room for maneuver and probably even less time. The Chetnik leaders realized that, over the short term, the Italians were their only major source of supplies and protection against German policies. It is significant that in December several formation leaders went out of their way to convince the Italians to reconsider or delay their evacuation from the second zone.[66] In Montenegro, where the officers did not have to contend with Ustaši or Partisans, they depended completely on Pirzio-Biroli's administration for their monthly dole of funds to support their troops.[67]

In a more general sense, Mihailović, his chief officer-delegates, and the leading civilian spokesmen for the Chetnik cause were all being placed on the defensive. Jevdjević and Trifunović found relations with the Italians increasingly difficult and were compelled to make promises which they could never enforce among the Chetnik rank and file. At the end of the year Serb bands were still threatening nearby Croat garrisons and starting fights with Ustaši troops at Mostar.[68] There was apparently little the civilian intermediaries could do to affect the behavior of the

---

[63] Plenča, *Medjunarodni Odnosi Jugoslavije*, pp. 145–46. The author's source is a report from a delegate of the Chetnik command, Captain Ivanisević, to Mihailović of 19 November 1942.

[64] Comando 2. Armata/Ufficio I, "Notiziario N. 45," 15 December 1942, *T-821*, roll 448, frame 398.

[65] Generale Spigo to Roatta, "N. 12194 del 11.11.1942," 11 November 1942, *T-821*, roll 64, frame 68; Deutsche General in Agram to Wehrmachtbefehlshaber Südost, "N. 0193/42 vom 7.12.1942," 7 December 1942, *T-501*, roll 268, frame 85.

[66] Kačavenda, "Kriza Četničkog Pokreta," p. 291.

[67] For instance, Krsto Popović to command of "Perugia" division, 19 August 1942, Zbornik, vol. 3, bk. 4, no. 222; Zarija Vuković (Second Chetnik Battalion) to commander of Zeta Flying Detachment, 29 October 1942, *Dokumenti o Izdajstvu Draže Mihailovića*, no. 54; command of National Liberation Army of Montenegro and Herzegovina to Supreme National Committee (Cetinje), 11 November 1942, *ibid.*, no. 55.

[68] Supreme Staff of Bosnian Chetnik Detachments (Luka Radić) to commander of Ustaši division at Banja Luka, 7 December 1942, cited by Topolović, *Pokreti Narodnog Otpora*, p. 39; report of Third Domobran "Zbor" of November 1942, *Zbornik*, vol. 4, bk. 8, no. 234.

·

Armed units. Second Army headquarters even reported that one of Jevdjević's collaborators from Mostar had conceded that he was "incapable of putting the brakes on his men because they are pervaded by a profound race hatred and dominated by desire for revenge." [69]

Jevdjević, because he was the chief negotiator with the Italians, came under strong attack when Roatta decided to arm Muslim and Croat anti-Partisan formations and insisted that the Chetniks curtail their political activities. Several Chetniks refused to carry out these commitments to Roatta, and in November two Chetniks came to Mostar in an attempt to assassinate him; another major civilian leader, Petar Samardžić, began to oppose him openly. [70] Mihailović himself became increasingly suspicious of the Italians and warned one of his subordinates that "the Italians are trying everywhere to come into contact with our people so they can use them for their own ends." [71] In November he also ordered one of his delegates, Major Djurić, not to negotiate with the Italians concerning the situation in Kosovo-Metohija because Roatta's officers had given indications of a willingness to sponsor Albanian Muslim armed formations. [72]

None of this meant, however, that Mihailović and his collaborators, military and civilian, were moving toward a break with the Italians. If anything, recent events demonstrate that collaboration had become something of a necessary evil. As Italian influence in Yugoslav occupation politics diminished and relations between Chetnik spokesmen and Second Army officers became more difficult, Mihailović's men tried a new way of bargaining, but in their view there was almost no immediate alternative to some form of cooperation with the Italians. The general had long since agreed to give tacit support to the collaboration of the Montenegrin officers and firmly rejected the requests of the British liaison staff that he begin sabotage operations against the Italians. [73]

Mihailović was finding himself in an increasingly difficult position vis-à-vis the Italians and his own nominal followers. In Herzegovina and Montenegro, the Chetnik strongholds, he opposed acts of resistance against the Italians, dealt with them for money and arms through Jevdjević, Djurišić, and the National Committee at Cetinje, and even proposed a major anti-Partisan drive to be carried out in conjunction with Second

[69] Comando 2. Armata/Ufficio I, "Notiziario N. 44 del 15 novembre 1942," 15 November 1942, T-821, roll 448, frame 382.

[70] Comando 1. Armata/Ufficio I, "Notiziario N. 44 del 15.11.1942," 15 November 1942, T-821, roll 448, frame 383; Comando 2. Armata/Ufficio I, "Notiziario N. 1 del 15 gennaio 1943," 15 January 1943, T-821, roll 448, frame 417.

[71] A message of November 1942 to Major Spasić, in Comando 2. Armata, "Premessa," 24 February 1943, T-821, roll 31, frame 373.

[72] Ibid.

[73] See the message of Captain Hudson, 15 November 1942, in F. W. D. Deakin, The Embattled Mountain (New York: Oxford University Press, 1971), pp. 152–53.

Army units. At the same time, he avoided personal contacts with Italian officers,[74] resisted Roatta's efforts to restrain the activities of the Chetniks, and contributed to undermining Jevdjević's position with the Italians by encouraging his followers, especially Major Ostojić and Captain Djurišić, to wage a campaign of terror against the Muslim population along the border of Montenegro and the Sandžak.[75] According to Mihailović, the Chetniks would begin operations against the Axis in the event of an Italian capitulation or a German invasion of Montenegro; in the meantime, they used their relatively secure position in Montenegro to carry on the civil war, especially against the exposed villages of the Muslim Sandžak.[76]

Outside the Chetniks' sphere Mihailović and the officers faced mounting difficulties. In several parts of Bosnia local Serb armed detachments had established treaties in the spring of 1942 with the Ustaši and the Germans; Chetnik headquarters in Montenegro had virtually no influence there, and Mihailović's schemes were challenged by both the Germans and the local Serb leaders. The Germans, although avoiding any immediate reprisals, left little doubt as to the eventual direction of their policies; General Lüters, named German general in Croatia on 16 November, began the new course when he directed the Croat military authorities to re-examine and dissolve the local treaties.[77] In mid-December Lüters went one step further and announced that the German command did not recognize any of the treaties concluded between Zagreb and the Bosnian Serbs.[78] Collaborationist civilian Chetniks like Jevdjević, who had tried unsuccessfully in September to intervene with the Germans on behalf of the Bosnian Serb formations, had even less influence now.[79]

Mihailović's efforts, beginning in the spring and summer of 1942, to use the numerous Serb armed bands in Croatian territory to rebuild the Chetnik movement had met insurmountable obstacles. By the end of

[74] *Ibid.*

[75] See, for instance, Ostojić to Djurišić, 10 November 1942, included among the intercepted messages in Comando 2. Armata, "Premessa," 24 February 1943, *T-821*, roll 31, frame 376.

[76] Ostojić reported that the Chetniks had just completely destroyed twenty-one Muslim villages and killed about thirteen hundred people.

[77] *KTB/OKW*, vol. 2, bk. 2, entry for 16 November 1942 (Lagebericht OKH); Befh. d. dt. Truppen in Kroatien/Ia to Wehrmachtbefehlshaber Südost, "Bindung mit fdl. gesinnten Kreisen in Serbien," 18 November 1942, *T-314*, roll 566, frames 357–58.

[78] Befh. d. dt. Truppen in Kroatien/Ic to Kdr. Gen. u. Befh. in Serbien, "Verträge mit pravosl. Freiwilligen Verbanden in Kroatien," 19 December 1942, *T-314*, roll 566, frame 732.

[79] Jevdjević had offered to instruct a Bosnian Chetnik force of about twelve thousand to behave loyally toward the Germans and protect the Sarajevo-Višegrad railway line. Glaise von Horstenau was firmly opposed. Deutsche General in Agram/Ia, "N. 05584/42 vom 9.9.1942," 9 September 1942, *T-501*, roll 265, frame 1018.

1942 most of the widely dispersed Serb formations in Bosnia, probably numbering over ten thousand followers, were either firmly tied to the unreliable agreements with the Ustaši or were beyond the reach of Mihailović's officer-emissaries. Repeated attempts, directed from Chetnik headquarters in Montenegro, to co-opt the bands and remove the local leaders probably hurt more than helped Mihailović's cause.

Several Bosnian Serb chiefs had established contact with Mihailović in late August and early September through the Chetnik delegate Captain Dragoslav Račić.[80] Jevdjević's efforts to organize them on a temporarily collaborationist basis by negotiating with the occupation authorities got nowhere. According to the Bosnian Serb leaders, most of Mihailović's delegates were killed or returned to Serbia; the remainder, like Račić, created considerable dissension when they attempted to subordinate the armed groups to the control of Mihailović's staff. At a conference of Bosnian Chetnik Detachments at Kulašim of 1 December 1942, one of the local heads, Stevan Botić, whom Račić had tried to purge in July, spoke out against the "intrigues" of the officers and accused Mihailović of withholding recognition of the local Bosnian leaders because he was "surrounded by Serbs and Montenegrins" who did not understand the situation in Bosnia.[81] While Mihailović's delegates insisted on the inadequacy of the Bosnian organization, several of the local original unit leaders demanded that the basically native and civilian organization be preserved. Finally, the conference passed a resolution that the Chetnik officers would come as "collaborators, not as tutors."

By the end of 1942, then, the Serb detachments in Bosnia had settled into a pattern of uneasy and in part necessary collaboration. Their major function was to buy the toleration of the Ustaši and Germans by accepting "police" duties and to protect the native Serb population by remaining strong enough to bargain for local spheres of influence. Several probably felt a moral bond and sympathy with Mihailović; few were willing or able to declare themselves openly as his followers. In Serbia there was virtually no independent military organization, and events showed that those who sought protection and future opportunities by attaching themselves to the Nedić administration could survive only if they refrained from all anti-German activity.

In the second half of 1942 Mihailović was not doing enough to satisfy the British [82] and had scored no noteworthy successes against Tito or

[80] Rade Radić to Mihailović, 1 December 1942, *Dokumenti o Izdajstvu Draže Mihailovića*, no. 118.

[81] Minutes of Inter-Detachment Conference of Bosnian Chetnik Units at Kulašim, 1 December 1942, *ibid.*, no. 119.

[82] Hudson was fully aware of the officers' cooperation with the Italians, thought Mihailović was essentially an opportunist, and even wondered whether the Chetniks

Pavelić. Most important, he had lost most of his organization in Serbia, failed to develop one in Bosnia, and had only about twenty thousand "troops" in Herzegovina and Montenegro, over whom he had no direct authority. These formations were as dependent on the Italians as their leaders were loyal to Mihailović. Collaboration meant a lease on life to the Chetnik officers—arms, supplies, and relative, if decreasing, freedom of action in their spheres; it also meant that the leaders had to play a constant double game and that their troops' activities were confined for the most part to the shrinking Italian zone and the immediately adjacent areas.

The main Chetnik contingents were trapped by rivalries within the occupation system and by the concessions they had made to the Italians. Their activities were restricted to Herzegovina and Montenegro, and they devoted most of their energy not to preparing for anti-Axis resistance or collaborating against the Partisans but to prolonging the struggle in the nearby ethnic borderlands against their national, largely civilian, enemies. In these areas, mainly the Croat and Muslim parts of Herzegovina and the eastern limits of Montenegro, the officers' policies compromised their relations with their Italian sponsors, considerably narrowed their potential base of support, and, in a more general sense, kept alive a civil war initiated by Axis policies and Ustaši excesses.

The mood of national and religious hatred and urge for revenge was a logical outcome of the events of 1941. Moreover, nothing that Mihailović or his collaborators could have done would have completely restrained the Serb bands. Until well into 1943, the entire Yugoslav resistance, both Chetnik and Partisan, was overwhelmingly Serb [83] and represented in a very basic way the armed response of the Serbs, especially in the western half of the country, to the tragedy of 1941. The crucial difference is that the Partisan leaders, for the most part young and free of confining ethnic loyalties, suffered numerous failures in their efforts to win over Croats and Muslims,[84] but the Chetnik officers, virtually all Serbs and

had made some sort of an overall anti-Partisan agreement with the Axis occupation authorities. Deakin, *Embattled Mountain,* pp. 152–54.

[83] Note Deakin's remark that, as late as the summer of 1943, the overwhelming majority of Partisans were Serbs. *Ibid.,* p. 106.

[84] Throughout the first half of the war, for example, the evidence from Partisan sources suggests that they had more than their share of problems trying to win over support from the Yugoslav Muslims. A Partisan document from Herzegovina of October 1941 explained that "for the time being, cooperation with the Muslims would be impossible." Staff of Herzegovinian National-Liberation Partisan Detachments, 2 October 1941, *Zbornik,* vol. 4, bk. 2, no. 4. In May 1942, when the main Partisan forces were forced to flee Foča, a report to Tito admitted that "the Muslims of Foča greeted the Italians enthusiastically." Chief of Supreme Staff of Yugoslav National-Liberation Partisan Detachments to Tito, 11 May 1942, *ibid.,* vol. 2, bk. 4, no. 27. In the Kosovo-Metohija area the Partisans did poorly with the Albanian Muslims. A letter written by the secretary of the local Kosovo-Metohija C.P.Y. committee stated that "as far as

schooled in a tradition which identified Serb military prowess and political hegemony with the Yugoslav idea, not only tolerated but took part in a campaign of revenge against non-Serb civilians who had nothing to do with the Partisans or the Ustaši.

The Chetnik officers rallied behind a Greater Serbian political program, attempted to put it into effect during the war, and apparently saw no contradiction between their Pan-Serb schemes and devotion to the Yugoslav idea. At the end of 1942 Chetnik conferences in Montenegro produced resolutions which spoke of a Balkan "Chetnik dictatorship" embracing "half of Albania, all of Bulgaria, half of Hungary, and Rumania up to the oil reserves." [85] Even Mihailović, according to a German report, had discussed the possibility of establishing a Greater Yugoslavia which would extend to the Black Sea by bringing Bulgaria into a Yugoslav customs union.[86]

Just as the Allies created an image of Mihailović and the Chetnik bands which bore little relation to reality, so the officers in Montenegro wildly exaggerated their political and military prospects. In all likelihood, they were far more impressed by the German defeats at Stalingrad and in North Africa than by their own reverses in Bosnia and Serbia. As for collaboration with the Italians, Mihailović could justify his actions by pointing to the strong probability that Italy would soon collapse militarily. When that occurred, the Chetniks would disown the Italians and defend Montenegro from a German invasion.[87] Similarly, British pressure for sabotage operations struck Mihailović as unreasonable but must also have reaffirmed his already strong conviction that the Allies had big plans for the Balkans. Before that happened the Chetniks had to secure exclusive Allied support for the future, and that meant crushing Tito once and for all. In 1943 Mihailović finally had his opportunity to participate in the destruction of the Partisan movement.

---

the Albanians are concerned, there is no difference between the Serb Chetniks and the Serb Partisans." Secretary of Kosovo-Mitrovitsa Provincial Committee, (?) November 1941, *ibid.*, vol. 1, bk. 9, no. 3. As late as August 1942 the Partisan organizers had had practically no luck with the Kosovo Muslims; a provincial committee report related that the Albanian Muslims, who made up about 70 percent of the population, were still a narrow minority within the party. Deakin (*Embattled Mountain*, p. 52) explains that in June 1943 Partisans moving through eastern Bosnia had to avoid hostile Muslim villages.

[85] Minutes of Chetnik Youth Organization Conference held at Sabović and presided over by Major Zaharije Ostojić and Captain Pavel Djurišić (30 November-2 December 1942), *Dokumenti o Izdajstvu Draže Mihailovića*, no. 4.

[86] Amt Ausland/Abwehr/Abt. Abwehr III to Aus. Amt/Pol. C, "N. 4024/42 vom 8.12.1942," 8 December 1942, *T-120*, roll 724, frame 321407.

[87] See Deakin, *Embattled Mountain*, p. 53.

VI
OPERATION
WEISS

:

Mihailović's next chance to contain or destroy the Communists came in early 1943, but this time he had to coordinate his strategy with the Italians, the Ustaši, and, above all, the Germans. The Germans had taken over command of military operations in Croatia and were expecting an Allied amphibious operation along the Aegean or Adriatic coasts. They were determined to carry through a grand anti-rebel action in order to secure their rear in the Balkans. After a short combined German-Ustaši drive in December 1942 succeeded only in pushing the Partisans out of part of western Bosnia,[1] it became clear that massive Italian support for a large, encircling operation was needed to crush the Tito movement completely. In the second half of December, the Germans announced to the Italians their plans for a vast operation in Independent Croatia and, without asking for Comando Supremo's approval, turned over all military responsibilities for the Balkans to the head of the South-East High Command, General Löhr.[2]

---

[1] Report of staff of Third National Liberation Division to First Bosnian National Liberation Shock Corps, 5 December 1942, *Zbornik*, vol. 4, bk. 8, no. 155; *KTB/OKW*, vol. 2, entries for 21 and 26 December 1942.

[2] Comando Supremo, "Argomenti militari speciali trattati nei colloqui presso il Quartiere Generale germanico nei giorni 18, 19 dicembre 1942," 19 December 1942,

The greater the supposed Allied threat to the Balkans, the more determined the Germans were to dispose of Mihailović as well as Tito. In early January General Löhr demanded that the Italians redeploy their own units to occupy the areas then patrolled by the Serb militia units and to prepare for the eventual disarmament of the Chetniks.[3] The Italians were being asked to reverse their policy of concentrating their forces along the Adriatic coast and risk a confrontation with Mihailović. Neither Ciano nor Roatta thought much of the German plan,[4] and, although Cavallero grudgingly agreed to it, the Italian command in Yugoslavia immediately began to sabotage it.

On 11 January Roatta issued final instructions for Operation Weiss but made no mention of Cavallero's promises to stop all arms deliveries to the anti-Partisan formations. He gave the confusing orders to "keep the M.V.A.C. [Voluntary Anti-Communist Militia] formations in the dark about the operations" but to employ them in at least one sector against Tito.[5] The initial directive was flexible enough to permit the use of "trustworthy individual [Chetniks]" to act as guides for the advancing Italians.

The Italians, then, were not willing to open hostilities against Mihailović but, on the eve of Weiss, had no plans for large-scale collaboration with him either. The Serb officers, on the other hand, had made no long-standing agreements with Roatta's headquarters for participation in Weiss but hurried into the operation at the last minute. At the beginning of the year one of Mihailović's top officers, Major Baćović, brought about two thousand Herzegovinian troops into an area recently evacuated by the Italians near Knin and Gracać,[6] while the former Belgrade journalist Milan Šantić opened talks with local Croat officials for a combined anti-Partisan action in western Bosnia. Mihailović had apparently not empowered Šantić to negotiate with the Italians or the Germans. As for their talks with the Croats, the Chetnik emissaries stated openly that their organization was the continuation of the Yugoslav royal army and demanded the right to settle accounts with certain local Ustaši who had been heavily involved in the Serb massacres. Only at the end of the first

T-821, roll 21, frame 975; OKW/WFSt/Op., N. 552273/42 g. K. Chefs., "Weisung N. 47 für die Befehlsführung und Verteidigung des Südostraumes," 28 December 1942, in Hitlers Weisungen, pp. 212–14.

[3] Ugo Cavallero, Comando Supremo: Diario 1940–1943 del Capo di S.M.G. (Bologna: Capelli, 1948), entry for 3 January 1943.

[4] Ciano, Diario, vol. 2, entry for 6 January 1943; Kasche to Ritter, "Telegramm N. 126 vom 8.1.1943," 8 January 1943, T-120, roll 395, frame 999/305504.

[5] Roatto to Ecc. Comandante del V. Corpo d'Armata, "Operazioni invernali," 11 January 1943, Zbornik, vol. 4, bk. 9, no. 211.

[6] Stellvertreter des. Allg. Verwaltungs Kommissars/Grossgespan der Bribir-Sidraga u. Gacko-Lika (David Sinčić), "Zusammenarbeit mit der Cetniks u. Cetniks als Jugoslawische Armee," 2 January 1943, T-501, roll 265, frame 503.

week of January did Chetnik headquarters realize that their anti-Partisan project had been saved by the Italians, who were arming various volunteer detachments for Weiss.

Mihailović's chief of staff, Major Ostojić, reported on 9 January not only that the Herzegovinians under Baćović were receiving arms and supplies from the Italians but that Djurišić's Montenegrins were getting the necessary support for a march to the north.[7] By the middle of the month the Chetnik formations were building up rapidly throughout the Italian occupation zone. In addition to a few thousand troops around Knin, Partisan sources identified another concentration, ranging from twelve hundred to fourteen hundred and mostly "newcomers from Herzegovina," near Gracać.[8] In Montenegro Stanišić hastily called on his subordinates at Nikšić, Danilovgrad, Podgorica, and Cetinje on 11 January to organize meetings in connection with the awaited march into Bosnia.[9]

Contrary to the Cavallero-Löhr agreements of early January, the Italians not only avoided a break with Mihailović but gave the Chetniks even greater amounts of arms. On 15 January Cavallero gave official sanction to what his generals in Yugoslavia had been doing for over a week when he approved the "temporary use" of the Montenegrin "volunteer units" on the condition that they operate on Croatian territory only for the duration of the anti-Partisan campaign.[10] Roatta, who was mainly interested in using Chetniks instead of Italians to fight Tito, seized the opportunity and offered the Montenegrin officers more support than ever before. Stanišić, in fact, soon had about four thousand troops ready for the campaign and got Pirzio-Biroli's permission to use Italian-controlled trains to move them north to Herzegovina.[11] At Mihailović's headquarters at Kolašin in southern Montenegro, the way now seemed clear for the Herzegovinians under Baćović and the Montenegrins under Stanišić and Djurišić to play a major role in the operations against Tito.[12]

[7] Ostojić to Mihailović and Ostojić to Djurišić, 9 January 1943, in Comando 2. Armata, "Appunti per colloqui dell' Ecc. con i capi cetnici," 8 March 1943, *T-821*, roll 31, frame 371. By this time both the Italians and Germans had succeeded in intercepting the Chetniks' radio messages. These messages appear in both the Second Army and German intelligence reports. Some of them were captured by the Partisans in the form of typed messages and later included in the publication of documents relating to Mihailović's trial in 1946. In addition, Vladimir Dedijer's diary contains a considerable number of these valuable Chetnik communications.

[8] Supplementary report of deputy chief of staff of National Liberation Army to supreme commander (Tito), 13 January 1942, *Zbornik*, vol. 2, bk. 7, no. 115.

[9] Stanišić to the commanders of the towns Nikšić, Danilovgrad, Podgorica, and Cetinje, 11 January 1943, *Dokumenti o Izdajstvu Draže Mihailovića*, no. 56.

[10] Comando Supremo to Comando 2. Armata, "N. 20181 del 15.1.1943," 15 January 1943, *Zbornik*, vol. 4, bk. 9, no. 218.

[11] Supersloda Operazioni to Governatorato Montenegro, 15 January 1943, *T-821*, roll 298, frame 211.

[12] Jevdjević to Mihailović, 22 January 1943, and Mihailović to Ostojic, 18 January

Not only did the Italians authorize the moving of large Chetnik formations into the zone of operations on Croatian territory but they also
appeared to be allowing Mihailović to act as coordinator, if not commander, of the anti-Partisan units. Jevdjević informed him of Italian
plans as soon as he learned of them from Second Army headquarters, and
Mihailović was therefore confident that the Montenegrins could move
unimpeded as far north as the south Dinaric area. He did not hesitate
to establish direct ties with the group of Herzegovinians in the Knin sector. In order to coordinate the tactics of the Montenegrin units with
Italian strategy, a delegate from General Djukanović's staff at Cetinje
was rushed to Split in an Italian plane on 19 January, the eve of Weiss.[13]

These preparations, however, were made at the last minute, and the
officers' formations, without any experience in large-scale combined
operations, were barely ready for the tasks the Italians had assigned to
them. Djurišić's formations depended completely on Italian arms and
transportation; on 18 January, only two days before Weiss began, they
still had not left Montenegro.[14] According to Ostojić, the unit leaders
had to ask the Italians for maps of the zone of operations before they
left,[15] and, with such a late start, there was little hope of their arriving at
this assigned sector, the area north of Prozor, before the end of January.[16]

When Operation Weiss began on 20 January, both the Italians and the
Chetnik leaders were still trying to position the anti-Partisan units in
such a way as to contribute to Tito's defeat while avoiding political or
military retaliation from Pavelić and the Germans. On the surface of
things, it appeared that Mihailovic's formations were a secondary, auxiliary contingent in a coalition whose superiority over the Partisans was
overwhelming. Tito's main units had, after all, established effective control only in certain parts of western Bosnia and numbered perhaps
twenty thousand to twenty-five thousand men.[17] General Löhr had at his

1943, in Comando 2. Armata, "Appunti per colloquio dell' Ecc. con i capi cetnici," 8
March 1943, T-821, roll 31, frames 371–72.

[13] Governatorato Montenegro to Comando XVIII. Corpo d'Armata, "N. 303 del 18
gennaio 1943," 18 January 1943, T-821, roll 298, frame 83; Comando XVIII. Corpo
d'Armata to Supersloda Operazioni, "I/54/M.V.A.C. del 20 gennaio 1943," 20 January
1943, T-821, roll 298, frame 179.

[14] Mihailović to Ostojić, 18 January 1943, in Comando 2. Armata, "Appunti per
colloqui dell' Ecc. con i capi cetnici," 8 March 1943, T-821, roll 31, frame 371.

[15] Ostojić to Djurišić, 18 January 1943, in Comando 2. Armata, "Appunti per colloqui
dell' Ecc. con i capi cetnici," 8 March 1943, T-821, roll 31, frame 371.

[16] Comando XVIII. Corpo d'Armata to Supersaoda Operazioni, "I/54/M.V.A.C. del 20
gennaio 1943," 20 January 1943, T-821, roll 298, frame 179.

[17] Ivan Lola-Ribar, Uspomene iz Narodno-Oslobodilački Borbe (Recollections from
the national liberation war) (Belgrade: Vojno Delo, 1961), p. 76; Jovan Marjanović
and Pero Morača, Naš Oslobodilački Rat i Narodna Revolucija (1941–1945) (Our war of
liberation and the national revolution, 1941–1945) (Belgrade: Izdavačko Preduzeće,

disposal five German divisions, four of which were active, three Italian divisions of the Fifth Army Corp, and the 369th Croat division.[18] On the first day of the operation, which had as its ultimate goal the pacification of the entire area from south of Zagreb to the Montenegrin border, about sixty-five thousand troops began pushing toward the Partisan concentration from four directions.[19]

Partisan strategy—and the Partisans had little choice in the matter—was to provide just enough resistance along the northern sector of the ring to permit the main body of troops to retreat south and force a breakthrough against the Italians and Chetniks. The Italian command, never enthusiastic about wasting troops in anti-rebel operations, tended to hold back, and Roatta encouraged the Chetniks to bear the brunt of the fighting, guessing that such a policy would further widen the gulf between Tito and Mihailović.[20] Therefore, the Herzegovinian and Montenegrin officers' formations played a significant military role in Operation Weiss and had to give way to increasing Italian supervision and control.

In spite of all of Mihailović's efforts to assume command, through Major Ostojić, of the participating anti-Partisan detachments, the officers quickly discovered that they were being forced to act as Roatta's auxiliary army. The Knin group was soon placed under the orders of General Gianuzzi of the "Bergamo" division, and the Montenegrins gathering slowly around Prozor were in turn placed under the command of the Sixth Army Corps.[21] Stanišić's troops, who were supposed to gather at Prozor for operations toward Tomislavgrad and Ravno, received orders to avoid "excesses" against the local Croats and Muslims and were also warned to "avoid . . . making contact with German or Croatian troops." [22] Most important of all, however, the Chetnik leaders had staked everything on Italian willingness to move about four thousand Montenegrin troops north to western Bosnia. Before Weiss was a week old, Roatta reneged on his promises, probably under German pressure,[23]

1958), p. 187; Branko Lazitch, *Tito et la révolution Yougoslave (1937–1959)* (Paris: Fasquelle, 1957), p. 95.

[18] Comando Supremo to Comando 2. Armata/Ufficio Operazioni, "Operazioni invernali combinate italo-tedesche-croate," 10 January 1943, *Zbornik*, vol. 4, bk. 9, no. 210.

[19] Vladimir Dedijer, *Dnevnik*, vol. 2 (Belgrade: Državni Izdavački Zavod Jugoslavije, 1946), entry for 22 January 1943.

[20] Supersloda Operazioni to Comando Supremo, 12 January 1943, *Zbornik*, vol. 4, bk. 9, no. 217.

[21] Comando XVIII. Corpo d'Armata/Ufficio Operazioni to Comando Divisione "Bergamo," "Operazione M.V.A.C.," 22 January 1943, *T-821*, roll 298, frames 144–46.

[22] Comando VI. Corpo d'Armata/Ufficio Operazioni to Comando Divisione "Murge," "Preavisso operativo," 22 January 1943, *T-821*, roll 298, frame 114–16.

[23] Italian and German documents are not clear on this. On 13 February Colonel Bailey, then in Montenegro, cabled the British that "recent arrangements made between the Chetniks and the Italians for transportation of Chetniks both from Nikšić

and halted all movement of the anti-Partisan units.[24] Without the prospect of a full-scale Chetnik buildup near Prozor, the Baćović group around Knin was isolated; the Italians recognized this and decided to limit the use of the Herzegovinians to small operations and to have them withdrawn immediately after Weiss to nearby Tenin.[25]

Before the Baćović group could extract itself by seeking Italian protection, Tito directed his field commanders to concentrate on the Herzegovinians;[26] by the end of January the Partisans had taken almost all the Chetnik strongpoints near Knin and had dealt the anti-Partisan formations a severe moral blow.[27] To the Italians, Baćović's Chetniks appeared poorly disciplined and inadequately led;[28] to Tito, Mihailović's troops were surprisingly easy prey, and the path seemed clear for operations against the small Montenegrin group near Prozor.[29] In the meantime, Baćović's Herzegovinians had suffered about two hundred dead, were described by the Italians as "tired, dirty, and shoeless,"[30] and were totally at Roatta's mercy for additional supplies.[31]

At Chetnik headquarters in Montenegro, the officers were bitter over the failure of the Italians to support the northern expedition, but, with both Partisans and Germans pushing south toward Herzegovina, they had little choice but to continue collaborating with Roatta's staff. Mihailović, for example, blamed the whole thing on the "perversity" of Roatta and Prizio-Biroli[32] but cautioned Jevdjević to maintain "the present policy toward the Italians" and "to stay calm . . . even after the Montenegrins leave the zone [of operations in Croatia]."[33]

and Kolašin to Bosnia were cancelled at the last minute, probably at German insistence. The Germans may not desire to have concentrated Chetnik forces in Bosnia." Deakin, *Embattled Mountain*, p. 180.

[24] Comando Supersloda to Comando XVIII. Corpo d'Armata, "N. 1339 del 25 gennaio 1943," 25 January 1943, *T-821*, roll 298, frame 131.

[25] Comando Divisione "Bergamo" to Comando XVIII. Corpo d'Armata, "Operazione M.V.A.C.," 26 January 1943, *T-821*, roll 298, frame 372.

[26] Directive of staff of First Proletarian Brigade, 27 January 1943, *Zbornik*, vol. 4, bk. 9, no. 135.

[27] Comando XVIII. Corpo d'Armata to Comando Aerogruppamento Zara, "N. 1525 del 27 gennaio 1943," 27 January 1943, *T-821*, roll 298, frame 338.

[28] Radivoje Ivanisević (Baćović's chief of staff) to Djujić, 28 February 1943, in Drago Gizdić, *Dalmacija, 1943–45* (Zagreb: Epoka, 1962–64), pp. 153–54.

[29] Tito to staff of First Proletarian Division, 27 January 1943, *Zbornik*, vol. 2, bk. 7, no. 167 Tito to staff of First Proletarian Division, 29 January 1943, *ibid.*, no. 172.

[30] Comando Divisione "Bergamo" to Comando XVIII. Corpo d'Armata, "Operazione M.V.A.C.," 1 February 1943, *T-821*, roll 298, frames 360–61.

[31] Roatta to Italmissione Zagabria, "N. 1661 del 30 gennaio 1943," 30 January 1943, *T-821*, roll 298, frame 849.

[32] Mihailović to Baćović, 31 January 1943, in Comando 2. Armata, "Appunti per colloquio dell Ecc. con i capi cetnici," 8 March 1943, *T-821*, roll 31, frame 374.

[33] Ostojić to Jevdjević, 29 January 1943, *Dokumenti o Izdajstvu Draže Mihailovića*, no. 439.

By early February the strains and tensions at Mihailović's headquarters and among his closest subordinates were unbearable. In addition to their shock at the early defeats at the hands of the Partisans and their total lack of confidence in Italian support, the officers began to see the growing likelihood of German penetration into Herzegovina and Montenegro.[34] Major Ostojić, in particular, began to warn that a confrontation with German troops was likely [35] and, in order to counter that possibility, advocated a tougher policy toward the Italians.

The immediate issue was guns and munitions, but the real question was whether or not Mihailović could afford to continue collaborating with the Italians. As for arms and supplies, the officers were unanimous in their conviction that any ruse to squeeze more support out of the Italians would be successful. Ostojić directed Baćović's chief of staff on 5 February, for instance, to "blackmail" the Italians for enough supplies to put the approximately four thousand Herzegovinians back in action; [36] Chetniks in the zone north of Foča received instructions to "force" the nearby Italian garrison to supply them with arms by claiming that three thousand Partisans were concentrating in the area.[37] Ostojić proposed destroying the railway line between Sarajevo and Mostar—"making it look like a Communist attack"—to induce the Italians to speed up arms deliveries for the Montenegrins, and Mihailović recommended sabotage operations against the lines from Sarajevo to Brod and Višegrad as well as against an electric power plant north of Split, "all of which [were to be] . . . camouflaged as Communist actions." [38]

Going even further, Ostojić began to suggest an open break with the Italians—by disarming them—and for a while there was a serious division over strategy between Mihailović and his chief of staff. By late January Ostojić had worked out a hasty plan to create a front against the Germans running south of Sarajevo and north of Mostar which they could hold, as he argued to Mihailović, with the aid of "Italian war booty." [39] Shortly thereafter he instructed Jevdjecić to "find out if the

[34] Ostojić to Jevdjević, 4 February 1943, in Comando 2. Armata, "Appunti per colloquio dell'Ecc. con i capi cetnici," 8 March 1943, T-821, roll 31, frame 372.

[35] For example, Ostojić to Ivanisević, 5 February 1943, in Comando 2. Armata, "Appunti per colloquio dell' Ecc. con i capi cetnici," 8 March 1943, T-821, roll 31, frame 374.

[36] Ibid.

[37] Ostojić to [?] [late February], 1943, in Comando 2. Armata, "Appunti per colloquio dell' Ecc. con i capi cetnici," 8 March 1943, T-821, roll 31, frames 374–75.

[38] Ostojić to Mihailović and Mihailović to Ostojić, 2 February 1943, in Comando 2. Armata, "Appunti per colloquio dell' Ecc. con i capi cetnici," 8 March 1943, T-821, roll 31, frame 375; Comando 2. Armata/Ufficio Operazioni to Comando 2. Armata/Ufficio I, "N. 1898 del 4 febbraio 1943," 4 February 1943, T-821, roll 294, frame 983.

[39] Ostojić to Mihailović, (late January), 1943, in Comando 2. Armata, "Appunti per colloquio dell' Ecc. con i capi cetnici," 8 March 1943, T-821, roll 31, frame 376.

Italians will fight if we present them with an ultimatum." [40] Mihailović, however, still gave priority to defeating Tito and warned his chief of staff at least twice in early February that they could not then afford to risk drastic actions against the Italians.[41] In the middle of Operation Weiss the officers wavered between strategies of resistance and collaboration.

The dilemma over strategy arose from the fact that Mihailović's units were becoming more deeply involved in a collaborationist struggle against the Partisans and more exposed to German hostility. Chetnik excesses against the civilian Croat population between Mostar and Prozor and the threat that the officers would somehow send more troops into Bosnia served as ammunition for typical German complaints.[42] This time, however, the Germans were more determined about the whole matter. Lüters once again gave strict orders to Pavelić's headquarters to avoid making any more treaties with Bosnian Chetniks,[43] South-East High Command gathered evidence on Mihailović's collaboration with the Italians,[44] and on 31 January O.K.W. asked Comando Supremo for a definitive statement of Rome's policies on the Chetnik question.[45]

During the first half of February, Comando Supremo, now headed by the anti-German General Ambrosio, broke decisively with the entire German strategy of relentless pursuit of Balkan guerrillas and thereby gave the Chetnik officers one more chance. Roatta refused to discuss disarming Mihailović's followers, and Ambrosio insisted that, if the anti-Chetnik action was to be carried out, it be done "with circumspection, not in haste"; [46] he later warned the new Second Army commander, General Robotti, that under no circumstances should German troops enter Herzegovina.[47] At Belgrade on 8 February, Robotti rejected flatly a joint action which was to begin on 15 February, agreed to help carry out the disarmament of the Chetniks only "at a most propitious moment,"

[40] Ostojić to Jevdjević, 4 February 1943, in Comando 2. Armata, "Appunti per colloquio dell' Ecc. con i capi cetnici," 8 March 1943, T-821, roll 31, frame 372.

[41] Mihailović to Ostojić, 2 and 9 February 1943, in Comando 2. Armata, "Appunti per colloquio dell' Ecc. con i capi cetnici," T-821, roll 31, frames 376–78.

[42] Kasche to Ritter, "Telegramm N. 488," 27 January 1943, T-120, roll 395, frames 999/30545, 6; chief of German liaison staff with Second Army (Colonel Dreschler) to command of Second Army, 27 January 1943, Zbornik, vol. 4, bk. 9, no. 235; Deutsche Bevoll. Gen. in Kroatien/Ia to OB Südost, "N. 619/43 vom 28.1.1943," 28 January 1943, T-501, roll 264, frame 899.

[43] Dt. Bevoll. Gen. in Kroatien to Hptquartier des Poglavnik, "Verträge mit Cetnikgruppen," 6 February 1943, T-314, roll 566, frame 711.

[44] KTB/OKW, vol. 3, entry for 31 January 1943.

[45] Ibid.

[46] Ibid., entry for 7 February 1943.

[47] Comando Supremo, "Colloquio con Ecc. Roatta e Robotti," 4 February 1943, T-821, roll 125, frame 810.

and denied vigorously that Italian-sponsored formations were responsible for recent outrages against Muslim civilians.[48]

Throughout these negotiations both Italian and Germans proposed courses of action on the Chetnik question based on considerations which had nothing to do with the military strength of Mihailović's organization. Rome's major concerns were opposing any German penetration of the Italian zone and avoiding all costly military operations, whether directed against Tito or Mihailović. The Germans saw the whole problem as a function of an expected Allied operation in the Balkans. Therefore, no matter how weak Mihailović was, an Allied landing would revive the Chetniks, giving the officers a clear advantage over Tito, or what was worse, would bring Tito and Mihailović together. On 16 February Hitler wrote Mussolini that an Allied invasion of the Balkans would unite "the Communists, Mihailović Partisans and all the other *comitagjes*" against the Axis "according to an Anglo-Saxon project."[49]

Despite Hitler's suspicions, Operation Weiss resembled more and more a civil war between Chetniks and Partisans, and the prospect of an Allied Balkan landing almost certainly made Mihailović and Tito give priority to eliminating each other. Moreover, in February the Partisans were clearly gaining the upper hand. In the early part of the month, an effort by Baćović and Djujić to go over to the counteroffensive in the Bos Grahovo sector of western Bosnia failed because of German opposition;[50] soon after, when the Italians decided to pull back, the Herzegovinian units had to withdraw with them.[51] By this time the Chetniks had failed in their attempt to use the western Bosnian operation as a springboard for recapturing the former stronghold at Drvar and uniting the Dinaric and western Bosnian formations.[52]

The important thing about these military operations is that the Chetniks, because they lacked supplies, had to avoid the Germans, and depended on Italian support; they lost all freedom of action and were

[48] Note of commander of Italian Second Army on Belgrade talks of 8 February 1943, *Zbornik*, vol. 4, bk. 10, no. 197.

[49] Hitler to Mussolini, 16 February 1943, *Les Lettres secrètes échangées par Hitler et Mussolini* (Paris: Editions de Pavois, 1946), pp. 149–54.

[50] Tito to Supreme Staff of Croatian National Liberation Detachments, 10 February 1943, *Zbornik*, vol. 2, bk. 8, no. 29; Comando XVIII. Corpo d'Armata to Comando Settare Dinara, "N. 2242 del 10 febbraio 1943," 10 February 1943, *T-821*, roll 298, frame 350.

[51] Comando XVIII. Corpo d'Armata to Supersloda Operazioni, "N. 2674 del 17 febbraio 1943," 17 February 1943, *T-821*, roll 298, frame 347; operation report of deputy chief of Supreme Staff of National Liberation Army to Tito, 18 February 1943, *Zbornik*, vol. 2, bk. 8, no. 51.

[52] Pop Djujić admitted this shortly after. Staff of Dinaric Chetnik division to commander of "Petar Kočić" brigade, 17 April 1943, *Dokumenti o Izdajstvu Draže Mihailovića*, no. 146.

functioning as auxiliary units attached to the Second Army. On numerous occasions the anti-Partisan formations had to attack and retreat alongside Italian units,[53] and in the Prozor sector, where the officers had hoped to concentrate about four thousand Montenegrins, the buildup was never fulfilled and Tito destroyed both the small Chetnik contingent and a good part of the "Murge" division.[54] The Partisans' capture of Prozor in mid-February gave Tito's followers a badly needed supply of Italian arms and opened the way for an assault on Mihailović's bastion in Herzegovina.[55]

At this phase of Weiss the officers recognized that the only way to stop Tito was to concentrate additional units in Herzegovina and thereby expose themselves even more to a future German action. Both Ostojić and Mihailović decided to take this chance; the chief of staff drew up plans for the creation of a Chetnik "front" along the Neretva and ventured as far north as Nevesinje, Herzegovina, to take personal command over the operation.[56] Mihailović hastened to get Djurišić's 2,500 men north toward Kalinovik in order to bolster Colonel Stanišić.[57]

Ostojić's plan, which was to keep all their troops south of the Neretva River so as to avoid being isolated by the advancing Partisans or the Germans, reflected an understandable caution but was opposed by both the unit leaders and the Italians. When Jevdjević agreed to an Italian order to send the formations across the river to the north bank, Mihailović's chief of staff called it a "scandal" and threatened to have Jevdjević removed.[58] Nor was resistance to Ostojić's strategy confined to civilians like Jevdjević. Bajo Stanišić reported to Mihailović on 18 February that all the Chetnik leaders in Herzegovina were opposed to Ostojić and supported the Italians' offensive strategy.[59] Other evidence also suggests

[53] For example, at Gornji Lapac. Comando Divisione "Sassari" to Comando XVIII. Corpo d'Armata, "N. 0466 del 11 febbraio 1943," 11 February 1943, *T-821*, roll 298, frame 685; Comando XVIII. Corpo d'Armata to Divisione "Sassari," "N. 2853 del 21 febbraio 1943," 21 February 1943, *T-821*, roll 298, frame 996.

[54] Ostojić to Captain Nikić, 4 February 1943, cited by Dedijer, *Dnevnik*, 2:122; Tito to staff of First Bosnian National Liberation Shock Corps, 16 February 1943, *Zbornik*, vol. 2, bk. 8, no. 44.

[55] Ostojić to Captain Nikić, 16 February 1943, *Dokumenti o Izdajstvu Draže Mihailovića*, no. 293.

[56] Ostojić to Major Pantić, 16 February 1943, *ibid.*, no., 269 *Sudjenje članovima Političkog i Vojnog Rukovodstva Organizacije Draže Mihailovića* (The sentence against the members of the political and military organization of Draze Mihailović) (Belgrade: Prosveta, 1945), p. 277.

[57] Mihailović to Stanišic, 17 February 1943, *Dokumenti o Izdajstvu Draže Mihailovića*, no. 59; Fitzroy Maclean, *Disputed Barricades* (London: Jonathan Cape, 1957), p. 210; Kruno Meneghello-Dinčić, "Les alliés et la résistance yougoslave," *Revue d'histoire de la Deuxième Guerre Mondiale* 2 (1962):16.

[58] Ostojić to Jevdjević, 17 February 1943, *Dokumenti o Izdajstvu Draže Mihailovića*, no. 299; Dedijer, *Dnevnik*, vol. 2, p. 132.

[59] Stanišić to Mihailović, 18 February 1943, cited by Živko Topalović, *Pokreti*

that several unit commanders thought the Italians were better informed on the military situation and favored Robotti's plan.[60]

At Chetnik headquarters in Nevesinje Ostojić asked whether the "[Chetnik] High Command or the Italians are giving orders" and issued a directive threatening death to anyone who carried out an order given by Jevdjević.[61] Ostojić found himself in a tug of war with the Italians over the tactical deployment of the Chetnik formations, lacked adequate information on their exact strength and location,[62] and was forced by the turn of military events to rely even more heavily on Second Army support. When Partisan units aproached the Neretva, Jevdjević reported that the troops were beginning to waver,[63] and Ostojić had little choice but to suggest more Italian air cover for an operation around Jablanica and to urge Major Pantić to request heavy artillery support in the same sector.[64]

Toward the end of February the efforts of the Chetnik officers to exercise effective control over the anti-Partisan contingents were straining relations with the Italians to the limit. The Italians were dissatisfied by the slow movement of Montenegrins north to the critical bauxite mining area around Mostar[65] and were bitter when a group of about seven hundred Muslim anti-Partisans, led by the Serb Chetnik Lukačević, disbanded at the first sign of fighting.[66] To the north, in western Bosnia, when the Chetnik intermediaries tried to talk the Italians into arranging for the return of Baćović's battered group to Herzegovina, they were turned down because the Germans were too close.[67] Baćović's chief of staff, Captain Ivanisević, even threatened to break off relations with the Italians, but to no avail.

As events were progressing, the officers had relatively little leverage with the Italians because they needed the continued support of Second Army headquarters more than the Italians needed the Chetniks. In the Mostar

---

Narodnog Otpora u Jugoslaviji, 1941–45 (Movements of national resistance in Yugoslavia, 1941–45) (Paris: n.p., 1958), p. 67.

[60] See, for example, the testimony of Perović in *Sudjenje članovima Političkog i Vojnog Rukovodstva Organizacije Draže Mihailovića,* pp. 266–67.

[61] Ostojić to all unit leaders, 17 February 1943, *Dokumenti o Izdajstvu Draže Mihailovića,* no. 300.

[62] For instance, Ostojič to Jevdjević, 20 February, and Ostojić to Radulović, 23 February 1943, *ibid.,* nos. 313, 336.

[63] Dedijer, *Dnevnik,* vol. 2, p. 132.

[64] Ostojić to Jevdjević, 19 and 20 February 1943, *ibid.,* pp. 133–34.

[65] Command of Italian Sixth Army Corps to command of Second Army, 18 February 1943, *Zbornik,* vol. 4, bk. 10, no. 234.

[66] Ostojić to Jevdjević, 23 February 1943, *Dokumenti o Izdajstvu Draže Mihailovića,* no. 332; Comando 2. Armata to Stato Maggiore R. Esercito/Ufficio Operazioni, "Collaborazione con elementi mussulmani," 8 May 1943, *T-821,* roll 288, frame 249.

[67] Captain Ivanisević to Mihailović, 25 February 1943, in Comando 2. Armata, "Intercettazione," 27 February 1943, *T–821,* roll 31, frame 379.

sector of Herzegovina, the Sixth Army Corps kept goading the Chetniks to commence offensive actions, and on 25 February General Amico issued an ultimatum threatening to break off collaboration if the anti-Partisan units did not seize the right bank of the Neretva immediately.[68] Ostojić, who was still complaining that he did not know "the strength and whereabouts of our people in Herzegovina," [69] tried to bluff the Italians by ordering a small group of Montenegrins to cross the river and return immediately.[70] Mihailović's chief of staff then changed his mind and supported a plan for a major offensive action to the north of the Neretva.

It made relatively little difference that Ostojić was suddenly supporting the offensive strategy of Jevdjević, Stanišić, and the Italians, for the Chetnik leaders, in this as in so many other instances, were making plans which went far beyond what the rank and file were able or willing to do. The Chetnik attack, launched on 27 February with the purpose of cutting off the Partisans' retreat from Jablanica to Prozor, failed to deal Tito a decisive blow.[71] Almost immediately the civilian spokesmen and Ostojić's headquarters, who were not well acquainted with the realities of the military situation, harshly criticized the unit leaders, especially Stanišić. On the day of the attack Jevdjević was complaining about the "slow progress" of Major Radulović's troops [72] and later referred to Stanišić's recently mobilized Montenegrins as "talkers rather than fighters." [73] Ostojić, although recently at odds with Jevdjević, now accepted entirely his assessment of the situation and sent Stanišić a harshly worded reprimand which denounced "the complete incompetence of [Stanišić's] command personnel." [74]

Ostojić and Jevdjević overreacted in a sense because, with Operation Weiss over a month old, the Partisans, although far from annihilated, were in serious trouble. By the end of February they had failed to cross the Neretva, could not move east because of resistance provided by Djurišić's group,[75] and had strained their resources in men and arms to

[68] Ostojić to Major Radulović, 23 February 1943, cited by Topalović, *Pokreti Narodnog Otpora*, p. 69.
[69] Ostojić to Radulović, 25 February 1943, *Dokumenti o Izdajstvu Draže Mihailovića*, no. 341.
[70] Major Radulović to Stanišić, 25 February 1943, *ibid.*, no. 61.
[71] Ostojić to Stanišić, 28 February 1943, Dedijer, *Dnevnik*, 2:143.
[72] Jevdjević to Ostojić, 27 February 1943, *ibid.*, p. 142.
[73] Jevdjević to Ostojić, 28 February 1943, *ibid.*
[74] Ostojić to Stanišić, 28 February 1943, *Dokumenti o Izdajstvu Draže Mihailovića*, no. 271; Maclean, *Disputed Barricades*, p. 210.
[75] Staff of Third National Liberation Division to Supreme Staff, 27 February 1943, *Zbornik*, vol. 4, bk. 10, no. 166; Order No. 18 of command of Montenegrin and Herzegovinian detachments, 25 February 1943, cited by Louis Adamič, *My Native Land* (New York: Harper, 1943), pp. 197–98.

the limit. German reports a week earlier had counted over 6,500 enemy dead and more than 2,000 captured; [76] new recruits were being mobilized along the way, but the shortage of arms was catastrophic. In some large units almost half the members were retreating without guns.[77] The officers were aware of this and could not understand how their troops could fail to deal quickly with such a weakened opponent. For obvious political reasons, Chetnik headquarters needed to defeat Tito as quickly as possible. Just as clear was the reason for Mihailović's plan to stop the Partisans as far north as possible.

When all these calculations failed, the Chetniks had to face the almost inevitable prospect of renewed fighting with the Partisans, a German penetration into Herzegovina and perhaps Montenegro, and increasingly difficult relations with the British. Mihailović saw no alternative in the near future to continued collaboration with the Italians and even admitted this to the new head of the British mission, Colonel Bailey, on 28 February. Bitterly and indiscreetly, he told Bailey that the Chetniks' enemies were, first of all, Tito, the Ustaši, the Muslims, and the Croats, and second, the Germans and Italians.[78] The British, he claimed, were pursuing their "state-strategic interests" in the Balkans, and the Italians were a better source of support.

Sharp words like these, which were symptomatic of the frantic mood at Mihailović's headquarters, only confirmed what the British already knew [79] and hastened the Chetniks' fall from favor with Churchill's government. Short of an almost immediate Balkan landing, however, there was little the British could do to extricate Mihailović from the military predicament of Operation Weiss. Over the short term, the Chetniks' fate depended far more on their ability to deal with the Axis Powers, especially the Germans. By the end of February, the officers had to contend with mounting pressure from Zagreb and Berlin and followed the anti-Partisan operations in Herzegovina with one eye on the Germans.

At the close of the first phase of Weiss, the German command in Croatia, frustrated by their inability to defeat Tito and prevent an ap-

---

[76] *KTB/OKW*, vol. 3, entry for 18 February 1943.

[77] Gizdić, *Dalmacija,* entry for 18 February 1943.

[78] Vojmir Kljaković, "Oslobodilački Rat Naroda Jugoslavije i Učešće Talijana u Ratu protiv Sovjetskog Saveza" (The Yugoslav people's war of liberation and the Italian participation in the war against the Soviet Union), *Jugoslovenski Istorijski Časopis* 4 (1964):40–41.

[79] The British knew of the collaboration between Mihailović's subordinates and the Italians from a number of sources, including the heads of their liaison missions, Hudson and Bailey, and some dissident Croat members of the exiled London government. See, for example, ambassador to Yugoslav government in exile (Biddle) to secretary of state, 2 January 1943, U.S., Department of State, *Foreign Relations of the United States* (hereafter cited as *FRUS*) *(1943),* vol. 2: *(Europe)* (Washington, D.C.: U.S. Government Printing Office, 1964), pp. 962–64.

parently large Chetnik concentration in Herzegovina, made a firm decision to take matters into their own hands. They sensed their own helplessness to cope successfully with Partisan and guerrilla groups, but they tended to exaggerate the threat posed by Mihailović and the Serb nationalist armed formations. As far as Hitler was concerned, Mihailović was a potentially menacing guerrilla leader ready to link his activities with an Allied Balkan landing. To the German command in Zagreb, more aware of the weaknesses of the Chetnik organization, Mihailović's troops and the armed bands under his moral leadership were gathering in excess numbers near the Mostar bauxite mines,[80] spreading anti-Axis propaganda among the Bosnian Serbs,[81] and in some instances even creating "friction" with German units.[82]

Among the German military in Yugoslavia, anxiety focused not so much on Mihailović's military potential but on the apparent anarchy among the Serb formations and the Italians' unwillingness to restrain them. Nonetheless, in Berlin the preference was for drastic action. Göring was concerned enough over the security of the bauxite mining operations to propose to Löhr that they throw together any available units to occupy the Mostar area "without regard for the Italo-German demarcation line." [83] On the same day, Ribbentrop told Alfieri, in assessing Roatta's pro-Chetnik policies, that the Italians had been "trying to drive out Satan with Beelzebub"; Hitler informed Löhr that German troops were to occupy the bauxite mines "at least temporarily" and, if necessary, without previously securing Comando Supremo's approval.[84]

The longer Weiss dragged on, the more anti-Partisan units the Italians permitted to gather in Herzegovina and, consequently, the more Berlin shifted its concern from Tito to Mihailović. At the end of February, the Germans had decided on a policy of force, with or without the cooperation of the Italians; political solutions, such as negotiating with Chetnik spokesmen or the Italians, were no more than temporary expedients or formalities. Neither the accords between Jevdjević and Zagreb which recognized the Neretva as a line of demarcation between German and

---

[80] *KTB/OKW*, vol. 3, entry for 19 February 1943; Sixth Domobran Division to Supreme Domobran Headquarters, 20 February 1943, *Zbornik*, vol. 4, bk. 10, no. 353; Deutsche Gesandtschaft in Agram to Aus. Amt./Pol. IV, "Telegramm N. 815 vom 22.2.1943," 22 February 1943, *T-120*, roll 395, frame 999/30510.

[81] Daily report of 718th Infantry Division, 19 February 1943, *Zbornik*, vol. 4, bk. 10, no. 245; 718. Inf. Div./Ia to Bfh. d. dt. Truppen in Kroatien, "N. 607 vom 27.2.1943," 27 February 1943, *T-315*, roll 2271, frame 936; 718. Inf. Div./Ic, "Lagebericht für die Zeit vom 17.2–26.2.1943," 28 February 1943, *T-315*, roll 2271, frame 941.

[82] *KTB/OKW*, vol. 3, entry for 23 February 1943.

[83] *Ibid.*, entry for 21 February 1943.

[84] Testimony of von Ribbentrop in International Military Tribunal, *Trial of the Major War Criminals (Proceedings)* (Nuremberg: International Military Tribunal, 1946), 10:391–93.

Chetnik troops [85] nor the military talks in Rome of 25–28 February, which produced no agreement at all,[86] changed Hitler's mind. In early March, when Comando Supremo rejected several German requests to withdraw the Chetniks operating around Mostar, O.K.W. ordered Löhr to send in German troops to disarm and capture them, forcibly if necessary.[87] Robotti was informed shortly after that the S.S. "Prinz Eugen" division would attack immediately toward Mostar and the bauxite mining region.[88]

Mihailović had fairly accurate information all along, through Jevdjević's ties with the Italians, about German plans regarding the Chetniks in Herzegovina.[89] In spite of this knowledge, the formations in Herzegovina continued to behave in an anarchic way and to defy the approaching Germans. The major and immediate cause of this behavior was the presence of about six thousand Chetniks in the vicinity of the Mostar bauxite mines.[90] Reports indicated that the Chetniks there were spreading anti-Croat propaganda and stirring up their troops with rumors that German units had clashed with anti-Partisan groups near Konjić; in the bauxite mining district, the small German garrison considered its position hopeless and the miners began to flee.[91] Elsewhere Chetnik groups used their temporary advantage to deliver ultimatums to small Ustaši garrisons.

The evidence suggests that the civilian intermediaries, like Jevdjević, and the officers at Ostojić's and Mihailović's headquarters, attempted to restrain this anti-Croat and anti-Axis behavior [92] but that the rank and file was simply out of control. Regardless of who was really responsi-

[85] Jevdjević to Ostojić, 23 February 1943, *Dokumenti o Izdajstvu Draže Mihailovića,* no. 381; Deutsche Bevoll. Kdr. Gen. in Kroatien/Ia to OB Südost, "Beurteilung der Lage: Mostar Bauxitgebiet," 25 February 1943, *T-501,* roll 264, frames 871–72.

[86] Comando Supremo, "Traccia di argomenti di prospettare nella udienza del 24 febbraio 1943," 24 February 1943, *T-821,* roll 125, frame 340; Comando Supremo, "Riunione a Palazzo Venezia del giorno 25 febbraio 1943," 26 February 1943, *T-821,* roll 125, frame 531; *KTB/OKW,* vol. 3, entry for 28 February 1943.

[87] *KTB/OKW,* vol. 3, entries for 3 and 5 March 1943.

[88] Robotti to command of Sixth Army Corps, 7 March 1943, *Zbornik,* vol. 4, bk. 2, no. 197.

[89] For example, Mihailović to Ostojić, 17 February 1943, in Comando 2. Armata, "Appunti per colloqui dell' Ecc. con i capi cetnici," 8 March 1943, *T-821,* roll 31, frame 374; Mihailović to Ostojić, 23 February 1943, in Deutsche General b. Hauptquartier der ital. Wehrmacht to Ambrosio, "Angehörte Funksprüche der Mihailovic Bewegung," 7 March 1943, *T-821,* roll 356, frame 112.

[90] Deutsche Bevoll. Gen in Kroatien/Ia to OB Südost, "Beurteilung der Lage: Mostar Bauxitgebiet," 25 February 1943, *T-501,* roll 264, frames 871–72.

[91] 718. Inf. Div./Ia, "Lage in Raume Mostar," 23 February 1943, *T-315,* roll 2271, frame 879; Deutsche Bevoll. Gen. in Kroatien to OB Südost, "Funksprüche Major Poche, Mostar," 25 February 1943, *T-501,* roll 267, frame 534; Kasche to Aus. Amt./Pol. IV, "N. 887 vom 26.2.1943," 26 February 1943, *T-120,* roll 395, frames 999/305, 299–300.

[92] See, for instance, Jevdjević to Ostojić, 24 February 1943, *Dokumenti o Izdajstvu Draže Mihailovića,* no. 387.

ble for the ostensible Chetnik "takeover" in Herzegovina, by early March both Ostojić and Mihailović recognized that a German raid was highly probable. With Tito's main forces still trapped north of the Neretva, Ostojić returned to his earlier defensive strategy and urged keeping all the Chetnik troops south of the river.[93] Determined not to "let the Italians lead us by the nose," Ostojić even fell back on his old scheme of disarming local Second Army units, to be accomplished "in twenty-four hours without firing a shot," in order to meet the Germans on more equal terms. Mihailović now saw things more or less the same way and pointed out that their field commanders had "to keep their eyes on the Germans so that they do not attack us from the rear." [94]

Toward the end of the first week of March, the Chetnik unit leaders in Herzegovina, in part because they sensed that the Partisans were on the verge of collapse [95] and in part because they were now more frightened by the impending German raid on Mostar, were concentrating on preserving their forces for the moment and preparing for an eventual general revolt against the Axis.[96] Mihailović gave orders not to concentrate excessively on the fight against Tito and told Jevdjević and Baćović not to worry about an immediate encounter with the Italians; [97] Ostojić went so far as to give instructions to a Chetnik officer in western Bosnia for "the moral and military preparation of the Army and people for the coming struggle against the occupation."

At precisely this moment, when the officers attached to Mihailović's staff and in the field were shifting their attention from the Partisan to the Germans, Tito dealt a decisive blow. The hard-pressed Partisan units, slowed down by their own wounded and encircled on all sides,[98] had little choice but to attempt a breakthrough toward Montenegro before they were overwhelmed by the Germans. On the night of 6 March the

---

[93] Ostojić to Mihailović, 3 March 1943, in Oberkommando/I Abt/Operationsbüro der Streitkräfte im Ostraum to Oberkommando der Streitkräfte Slowenien-Dalmatien, "Abgehörte Funksprüche der Mihailović-Bewegung," 20 March 1943, *T-821*, roll 356, frame 115. This is a German translation of an Italian interception.

[94] Mihailović to Ostojić, 3 March 1943, in Oberkommando/I Abt./Operationsbüro der Streitkräfte im Ostraum to Oberkommando der Streitkräfte Slowenien-Dalmatien, "Abgehörte Funksprüche der Mihailović-Bewegung," 20 March 1943, *T-821*, roll 356, frame 115.

[95] For example, Stanišić to Mihailović, 5 March 1943, *Dokumenti o Izdajstvu Draže Mihailovića*, no. 65.

[96] Staff of Konjić group (Lukačević) to column commanders, 5 March 1943. Dedijer, *Dnevnik*, 2:200.

[97] Mihailović to Baćović, March 9, 1943, in Oberkommando/I Abt./Operationsbüro der Streitkräfte im Ostraum to Oberkommando der Streitkräfte Slowenien-Dalmatien, "Abgehörte Funksprüche der Mihailovic-Bewegung," 23 March 1943, *T-821*, roll 356, frame 124.

[98] Tito to staff of Fourth Operations Zone of National Liberation Army in Croatia, 2 March 1943, *Zbornik*, vol. 2, bk. 8, no. 109.

main Partisan concentration, numbering about four thousand to five thousand troops and believed by Chetnik officers to be weakened beyond repair,[99] began to force their way across the Neretva near Jablanica.[100] The officers' troops were taken totally by surprise. Lukačević, for example, who spent the previous week trying to keep out of the way of the aproaching Germans, reported that "a very small Communist group succeeded in crossing the Neretva at Jablanica by spreading panic among the garrison troops and creating so much confusion that some units began to shoot at each other." [101]

More important, what began as a local breakthrough quickly turned into a rout of the Chetniks on the southern bank of the river.[102] By the middle of March, the entire main Partisan force had crossed the Neretva, and Tito had pulled himself temporarily out of the encircling ring and was now more convinced than ever that he could handle Mihailović militarily. After the initial encounters with the Montenegrin formations, the Second Proletarian Division reported that Mihailović's "army is of rather poor quality and that the Chetniks, as special military formations, cannot provide any strong resistance unless they are aided directly by the troops of the occupation forces." [103]

As evidence accumulated that the Chetniks were poorly equipped and did not enjoy the unswerving loyalty of many of their recently mobilized troops, the Partisans quickly elected a strategy of a full-scale anti-Mihailović offensive in Montenegro. Peko Dapčević's Second Proletarian Division issued instructions calling for actions directed almost exclusively against the Chetniks; [104] they soon captured a Chetnik propaganda team and discovered the whereabouts and strength of Mihailović's headquarters near Kolašin in southern Montenegro.[105]

While the Chetnik troops in Herzegovina were being thrown 'back by Partisan pressure, the officers and civilian leaders at first barely understood the gravity of the situation and appear to have been more concerned about a showdown with the Germans. Jevdjević, as usual tried to inter-

---

[99] For instance, Radulović to Stanišić, Jevdjević, and Baćović, 6 March 1943, *Dokumenti o Izdajstvu Draže Mihailovića*, no. 68.

[100] Marjanović and Morača, *Naš Oslobodilački Rat i Narodna Revolucija*, p. 196; Obrad Egić, *Ratni Dnevnik 2. Proleterske Dalmatinske Brigade* (War diary of the Second Proletarian Dalmatian Brigade) (Zagreb: Stvarnost, 1667), entry for 6 March 1943.

[101] Lukačevic to [?], 7 March 1943, *Dokumenti o Izdajstvu Draže Mihailovića*, no. 274.

[102] Tito to staff of Ninth National Liberation Shock Division, 7 March 1943, *Zbornik*, vol. 2, bk. 8, no. 146.

[103] Second Proletarian Division to Supreme Staff, 8 March 1943, *Zbornik*, vol. 3, bk. 11, no. 43.

[104] Order of Second Proletarian Division, 11 March 1943, *Zbornik*, vol. 4, bk. 2, no. 80.

[105] Second Proletarian Division to Supreme Staff of National Liberation Army, 16 March 1943, *Zbornik*, vol. 4, bk. 11, no. 81.

vene with the Germans at Sarajevo: he denied any complicity with Chetnik activities in the Mostar area and promised that the Herzegovinian formations would never oppose German troops.[106] By this time, however, the issue was beyond negotiation, and on 11 March Mussolini finally gave approval to the S.S. "Prinz Eugen" division's temporary occupation of the bauxite mining area.[107] When the Chetnik leaders discovered that German troops were occupying Mostar they flew into a panic [108] but had no realistic prospects of resistance. The day before the Germans were scheduled to arrive Ostojić, who had been suggesting possible countermeasures since the beginning of the year, had to ask Mihailović for instructions on how to deal with the situation.[109]

By the end of the third week of March, when the second phase of Weiss had ended, the officers had failed to hold the Neretva "front" against either Tito or the Germans. Mihailović was far more concerned with the threat posed by German troops in the Mostar area, although the latter made no attempt to disarm or attack nearby Chetnik formations. At this point the fighting in Herzegovina was almost exclusively between the Chetniks and the Partisans. The Italians were as usual unenthusiastic about carrying through the anti-rebel action, and the Germans were frustrated with the apparently meager results of Weiss and unwilling to push any further south before resting their units.[110]

Tito used this pause in military operation by the occupation powers to break up and destroy the Chetniks in Herzegovina and Montenegro. Initial operations were directed against Major Ostojić's headquarters at Nevesinje; Stanišić's Montenegrins were not up to the task of protecting the city, and Ostojić had to call on both Djurišić and Baćović to move their men there immediately.[111] The Chetnik leaders were badly divided on questions of strategy and had lost all faith in their troops. Jevdjević went so far as to propose to the Italians that they request "temporary" aid from the Germans to salvage the situation at Nevesinje.[112] He was

---

[106] Comando 2. Armata/Ufficio Informazioni, "13 marzo 1943," 13 March 1943, *T-821,* roll 297, frame 369.

[107] *KTB/OKW,* vol. 3, bk. 1, entry for 11 March 1943.

[108] Jevdjević threatened "a unanimous revolt, led by fifty thousand troops, in Bosnia, Herzegovina, Montenegro, and the Sandžak." Comando 2. Armata/Ufficio Operazioni, "13 marzo 1943," 13 March 1943, *T-821,* roll 297, frame 370.

[109] Ostojić to Mihailović, 13 March 1943, in Oberkommando/I Abt./Operationsbüro der Streitkräfte im Ostraum to Oberkommando 2. Armee, "Abgehörte Funksprüche der Mihailović-Bewegung," 21 March 1943, *T-821,* roll 356, frame 127.

[110] See, for example, the German rejection of an Italian request for an attack on the Partisan rear around Nevesinje. Gen. d. Inf. Lüters to 718. Inf. Div., "22.3.43," 22 March 1943, *T-315,* roll 2271, frame 1142.

[111] Ostojić to Stanišić, 18 March 1943, *Dokumenti o Izdajstvu Draže Mihailovića,* no. 281.

[112] Command of Sixth Army Corps to command of Second Army, "N. 4214 of March 20, 1943," 20 March 1943, *Zbornik,* vol. 4, bk. 11, no. 254.

opposed by Mihailović, who insisted that the Chetniks would be better off dying in battle against the Partisans than being slaughtered by the Ustaši and the Germans.[113] Major Baćović's units, who finally succeeded in making their way to Herzegovina after three months of fighting as far north as the Knin sector, had simply exhausted themselves and, according to General Djukanović, "lost so many men [near Nevesinje] that they had to retreat." [114] Jevdjević conceded to Mihailović that Nevesinje was lost and that Baćović's troops were "very tired and want to get out of the fight."

What took place in Herzegovina in March and April of 1943 was more than just a series of military reverses: it was a major crisis of morale and the failure of a whole strategy for the officers. At the end of March and the beginning of April, when the Partisans succeeded in seizing virtually every Chetnik stronghold in Herzegovina,[115] Tito was suddenly in a position to turn the tables on Mihailović and attempt the total annihilation of the Chetniks before the expected Allied landing. Partisan directives now called for a concentration of all available forces against Mihailović in Herzegovina; [116] the same instructions to the few remaining groups in western Bosnia ordered "defensive" tactics against the Ustaši so they could use nearly all their strength against the Chetniks there. Partisan strategy followed the same general guidelines throughout western Yugoslavia. In April, Tito informed Ranković that "the situation in Montenegro is clearly better than we thought," and revealed that he was working out a "strategic plan" for the exclusive purpose of dealing "a decisive blow against the Montenegrin Chetniks." [117] Here the Partisans not only tended to avoid the Italians but had specific instructions to avoid "launching aggressive operations against the Chetniks of [the Montenegrin federalist leader] Krsto Popović, and to throw all their weight against the pro-Mihailović Chetniks.[118]

After his efforts to wage a full-scale, Partisan-dominated war of resistance and to force a break with the monarchist officers at the end of 1941, Tito's decision to exploit a temporarily favorable situation to

[113] Mihailović to Stanišić, 1 April 1943, in Oberkommando/I Abt./Operationsbüro der Streitkrafte im Ostraum, "Abgehörte Funksprüche der Cetniks," 9 April 1943, T-821, roll 356, frame 150.

[114] Head of Supreme National Command, 27 March 1943, Dokumenti o Izdajstvu Draže Mihailovića, no. 75.

[115] Tito to Second Proletarian Division, 23 March 1943, Zbornik, vol. 2, bk. 8, no. 193; Tito to First Proletarian Division, 24 March 1943, ibid., no. 197; Tito to staff of National Liberation Army in Croatia, 4 April 1943, ibid., bk. 9, no. 14.

[116] Tito to First Bosnian National Liberation Shock Corps, 30 March 1943, ibid., bk. 8, no. 216.

[117] Tito to Ranković, April (?), 1943, ibid., bk. 9, no. 45.

[118] Political Commissar of Third Shock Division to Provincial Committee of C.P.Y. in Montenegro, Kotor, and the Sandžak, 20 April 1943, ibid., vol. 3, bk. 5, no. 4.

eliminate Mihailović was his most daring move. The Partisan leaders recognized that the Chetnik troops were the weak link in the haphazardly thrown together anti-Partisan coalition and that Mihailović was blocking their way out of the German zone of operations and into Montenegro and the Sandžak. Moreover, Tito must have realized that the Germans, although still determined to rid their Balkan rear of all guerrilla groups, would look with some favor on a Partisan campaign against Mihailović. Finally, if the Chetniks wanted to see Tito eliminated before an Allied amphibious operation in the Balkans, the Partisans also wanted to deal Mihailović a decisive blow before such an Allied action revived the Chetniks. It is important to bear in mind that at this time both the Partisans and Germans expected that an Allied landing would work mainly to the advantage of Mihailović.[119]

Both Tito and the Germans were in a rather desperate situation and shared, at least temporarily, a common interest in a Chetnik defeat. Tito attempted to exploit this by offering the Germans a temporary armistice. The negotiations were carried out by the intermediary Hans Ott, a German formerly engaged in Croatian coal and bauxite mining operations whom the Partisans had captured near Livno the previous summer. Ott had been active in German-Partisan negotiations for the exchange of prisoners[120] and had good ties with Partisan headquarters. General Löhr, for example, had enough confidence in Ott to recommend using him in December 1942 "for the purpose of gathering information"; Kasche reported in the spring that Ott's activities had provided the Germans with a "view of the internal and military structure of the Partisan [movement] . . . which we could not have gotten any other way."[121]

Sometime in mid-March, or shortly after Tito's breakthrough into Herzegovina, Partisan negotiators suddenly suggested to Ott the possi-

---

[119] Berlin, of course, was very worried about this. German documents dating from December 1942 demonstrate that the German military authorities in the Balkans were deeply suspicious of the Montenegrin Chetniks because of a plan attributed to Mihailović to seize the whole province from the Italians in conjunction with an Allied action along the Adriatic. Third National Liberation Shock Division to Supreme Staff, 11 December 1942, *ibid.*, vol. 4, bk. 8, no. 171. As for the Partisans, Deakin mentions (*Embattled Mountain*, p. 62) that they were terribly concerned, well into the summer, that the British and Americans would invade the Balkans before recognizing Tito and breaking with Mihailović.

[120] Der Deutsche General in Agram, "Aufzeichnung über Angaben des deutsche Staatsangehöriger Hans Ott Leiter der Bohrarbeiten der Hans-Leichtmetall-Werke in Livno," 15 August 1942, *T-501*, roll 265, frame 974; Kasche to Ribbentrop, "N. 1333 vom 30.3.1943," 30 March 1943, *T-120*, roll 212, frame 162441; Wilhelm Hoettl [Walter Hagen], *The Secret Front* (London: Weidenfeld and Nicolson, 1953), p. 168.

[121] Nezavisna Država Hrvatska/Ministarstvo Vanjskih Poslova (Independent State of Croatia Ministry of Foreign Affairs), "Besprechungen General Glaise-Generaloberst Löhr," 15 December 1942, *T-501*, roll 267, frame 437; Kasche to Ribbentrop, "N. 1333 vom 30.3.1943," 30 March 1943, *T-120*, roll 212, frame 162441.

bility of a temporary arrangement whereby they would call off hostilities against the Axis occupation troops in return for a "free hand" to settle accounts with Mihailović.[122] In order to convince the Germans of the sincerity of his proposals, Tito accelerated the talks by sending two personal delegates to Zagreb. The key Partisan negotiator, who called himself Doctor Petrović, turned out to be Vladko Velebit, a leading Croatian Communist and Tito's source of communications with Moscow during the first year of the war.[123]

Velebit repeated the proposals and quickly convinced Kasche that the Germans had something to gain by making an arrangement with Tito. As far as the Germans were concerned, a Partisan drive into Montenegro and the Sandžak could not be stopped immediately, and Tito's evident desire to finish off the Chetniks quickly was consistent with one of the basic goals of Weiss.[124] Realizing that they could expect little support for such a project from the Foreign Office, Glaise tried to enlist Himmler's cooperation by bringing up the matter with the Secret Service.[125] According to Kasche, "General Glaise Horstenau would welcome any means to bring to an end the Partisans' resistance, [even including] a political solution." [126] The rest of the German military, the Croats, and the Italians saw the problem in much the same way. Lorković, the foreign minister, favored any solution which would call a halt to Partisan activities in Croatia; Casertano was firmly behind the project, and General Lüters, although claiming he was neutral "in any political question," raised no objections.[127]

Each side, then, was negotiating from what it believed was a weak position. The Germans saw the proposal as a convenient way to accomp-

[122] Kasche to Aus. Amt./Pol. IV, "N. 1174 vom 17.3.1943," 17 March 1943, *T-120*, roll 212, frame 162441.

[123] Velebit was the son of an Austrian officer and became a Communist, like several others, during his student days at Belgrade University. Until early 1942 his wireless at Zagreb was Tito's only means of contact with Moscow. In April of that year, Velebit, who had even joined the Catholic Church to protect himself, left the capital and joined Partisan headquarters at Foča. At the end of 1943 he flew to Cairo with Maclean and Deakin for talks with the British. Deakin mentions (*Embattled Mountain*, p. 61) that Velebit was "reticent about the past." During most of 1944 he served as Tito's principal liaison officer with the British in Italy and was present at the Tito-Churchill meeting at Naples in August. In 1952 he was appointed Yugoslav ambassador to England.

[124] Kasche to Aus. Amt./Pol. IV, "N. 1303 vom 26.3.1943," 26 March 1943, *T-120*, roll 212, frame 162434; Kasche to Ribbentrop, "N. 1333 vom 30.3.1943," 30 March 1943, *T-120*, roll 212, frame 162442.

[125] Hoettl, *Secret Front*, p. 170. Hoettl (Hagen) was a senior officer in Branch VI (South) of the Secret Service.

[126] Kasche to Ribbentrop, "N. 1333 vom 30.3.1943," 30 March 1943, *T-120*, roll 212, frame 162440.

[127] Kasche to Aus. Amt./Pol. IV, "N. 1303 vom 26.3.1943," 26 March 1943, *T-120*, roll 212, frame 162434.

lish at least one of the goals of Weiss. The Partisans' predicament, and this cannot be emphasized too strongly, was very serious. In spite of the recent victories of the Partisans against Mihailović, Tito had absorbed losses which must have approached half of his main force, and he must have feared that the gains of 1942 in Croatia, especially in western Bosnia, had been permanently lost. Moreover, the Partisan leaders, like the Germans, not only recognized that Mihailović was weak militarily but feared that the expected Allied Balkan landing would give the officers effective British backing and revive the Chetniks. The British still maintained liaison officers only with Mihailović and were advocating that the Partisans and Chetniks join forces, a course of action which neither Tito nor Mihailović would support. Interestingly enough, the Germans noticed that Tito's radio transmissions had taken an increasingly anti-British line since early 1943.[128] Furthermore, the Partisans' hard-pressed troops were still getting no appreciable support from Moscow, either diplomatic or in the form of supplies, in spite of Tito's urgent appeals since January.[129]

What is significant about Tito's efforts to arrive at an understanding with the Germans is that the community of aims between the Partisans and Germans was very accidental and inevitably short-lived and that Tito was asking for temporary freedom of action against Mihailović rather than the sort of ongoing collaboration which the Chetniks developed with the Italians. Tito's tactics were very similar to Mihailović's in Serbia in November of 1941, and, although the situation had changed drastically, they produced the same results. In the middle of April General Lüters issued orders for operations in May directed against both the Partisans and the Chetniks;[130] shortly thereafter, Ribbentrop conveyed strict orders to Kasche to abandon the talks with Tito.[131]

Militarily, the overriding difference between the two Yugoslav guerrilla groups was that, while Tito was certainly very interested in some toleration from the Germans, Mihailović's movement had developed in

---

[128] *Ibid.;* Hoettl, *Secret Front,* p. 170.

[129] See, for instance, the message from Tito to Moscow of 31 January in Maclean, *Disputed Barricades,* pp. 206: "I must once again ask you if it is really quite impossible to send us some sort of help. . . . Typhus has now begun to rage here. . . . Do your utmost to help us." The negative reply came on 11 February. Kasche observed that "the absence of any Russian help has damaged [the Partisans'] trust in Russia." It is possible, of course, that Velebit made disparaging statements about the Russians in order to convince the Germans in Zagreb that Tito was acting independently. It is also possible, and the evidence here is more solid, that the Yugoslav Partisans' bitterness toward the Russians was entirely sincere. Stalin, it should be added, had even expressed disapproval of Tito's negotiations with the Germans for the exchange of prisoners.

[130] Kdr. Gen. u. Bfh. in Serbien/Ia to 104. Jäger Division, "Unternehmen Schwarz," 14 April 1943, *T-501,* roll 250, frame 272.

[131] Ribbentrop to Kasche, "N. 502 vom 21.4.1943," 21 April 1943, *T-120,* roll 212, frame 162483.

such a way that it could not act effectively without considerable support from the Italians. When the Partisans overran Herzegovina in March and April, the officers were shocked and angered at the fact that Robotti's Second Army not only failed to offer substantial aid but appeared to be deserting the Chetniks altogether. Immediately after the Partisans took Nevesinje (23 March) the Sixth Army Corps pulled its troops out of nearby Gačko and forced the anti-Partisan units to retreat with them.[132] Weakened by the Italians' quick withdrawal, Stanišić's recently mobilized Montenegrins failed, according to one Partisan report, to "put up any resistance and fled in panic back to their homes." [133] By the time Tito's Third Shock Division entered Gačko, their intelligence reports were speaking confidently of a "deepening moral crisis in the Chetnik movement."

When the Partisans began to push ahead toward Bileća in early April, Stanišić's troops had lost all hope of Italian support.[134] Efforts of Jevdjević, Major Radulović, and Baćović to get some help for Stanišić from the Italian Sixth Army Corps failed.[135] General Robotti's command posts not only refused to provide arms but left the Chetniks in the lurch again by quickly evacuating Bileća and Stolac.[136]

In the Kalinovik-Foča area, the eastern sector of the zone of operations, Djurišić's efforts to use his Montenegrins to prevent a Partisan breakthrough toward Serbia and the Sandžak were stalled by wavering Italian cooperation. Djurišić's units, numbering something over 2,000 men, were badly mauled in mid-March near Kalinovik and had to fall back toward the Drina River.[137] At the end of the month, he had an assortment of about 4,500 Bosnians and Montenegrins at Foča, the Partisan stronghold of early 1942, but was in such desperate need of supplies that he ordered his followers at nearby Kolašin to attack an Italian garrison at Plevlje if they refused to turn over machine guns and ammunition immediately.[138] At Foča some of the Chetniks pulled back behind the river; [139] the

[132] Third National Liberation Shock Division to Supreme Staff of National Liberation Army, 24 March 1943, *Zbornik*, vol. 4, bk. 11, no. 122.

[133] Tenth Herzegovinian National Liberation Shock Brigade to Dušan Grka, 24 March 1943, *ibid.*, no. 124.

[134] Report of Italian intelligence officer (Lieutenant Sanazzi?) at Bileća, 3 April 1943, *ibid.*, bk. 12, no. 183.

[135] Report of Italian intelligence officer (Major Guarnacci), 3 April 1943, *ibid.*, no. 182.

[136] Mihailović to Stanišić, 4 April 1943, in Oberkommando/I Abt./Operationsbüro der Streitkräfte im Ostraum, 17 April 1943, *T-821*, roll 356, frame 158.

[137] Command of Sixth Army Corps to command of Second Army, 16 March 1943, *Zbornik*, vol. 3, bk. 5, no. 142; Gizdić, *Dalmacija*, entry for 18 March 1943.

[138] Djurišić to Kolašin staff, 22 March 1943, in Der Deutsche General b. Hauptquartier des ital. Wehrmacht to Comando Supremo, "Abgehörte Funksprüche der Bewegung Mihailović, 30 March 1943, *T-821*, roll 356, frame 127.

[139] First Proletarian Division to First Brigade, 29 March 1943, *Zbornik*, vol. 4, bk. 2, no. 148.

Italians announced that they were abandoning most of the Sandžak and withdrew the bulk of their troops from Foča itself.[140] By mid-April Djurišić's strength had dropped to less than 3,000, and the Chetniks spent the rest of the month fighting a seesaw battle with the Partisans along the Drina around Foča. At best, though, this was a holding action and, of course, had no effect on the officers' loss of their bastion in Herzegovina.

In Montenegro, which was rapidly becoming their last zone of influence, the Chetniks had as yet suffered no major military reverses but were nonetheless in serious trouble. In areas bordering on Montenegro and populated primarily by Muslims, the officers faced, as a result of their own actions, overwhelming civilian hostility. In the heavily Albanian Muslim region just north of Kosovo Polje, a virtual religious war had been going on for almost two years between the Albanians and the Montenegrin Serbs.[141] In the largely Muslim Sandžak, immediately east of Montenegro, Djurišić's outrages during 1942 made the area a fertile recruiting ground for Germans and Partisans later in the war.[142]

The Chetnik officers had also forfeited their credit among the Montenegrin Serbs. Montenegro was exhausted from the bloody civil war in 1941, and the officers' detachments in this part of Yugoslavia had identified themselves with a collaborationist line more openly than anywhere else. The best units had already been used up in Stanišić's and Djurišić's campaigns to the north, and additional mobilization was virtually out of the question. In April, for instance, when General Djukanović ordered about a thousand recently mobilized peasants moved in trucks to Nikšić, at the last minute the recruits refused to leave.[143] This incident reflected not only a general war-weariness but a noticeable lack of willingness among many of the detachments to fight except near their own villages. The Chetniks throughout the western half of Yugoslavia behaved like a collection of uncoordinated village self-defense units in spite of all the efforts of the officers and politicians to impose ambitious and mobile strategies upon them. In late April, for example, Stanišić admitted that the predominantly Herzegovinian "Foča" Brigade objected to plans which called for their continuing military operations in Montenegro and demanded to return to their native province instead.[144]

[140] Tito to staff of First Proletarian Division, 8 April 1943, *ibid.*, vol. 2, bk. 9, no. 28.

[141] Deutsches General Konsulat Tirana to Deutsche Botschaft Rom, "Lage in Albanien," 9 February 1943, *T-120*, roll 2908, frames 6181H/E464398–400.

[142] Kdr. General u. Bfh. in Serbien, "Merkblatt über den Sandzak," 25 April 1943, *T-501*, roll 250, frames 251–52; Comando Supremo, "Notizie dal Montenegro," 2 March 1943, *T-821*, roll 248, frames 33–34.

[143] Command of Sixth Army Corps to command of Second Army, 19 April 1943, *Zbornik*, vol. 3, bk. 5, no. 149.

[144] Stanišić to [?], 28 April 1943, in Oberkommando/I Abt./Operationsbüro der

The growing disintegration of the Chetnik rank and file, then, was evident throughout former Yugoslavia. In Herzegovina, where Mihailović had been forced to stake everything, there was a full-scale revolt from below. Native detachments refused to fight for the officers in Montenegro, Baćović's troops were exhausted, and Jevdjević began to report a growing sense of despair among the Herzegovinian anti-Partisan Serbs.[145] Trying to revive their morale by purging the less dedicated elements, Jevdjević called on all the unit leaders to assemble at Mostar to determine who was able to launch another operation against Partisan-occupied Nevesinje. At the same time he issued leaflets denouncing the troops for their cowardly behavior in the recent fighting.[146] Mihailović, on the other hand, could do little more than order Baćović to spread the rumor that five thousand Chetniks were coming from Serbia to reinforce the Herzegovinians.[147]

At this point the Chetnik leaders had already overmobilized the civilian population and could no longer count on sizeable reinforcements. Mihailović's instructions to the officers in western Serbia to send troops immediately through the Sandžak produced meager results.[148] The mobilization, carried out mostly in the villages of northwestern Serbia, was completed with such haste and cruelty that several men who refused to go were murdered on the spot;[149] in early May two Serb Chetniks, Keserović and Gordić, arrived in Montenegro with a combined strength of perhaps twelve hundred troops. At the same time, Chetnik efforts at Mostar, Herzegovina, to replace losses with new recruits got nowhere.[150] When they ordered the forced mobilization of all local Serbs between ages sixteen and sixty, General Robotti intervened to stop them.[151] Moreover, Jevdjević lacked the money to purchase provisions for the troops they still had.[152]

Streitkräfte im Ostraum, "Abgehörte Funksprüche der Cetniks," 6 May 1943, *T-821*, roll 356, frame 184.

[145] Jevdjević to Mihailović, 3 April 1943, in Der Deutsche General b. ital. Wehrmacht to Comando Supremo, "Abgehörte Funksprüche der Mihailović-Bewegung" (early April), 1943, *T-821*, roll 356, frame 130.

[146] Nezavisna Država Hrvatska/Obće Upravnog Povjerenictvo to Comando 2. Armata, "Foglio volante di cetnici di Mostar," 8 May 1943, *T-821*, roll 297, frames 170–72.

[147] Jevdjević to Mihailović, 3 April 1943, in Der Deutsche General b. Hauptquartier der ital. Wehrmacht to Comando Supremo, "Abgehörte Funksprüche der Mihailović-Bewegung" (early April), 1943, *T-821*, roll 356, frame 130.

[148] See the testimony of Dragutin Keserović in *Sudjenje članovima Političkog i Vojnog Rukovodstva Organizacije Draže Mihailovića*, pp. 210–11.

[149] Tassa Dinić (Nedić's minister of the interior) to Kdr. General u. Bfh. in Serbien, "Mobilisation des Draza Mihailovic," 3 May 1943, *T-501*, roll 256, frames 898–99.

[150] Bfh. d. Dt. Truppen in Kroatien/Ia to OB Südost, "N. 2316/43 vom 11.5.1943," 11 May 1943, *T-314*, roll 566, frame 777.

[151] Comando 2. Armata/Affari Civili to Comando VI. Corpo d'Armata, "N. 5947/AC del 8 maggio 1943," 8 May 1943, *T-821*, roll 294, frame 468.

[152] Jevdjević to Chetnik High Command, 3 May 1943, in Oberkommando/I Abt./

Mihailović and his officer subordinates had concentrated about twenty thousand of their best troops in Herzegovina,[153] made their grand military effort, collaborationist in practice but also anti-Axis in long-range intent, and failed. Henceforth, mobilization procedures were generally unsuccessful, and units simply broke up, either because the men wanted to return home or to join the Partisans. Detachments which did hold together oftentimes could not be coaxed to leave the area around their own villages. This overall trend was evident in the former Chetnik strongholds, Herzegovina and Montenegro, and in Serbia, where there was as yet no significant Partisan revival. In Bosnia, where about ten thousand Serbs were organized in a number of territorial units and Mihailović never succeeded in establishing his authority, the same trends were even more evident. Around Sarajevo a whole brigade attempted to desert and return home.[154] In western Bosnia, where Pop Djujić was the major leader, the men refused to engage in mobile operations [155] and, according to one Italian assessment, were good for little else but plunder.[156]

In most instances, the breakup was due to war-weariness. Some of the Chetnik troops, however, deserted and joined the Partisans. In Herzegovina, there was clearly a crisis of morale in which the officers could not cope with either the war-weary or the radicalized. Tito, after all, in spite of his shifting tactics, was fighting what appeared to be a relentless war against the Axis occupation and the Quislings; Mihailović, although his long-haul goals were anti-Axis and his relations with his Italian patrons were never good, was engaging in collaboration which everyone could

---

Operationsbüro der Streitkräfte im Ostraum, "Abgehörte Funksprüche der Cetniks," 12 May 1943, *T-821*, roll 356, frame 188.

[153] Josef Matl ("Jugoslawien im Zweiten Weltkrieg," in *Jugoslawien*, ed. Werner Markert [Cologne: Bohlau Verlag, 1954], p. 105) uses the figure 19,000; a recent Yugoslav survey (Ahmet Djonlagić et al., *Yugoslavia in the Second World War*, trans. Lovett F. Edwards [Belgrade: Medjunarodna Stampa, 1967], p. 113) mentions 20,000. These figures are certainly more or less accurate. An Italian document of late February gave the strength of the anti-Partisan units in Herzegovina as 20,514. Comando 2. Armata, "Riepilogo Situazione Forze M.V.A.C.," 28 February 1943, *T-821*, roll 31, frame 218. Also, a Croat division-level report of late March rated the Chetniks at from 17,000 to 20,000. Croatian Sixth Infantry Division, "N. 3121," 27 March 1943, *Zbornik*, vol. 4, bk. 2, no. 340. At the Rome talks of 3–4 March Robotti tossed out the figure 25,000 but was not specific about which Chetniks that number included.

[154] Report of Italian intelligence officer (Major Guarnacci ?) to command of Sixth Army Corps, 3 April 1942, *Zbornik*, vol. 4, bk. 12, no. 182.

[155] See the account of Djujić's speech of early March in Comando 2. Armata/Ufficio I, "Notiziario N. 4," 15 April 1943, *T-821*, roll 448, frame 456.

[156] Comando 2. Armata/Ufficio Operazioni, "Situazione ed Armamente della Formazione M.V.A.C. alle dipendenze del XVIII C.A.," 18 April 1943, *T-821*, roll 294, frame 883.

see. Moreover, some the Herzegovinian and Montenegrin troops were actually Partisans of 1941 who joined the officers in 1942 to save their own lives. There was something of a "floating" resistance, then, which passed from one leadership to the next but whose sympathies were always solidly anti-Axis. By the middle of 1943, this hard-core resistance passed almost entirely out of the officers' hands and into Tito's ranks.

VII
THE CRISIS
OF THE CHETNIK
LEADERSHIP

·

The events of the spring not only demonstrated that the Chetnik rank and file did not represent a solid military force but also pointed to serious inadequacies at the top of Mihailović's fragile organization. During Operation Weiss the officers and civilian spokesmen never had a firm hold on their followings, and through the summer of 1943 a series of factors conspired to isolate and discredit the leadership until, on the eve of Italy's capitulation, there was neither coherent direction nor agreement on future action. The entire period from the close of "Weiss" to Italy's exit from the war marked the definitive collapse of the non-Communist resistance in Yugoslavia. Significantly enough, the Serb armed groups, whether Italian-sponsored or not, were never really overwhelmed militarily and were probably about as numerous in late 1943 as they were in the early part of the year. What failed was the leadership. Officers lost control of their detachments and turned against each other over questions of authority and strategy. At the same time, the officers could no longer exercise predominant influence over the civilian unit leaders and spokesmen. Finally, Mihailović lost the effective support, through one means or another, of practically all his major subordinates

140

and by the end of the summer found himself almost totally isolated from the remains of the movement in the western half of Yugoslavia.

A good deal of the responsibility for the crisis belonged to Mihailović from the very beginning. Unlike the Partisans, the Chetniks never, with the exception of the early months of 1943, organized their main forces as a fairly compact unit, and, unlike Tito, Mihailović stayed away from the troops. During the culminating phase of Weiss and immediately after, he did move north from his headquarters in southern Montenegro but returned in mid-April [1] and never assumed a firm direction of the military operations. Even more significant, as he admitted at his trial in 1946, Mihailović was moving about so frequently that he had to let his chief of staff, Ostojić, give all the orders.[2] Available evidence suggests that by mid-March not even Ostojić was in constant contact with the officers in the field.[3]

Major Ostojić, while ostensibly in direct command of operations, proved unable to cope with the confusing and rapidly shifting situation. At first, he insisted on an unpopular, basically defensive strategy, violently attacked Jevdjević's right to get involved in military matters, and then blamed practically all of the officers for the defeats. Jevdjević, on the other hand, tended to support the Italian strategy and finally, without approval from Mihailović, tried to negotiate for military collaboration with the Germans. Mihailović was unable to impose a firm political line on his civilian supporters or to direct through Ostojić the tactics of the officers. At his trial he admitted as much when he criticized Djurišić's slow movement to Kalinovik and the whole behavior of Jevdjević, "an unbalanced sort of man whom nobody could restrain."[4]

The outbursts of charges and countercharges and the disputes over strategy and tactics probably tell us very little about who was least competent to direct the Chetnik troops but do illustrate in a striking way the basic fact that no one in the officers' camp exercised compelling authority over the armed detachments. Mihailović failed to take charge personally and did not distribute authority clearly among his subordinates; Ostojić's actions exacerbated rather than directed the officers. Jevdjević,

---

[1] Mihailović left his headquarters at Lipovo and moved to Kalinovik on 17 March, then went to Konjić, had transferred his staff to Foča by 6 April, and returned to Lipovo on 13 April. He left his headquarters on 19 April. See F. W. Deakin, *The Embattled Mountain* (New York: Oxford University Press, 1971), pp. 190–94.

[2] *The Trial of Dragoljub-Draža Mihailović*, p. 171.

[3] An examination of the Chetnik messages intercepted and decoded by the Germans and Italians shows that after the Partisans crossed the Neretva there was a sudden decline in the amount of communication between Ostojić and the unit commanders. The headquarters of the Chetnik chief of staff at Nevesinje was taken by the Partisans on 23 March.

[4] *The Trial of Dragoljub-Draža Mihailović*, pp. 167–68.

whose influence was more or less confined to Herzegovina and rested in large measure on his ties with Italians, fared worst of all.

The crisis of leadership among the Herzegovinian and Dalmatian anti-Communist Serbs was the most open and immediately became evident. In addition to their military reverses, the Chetnik leaders, both officers and civilians, were compelled after February to decide on the succession to the nominal leadership of the recently deceased Birčanin. Mihailović apparently could not or did not resolve the matter immediately, and throughout the spring a struggle took place between two groups, one led by Jakša Račić, a familiar figure at the court in the prewar years, Professor S. Alfierević, the Orthodox priest Sergije Urukalo,[5] and another combination dominated by Jevdjević and Major Baćović.[6] Indicative of the strained relations between Chetnik headquarters in Montenegro and Jevdjević is the fact that, although Jevdjević was easily the dominant civilian figure among the Serb nationalists in the Italian zone, Mihailović finally sided with the Račić group.[7] Challenged politically by other civilians and more uncertain than ever of Mihailović's support, Jevdjević had little alternative but to rely on the Italians; when in early April Robotti consented to a German plan for a visit to Mostar by the notorious Grand Mufti of Jerusalem, Jevdjević's reputation among the Serb nationalists suffered an irreparable blow.[8]

Jevdjević's loss of standing, probably stemming ultimately from his feud with Major Ostojić, was symptomatic of the growing difficulties between the officers and civilians. In Dalmatia and the adjoining Dinaric area, two leading Chetnik clergymen, Urukalo and Djujić, both strongly collaborationist,[9] were sharply ordered by Mihailović's delegate-officer Ivanisević to avoid any contacts with the Italians not previously approved by Chetnik headquarters.[10] In Bosnia, where the officers never succeeded in bringing all the Serb armed bands under Mihailović's direction, the situation was totally anarchic. Some formations broke up, while others simply deserted to return home; whatever the local leaders and their

[5] Drago Gizdić, *Dalmacija, 1943–45* (Zagreb: Epoka, 1962–64), entries for 3 and 20 February 1943.

[6] See the letter of the Split Chetnik Djuro Vilović to Mihailović of 1 March, 1943, cited in *ibid.*, entry for March 1, 1943.

[7] *Ibid.*, p. 130.

[8] Comando 2. Armata/Affari Civili to Comando VI. Corpo d'Armata, "N. 4039/AC del 2 aprile 1943," 2 April 1943, *T-281*, roll 294, frame 592.

[9] Djujić's collaboration with the Italians went back to the summer of 1941. Urukalo had recently tried to reconstitute the Chetnik formations by having new detachments "legalized" by Robotti's command. Ivanisević to Mihailović, 23 March 1943, in Der Deutsche General b. Hauptquartier der ital. Wehrmacht to Comando Supremo, "Abgehörte Funksprüche der Bewegung Mihailović," 30 March 1943, *T-821*, roll 356, frame 127.

[10] Ivanisević to Mihailović, 25 April 1943, Gizdić, *Dalmacija*, p. 258.

rank and file did, Mihailović's delegates could not stop them. In the Ozren sector of eastern Bosnia, the Serb bands, contrary to the overall trend, fought a bitter struggle with the Germans, Croats, and armed Muslim groups throughout April and rejected proposals of the chief Chetnik delegate, Rade Radić, "to stop the pillage of civilians, restore order and discipline in the ranks and avoid all hostile acts against the Croatian and Muslim civilian populations." [11] Indeed, in Bosnia the local Serb leaders, almost all of whom were civilians, opted for short-term strategies of resistance or collaboration independently, according to local circumstances and without any endorsement from Mihailović's representatives.

Shortly after Operation Weiss, then, Montenegro was the only part of western Yugoslavia where the officer leadership remained relatively intact, but even here Mihailović had already used up the best formations and had to contend with an immediate struggle with the nearby main body of Partisans and the almost certain prospect of a German action. Whatever doubts the officers had about the German plans were swept away as early as mid-April, when they received information from the Italians that Hitler had ordered the invasion of Montenegro. [12]

Operation Schwarz was actually a very hasty effort on the part of the Germans to revive the final, culminating phase of the original Weiss strategy and to clear the Adriatic coast and hinterland of the badly mauled Partisans and Chetniks. With German resistance crumbling in Tunisia, Berlin was more frightened than ever of an imminent Allied action in the Balkans, and called for an anti-rebel drive which their troops were barely able to carry out and with which the Italians refused from the beginning to cooperate. [13] Therefore, more than ever before, the officers found themselves caught between the conflicting occupation policies of the Axis Powers; with little immediate alternative, they braced themselves for the inevitable German raid and kept negotiating with the Italians for supplies and protection. [14]

Despite all the warnings coming from the Italians, the Montenegrin Chetniks were in no position to offer serious resistance to the German

[11] Command of Bosnian Chetnik Detachments, 15 April 1943, *Dokumenti o Izdajstvu Draže Mihailovića,* no. 199.
[12] Urukalo to Mihailović, 11 April 1943, Gizdić, *Dalmacija,* p. 225; High Command of Mihailović, 13 April 1943, in Oberkommando/I Abteilung/Operationsbüro der Streitkräfte im Ostraum, "Abgehörte Funksprüche der Cetniks," 26 April 1943, *T-821,* roll 356, frame 108.
[13] Comando Supremo, "Convegno italo-tedesco," 4 April 1943, *T-821,* roll 21, frame 1015.
[14] Radulović to Mihailović, 23 April 1943, in Der Deutsche General bei ital. Wehrmacht to Comando Supremo, "Abgehörte Funksprüche der Mihailović-Bewegung," 26 April 1943, *T. 821,* roll 356, frame 177.

units and had all they could do to avoid capture. In the Foča sector small Chetnik groups, some with papers proving their "legal" status in Serbia, were easily arrested in early May.[15] Virtually everywhere the officers were completely paralyzed, lacked specific instructions from Mihailović, and sought out Italian protection if they could. Lukačević, one of the arrested leaders at Foča, was released only when the Italian authorities protested, but he had no armed following thereafter.[16] Major Baćović, after hearing about the German raid on Foča, tried to move his troops to nearby Kalinovik, was stopped by the Italians, who wanted to avoid Chetnik-German clashes, and finally had to ask Mihailović what to do if the Germans attacked him.[17] Jevdjević moved quickly from the sensitive Mostar area to Italian-annexed Dubrovnik.[18]

In mid-May the Germans, without announcing their specific plans to the Italians, entered the Sandžak and eastern Montenegro.[19] Djurišić pulled back to Kolašin with about five hundred men and joined forces with a recently arrived Serb group led by Keserović;[20] at Kolašin on 12 May he called for an assembly of the officers, but only a few days later Djurišić was seized by units of the German First Mountain Division.[21] When the Italians again protested the capture of their supposed ally, O.K.W. intervened and ordered that Djurišić be removed immediately to a P.O.W. camp in Germany.[22]

Almost immediately after Schwarz had begun, the entire Chetnik leadership in Montenegro was broken up and immobilized. Djurišić was a German prisoner; Stanišić became ill and had to turn over his command temporarily to Major Djordje Lašić,[23] and Mihailović himself was almost captured during the Kolašin raid and had to flee toward western Serbia in June.[24] The remainder of their armed detachments were

[15] Commander of Zlatibor Chetnik Formation (Captain Dušan Radović), 4 May 1943, *Dokumenti o Izdajstvu Draže Mihailovića*, no. 664; KTB/OKW, III, entry for 5 May 1943.

[16] Lukačević to Stanišić, 12 May 1943, in Oberkommando/I Abteilung/Operationsbüro der Streitkräfte im Ostraum, "Abgehörte Funksprüche der Cetniks," 22 May 1943. T-281, roll 356, frame 205.

[17] Baćović to Mihailović, May 6, 1943, in Oberkommando/Operationsbüro der Streitkräfte im Ostraum, "Abgehörte Funksprüche der Cetniks," 14 May 1943, T-821, roll 356, frame 190.

[18] Befh. d. Dt. T. in Kroatien/Ic to OB Südost, "N. 2094/43 vom 13.5.1943," 13 May 1943, T-314, roll 566, frame 770.

[19] OB Südost/Ia to OKW/WFSt, "Tagesmeldung," 14 May 1943, T-311, roll 175, frame 1440.

[20] KTB/OKW, III, entry for 14 May 1943.

[21] OB Südost/Ia to OKW/WFSt, "Tagesmeldung," 14 May 1943, T-311, roll 175, frame 1440; Milan Bandović, *Knjiga o Draži*, 2: 300.

[22] OB Südost/Ia, "Kriegstagebuch (Mai 1943)," 18 May 1943 (Anlage 87), T-311, roll 175, frame 43.

[23] Bulletin of First Proletarian Division, 13 May 1943, *Zbornik*, vol. 4, bk. 13, no. 58.

[24] Živko Topalović, *Pokreti Narodnog Otpora u Jugoslaviji, 1941–45* (Paris: n.p., 1958), p. 74.

thoroughly disorganized and scattered. The Germans, despite repeated efforts, never did encounter a large body of Chetniks and succeeded in capturing only a few thousand of Mihailović's followers in Montenegro.[25] Without any effective military leadership, the Mihailović movement in Montenegro was probably saved from total destruction only by the difficult mountainous and woody terrain and the Italians' steadfast refusal to cooperate with the Germans. South of Mostar, Italian Sixth Army Corps units evacuated Chetniks in lorries,[26] and, in some instances, Pirzio-Biroli's officers warned them of impending German attacks.[27] Toward the end of May, Sixth Army Corps headquarters even ordered its troops not to cooperate with the Germans against the Chetniks.[28]

For a short while several of Mihailović's supporters thought that the Italians could be used once more to obstruct politically the German penetration of the Italian occupation sphere. Jevdjević predicted that Rome could force the Germans to release captured Chetniks and to withdraw from Foča.[29] Baćović reported that the Italians somehow were going to stop the German drive into southern Montenegro.[30]

These and similar calculations were actually the products of desperation rather than a realistic assessment of the course of events. Almost immediately the S.S.-"Prinz Eugen" Division easily penetrated the line that the Italians had promised would constitute the southern limit of the German advance,[31] and both Jevdjević and Baćović lost their illusions about Italian support.[32] At this point, almost all of Mihailović's supporters were overcome with a sense of futility and demoralization. Baćović finally informed Mihailović that he had changed his plans to avoid

[25] A report in late May from the German minister at Zagreb to Berlin placed the number of hitherto disarmed Chetniks in Montenegro at only sixteen hundred. Deutsche Gesandtschaft in Agram to Aus. Amt./Pol. IV, "Telegramm N. 2153 vom 24.5.1943," 24 May 1943, T-120, roll 212, frame 245/162557. A recent Yugoslav source, however, doubles that figure. Zbornik, vol. 2, bk. 9, p. 248, n. 4.

[26] Deutsche Gesandtschaft in Agram to Aus. Amt./Büro d. Staatssek., "Telegramm N. 2047 vom 17.5.1943," 17 May 1943, T-120, roll 212, frame 245/162549.

[27] Deutsche Gesandtschaft in Agram to Aus. Amt./Pol. IV, "Telegramm N. 1996 vom 14.5.1943," 14 May 1943, T-120, roll 212, frame 245/162532.

[28] Commander of Sixth Army Corps, "N. 1685," 20 May 1943, Zbornik, vol. 4, bk. 13, no. 236.

[29] Jevdjević to Ostojić, 16 May 1943, in Oberkommando/I Abteilung/Operationsbüro der Streitkräfte im Ostraum, "Abgehörte Funksprüche der Cetniks," 25 May 1943, T-821, roll 356, frame 210.

[30] Baćović to Mihailović, 19 May 1943, in Oberkommando/I Abteilung/Operationsbüro der Streitkräfte im Ostraum, "Abgehörte Funksprüche der Cetniks," 25 May 1943, T-821, roll 356, frame 210.

[31] Second Proletarian Division (Peko Dapčević) to Supreme Staff, 20 May 1943, Zbornik, vol. 4, bk. 13, no. 105.

[32] Jevdjević to Mihailović, 19 May 1943, in Oberkommando/I Abteilung/Operationsbüro der Streitkräfte im Ostraum, "Abgehörte Funksprüche der Cetniks," 29 May 1943, T-821, roll 356, frame 216.

"a fight with the Germans so as to preserve our strength"; [33] Jevdjević, who had always inclined toward a collaborationist solution, suddenly advocated that the Chetniks "attack . . . for reasons of prestige or else the people will go over to the Partisans." [34] Jevdjević was completely out of touch with reality: by now even the officers' detachments in Montenegro could do little more than break up into small groups to avoid capture. By 20 May, for instance, Major Radulović, reporting to Mihailović from the area around Nikšić where the Germans had just attacked, said that the Chetniks there were "completely destroyed" and had "no more striking power"; "the people" he said, "were dominated by a terrible sense of defeat." [35]

The remainder of the Montenegrin Chetnik leaders tried to fend for themselves. Lašić was no more able than Radulović to risk suicidal attacks, and one of his subordinates still proposed that they negotiate the liberation of the captured Chetniks "by intervening immediately with [Pirzio-]Biroli." [36] In western Montenegro, the troops of the federalist leader Krsto Popović were withdrawing rapidly toward the coast "out of fear that they would be mistaken for [Mihailović's] Chetniks and disarmed by the Germans." [37]

During the summer of 1943 the tenuous alliance between the Mihailović-dominated National Committee and the Montenegrin separatist leaders broke down completely. Popović's detachments made no contribution to the campaign in Herzegovina,[38] and his political followers showed more interest in propagandizing for an independent Montenegro than supporting Yugoslav unity under a Serb dynasty.[39] In May one of Popović's leading civilian spokesmen, Sekula Drljević, even went to Zagreb to promise Pavelić the allegiance of six thousand federalist troops if Zagreb annexed Montenegro as "an autonomous unit" as soon as the Italians left the war.[40]

[33] Baćović to Mihailović, 19 May 1943, in Oberkommando/I Abteilung/Operationsbüro der Streitkräfte im Ostraum, "Abgehörte Funksprüche der Cetniks," 29 May 1943, T-821, roll 356, frame 215.

[34] Jevdjević to Mihailović, 19 May 1943, in Oberkommando/I Abteilung/Operationsbüro der Streitkräfte im Ostraum, "Abgehörte Funksprüche der Cetniks," 29 May 1943, T-821, roll 356, frame 216.

[35] Radulović to Mihailović, 20 May 1943, in Der Deutsche General b. ital. Wehrmacht to Comando Supremo, "Abgehörte Funksprüche der Mihailović-Bewegung," 30 May 1943, T-821, roll 356, frame 202.

[36] Captain Leka Vujišić to Lašić, 28 May 1943, Zbornik, vol. 3, bk. 5, no. 186.

[37] Sixth Army Corps to Command of Second Army, 22 May 1943, ibid., no. 195.

[38] General Djukanović, 10 April 1943, Dokumenti o Izdajstvu Draže Mihailovića, no. 202.

[39] Stato Maggiore R. Esercito/S.I.E., "Montenegro-Crisi del movimento nazionalista," 13 May 1943, T-821, roll 248, frame 11; Comando 2. Armata, "Notiziario N. 5," 15 May 1943, T-821, roll 448, frame 470.

[40] Deutsche Gesandtschaft Zagreb to Deutsche General in Kroatien, "N. 818/43 vom 26.5.1943," 26 May 1943, T-501, roll 267, frame 1036.

Most of the Montenegrin Chetniks were captured, disappeared into the woods, or joined the Partisans. Those who remained loyal to Mihailović, perhaps a few thousand, broke up into a half a dozen groups and moved into the Sandžak in June.[41] This last group escaped repeated German efforts to disarm them but found themselves surrounded by a firmly hostile Sandžak Muslim population [42] and were defeated in just about every other sense. In Montenegro proper the situation was so chaotic that General Löhr and Pirzio-Biroli, in a meeting at Saloniki on 2 June, could not establish whether the German figure of twelve thousand or the Italian estimate of seven thousand represented the number of still uncaptured Chetniks.[43]

General Djukanović's staff made several efforts to replenish the Chetnik ranks and issued instructions to constitute new units on a local, clan basis, but these attempts proved futile.[44] The civilian population was war-weary and unwilling to be mobilized forcibly by Djukanović's agents, and the officer leadership had almost completely disappeared or been immobilized as a result of the German raids. Mihailović himself spent a short time in the nearby Sandžak but only for the purpose of moving his staff to Serbia in June. His most trusted unit leader, Djurišić, had been removed, the federalist allies led by Popović had proven useless, and the remaining officers were in no position to reorganize the scattered bands. Italian intelligence rated Lašić's following in late June at about six hundred.[45] Even more telling proof of the internal disintegration is the evidence from Italian sources that, in addition to the falling out between the pro-Mihailović and separatist officers, some of the remaining Chetnik leaders complained openly about Mihailović's leadership and even resorted to threats against the lives of his agents.[46]

[41] OB/Sudost/Ia to OKW/WFSt, "Tagesmeldung," 6 June 1943, *T-311*, roll 175, frame 1334; Governatorato del Montenegro/Ufficio I, "Foglio Notizie N. 86," 21 June 1943, *T-821*, roll 287, frame 119; Comando Supremo, "Notizie dal Montenegro," 22 June 1943, *T-821*, roll 248, frame 4; Comando Supremo to Mussolini, "Novità del giorno 23 guigno 1943," 23 June 1943, *T-821*, roll 125, frame 234.

[42] Deutsche Gesandtschaft in Agram to Aus. Amt./Pol. IV, "Telegramm N. 2087 vom 19.5.1943," 19 May 1943, *T-120*, roll 212, frame 245/162553.

[43] Governatorato del Montenegro, "Riassunto del colloquio di Salonicco," 2 June 1943, *T-821*, roll 31, frame 237.

[44] Governatorato del Montenegro/Ufficio I, "Foglio Notizie N. 88," 25 June 1943, *T-821*, roll 287, frame 112.

[45] Governatorato del Montenegro/Ufficio I, "Foglio Notizie N. 86," 21 June 1943, *T-821*, roll 287, frame 119.

[46] By the end of June, the Italians at Cetinje noticed increasingly frequent "internal disputes and squabbles" among the remains of the Chetniks, "due in part . . . to an as yet not clearly identified anti-Mihailović trend." Rumors were widespread that the Serb Chetnik Masan Djurović, who had recently come to Montenegro, had been murdered by Keserović's people. Soon another delegate, Nikola Kjanović, was threatened by "Chetnik elements of the Zlatar region." Governatorato del Montenegro/

The dissolution of the officers' movement in Montenegro and Mihailović's flight to Serbia nullified the efforts to build up the Chetnik organization in the western half of Yugoslavia. Virtually everywhere, the armed formations broke up or pursued independent courses of action. Former leaders of the first rank, both civilian and military, lost influence over these bands, and a new group emerged, usually local civilian notables, who tended to drift toward collaboration. The "old" collaborationists, especially Djukanović, Jevdjević, and Djujić, saw their entire program of short-term understandings with the Italians collapse in late May when Mussolini finally gave in to German pressure and ordered General Robotti "to cooperate as quickly as possible with the Germans in the disarmament of the Chetnik formations." [47] The Italians immediately placed Jevdjević under house arrest,[48] agreed to the German 373rd Division's permanent occupation of Mostar,[49] and, on 1 June, officially ceased all aid to the remaining Herzegovinian Chetniks.[50]

General Piazzoni of the Sixth Army Corps summed up the situation in Herzegovina at the end of June with the remark that the Chetniks occupied "a more or less intermediary territory [between the Germans and the Italians] which one might call No Man's Land." [51] Perhaps six to seven thousand of the officers' troops remained uncaptured in the hills, but they were powerless to resist the Germans, to collaborate further with the Italians, or to compete successfully with the Partisans for the sympathy of the anti-Axis elements in the civilian population. Moreover, they were almost leaderless. Major Baćović, the only remaining officer of some significance, was probably fleeing toward the east, was believed by Pirzio-Biroli to have run out of supplies,[52] and in early June asked Mihailović for an immediate meeting in eastern Bosnia.[53]

Ufficio I, "Foglio Notizie N. 88," 25 June 1943, *T-821,* roll 287, frame 113; Governatorato del Montenegro/Ufficio I, "Foglio Notizie N. 93," 6 July 1943, *T-821,* roll 287, frame 90.

[47] Superesercito Operazioni to Comando 2. Armata/Ufficio Operazioni, "N. 10291 del 31.5.1943," 31 May 1943, *T-821,* roll 31, frame 332.

[48] Comando 2. Armata/Ufficio Informazioni to Comando VI. Corpo d'Armata, "N. I/14681 del 24.5.1943," 24 May 1943, *T-821,* roll 31, frame 245; Comando 2. Armata/Ufficio Informazioni to Italmissione Zagabria, "N. I/23714 del 20.8.1943," 20 August 1943, *T-821,* roll 287, frame 141.

[49] Comando Divisione "Marche" to Comando Lettore Mostar, "Accordi fra il gen. di div. Amico . . . e il Ten. Generale Zellner (373. Div.)," 28 May 1943, *T-821,* roll 294, frame 813.

[50] This is confirmed by a German source. SS. Frw. Geb. Div. "Prinz Eugen"/Ia to Befh. d. dt. Truppen in Kroatien, "Verbindengsaufnahme mit ital. VI. Armeekorps," 13 August 1943, *T-314,* roll 556, frame 316.

[51] Kommando der VI. Armeekorps/Generalstab to Kommando der 2. Armee, "Die politische Lage Ende Juni 1943," 1 July 1943, *T-821,* roll 347, frame 831.

[52] Governatorato del Montenegro (Pirzio-Biroli), "Riassunto del Colloquio di Salonicco, 2 June 1943, *T-821,* roll 31, frame 328.

[53] Baćović to Mihailović, 8 June 1943, in Der Deutsche General b. ital. Wehrmacht

In some instances, local leaders emerged to fill the gap, but their behavior was so inconsistent that, if anything, they further disrupted what remained of the Chetniks' political cohesion. In the Nevesinje sector, for example, the politician and long-standing collaborator Petar Samardžić probably established ties with the Partisans and actually threw his men against the Germans in a brief clash of mid-June;[54] he soon agreed to turn over his arms provided that the Germans promise not to permit the return of the Ustaši.[55] Even more striking was the sudden turn of events in the Ozren Mountains sector of eastern Bosnia: there the armed Serb bands, who fought pitched battles with Germans and Ustaši in April, by July were engaged in a desperate struggle with the Partisans and by the end of the month were receiving arms and supplies from the 369th Croat Legion Division.[56]

Although the overall trend was toward collaboration, enough Chetnik groups made deals with, went over to the Partisans, or continued the old pattern of raids on nearby Croat and Muslim civilians to keep the occupation authorities permanently suspicious of all Serb leaders. As already indicated, the local heads often chose collaboration or made an armistice of sorts with the Germans only after they were forced to. Furthermore, although many individual armed groups came to terms with the occupation regime, collaborators of long standing, like Uroš Drenović, failed to reassert any sort of central direction.[57] Many armed detachments simply dissolved or pursued independent courses of action. In the vicinity of the Romanije Mountains, the Chetniks split up into pro- and anti-Partisan groups;[58] in the Kalinovik sector evidence suggests that a former Chetnik officer who had just gone over to the Partisans was responsible for the murder of other still loyal supporters of Mihailović.[59] In other areas, like the extreme southeastern parts of Bosnia, the bands remained in contact

to Comando Supremo, "Abgehörte Funksprüche der Mihailović-Bewegung," 5 July 1943, *T-821*, roll 356, frame 242.

[54] Comando 2. Armata/Ufficio I, "Notiziario N. 7," 15 July 1943, *T-821*, roll 448, frame 494.

[55] Governatorato del Montenegro/Ufficio I, "Foglio Notizie N. 95," 10 July 1943, *T-821*, roll 287, frame 81.

[56] Comando Supremo/SIM, "Croazia-Tentativi di accordi fra le autorità germaniche e i cetnici erzegovisi," 10 August 1943, *T-281*, roll 347, frames 632–33; 369 (Kroat.) Inf. Div./Ia to Berh. d. dt. Truppen in Kroatien, "Abgabe von Munition an Cetniks," 17 August 1943, *T-314*, roll 554, frame 603; Befh. d. dt. Truppen in Kroatien/Ia to Dt. Eis. Sichr. Stab Kroatien, "N. 3795/43 vom 21.7.1943," 21 July 1943, *T-314*, roll 566, frame 682.

[57] Drenović once more attempted to create a unified Bosnian Chetnik command in early June. Minutes of meeting of Drenović, Vukasin Marčetić, and Jovo Mišić, 3 June 1943, *Dokumenti o Izdajstvu Draže Mihailovića*, no. 130.

[58] Governatorato del Montenegro/Ufficio I. "Foglio Notizie N. 97," 14 July 1943, *T-821*, roll 287, frames 70–77.

[59] *Ibid.*

with Chetniks in Serbia and continued to fight the anti-Muslim civil war.[60]

Although none of the major Chetnik leaders in western Yugoslavia joined Tito in 1943, some of their former followers had, which put them in an impossible position. Baćović, for instance, although proposing to the Italians joint operations against the Partisans at Kotor and Split in July,[61] had been recently suspected of establishing ties of "toleration and indirect collaboration with the Partisans."[62] Jevdjević also aroused suspicion when he smuggled out a letter to some of his Herzegovinian supporters warning them not to follow Samardžić's example of collaboration with the Germans.[63]

Pop Djujić, whose long record of cooperation with the Italians and clerical status enabled him to avoid reprisals from the occupation authorities in the early summer, nonetheless saw his position deteriorate steadily. Although he fought the west Bosnian Partisans all summer, he had to work hard to win Italian backing against German proposals for the disarmament of the Dinaric Chetniks.[64] In early June the best General Robotti could do was convince Löhr that it would be better to disarm Djujić's formations "progressively," or after a respite of a few months.[65] At the same time, though, the Italian Eighteenth Army Corps was instructed to reduce gradually their supply of foodstuffs to the Dinaric Chetniks,[66] and a month later, when Djujić's troops had to withdraw after suffering heavy losses at the hands of the Partisans near Bos Grahovo, Robotti demanded an explanation.[67]

Toward the end of the summer a combination of German pressure, con-

[60] OB/Südost/Ia to OKW/WFSt, "N. 4578/43 vom 2.7.1943," 2 July 1943, *T-311,* roll 175, frame 1259; OB Südost/Ia to OKW/WFSt, "Tagesmeldung," 22 August 1943, *T-311,* roll 175, frame 1147.

[61] Comando 2. Armata/Informazione to Comando VI. Corpo d'Armata, "N. 21403 del 31.7.1943," 31 July 1943, *T-821,* roll 288, frame 393.

[62] Comando VI. Corpo d'Armata to Comando 2. Armata/Informazione, "N. 8730 del 1.7.1943," 1 July 1943, *T-821,* roll 288, frame 497; Comando VI. Corpo d'Armata/ Informazione to Comando 2. Armata, "N. 102003/I del 30.7.1943," 30 July 1943, *T-821,* roll 289, frame 597.

[63] Comando 2. Armata/Ufficio, "Notiziario N. 8 del 15.8.1943," *T-821,* roll 448, frame 505.

[64] Comando XVIII. Corpo d'Armata to Comando 2. Armata/Informazioni, "N. 9325/ I del 7.8.1943," 7 August 1943, *T-821,* roll 289, frame 242.

[65] Governatorato del Montenegro, "Riassunto del colloquio di Salonicco," 2 June 1943, *T-821,* roll 31, frames 329–30.

[66] Comando 2. Armata/Ufficio Informazione to Comando XVIII. Corpo d'Armata, "N. I/19115 del 8.7.1943," 8 July 1943, *T-821,* roll 289, frame 206.

[67] Comando XVIII. Corpo d'Armata to Comando 2. Armata/Operazioni, "N. 10400/ Op. del 1.8.1943," 1 August 1943, *T-821,* roll 289, frame 252, 3; Comando 2. Armata/ Informazioni to Comando XVIII. Corpo d'Armata, "N. I/21567 del 2.8.1943," 2 August 1943, *T-821,* roll 289, frame 48; Comando XVIII. Corpo d'Armata/Ufficio Operazioni to Comando 2. Armata, "N. 10892/Op. del 14.8.1943," 14 August 1943, *T-821,* roll 289, frame 47.

tracting Italian supplies, and a long, costly struggle with the Partisans was wearing down the Dinaric Chetniks and undermining Djujić's authority. Persistent rumors and information from captured Partisans pointed to a noticeable defection from Djujić's ranks to Tito; [68] another Chetnik, Djuro Plečas, whom Mihailović had appointed as a delegate for western Bosnia and who was apparently on bad terms with Djujić, was suddenly and mysteriously killed in August.[69] On the eve of Italy's capitulation Djujić tried once more to assure some support or at least toleration in his rear by going to Knin to promise the headquarters of the Eighteenth Army Corps his "sincere friendship and cooperation with the Italian people." [70] By this time, however, the Italians were barely the masters of the situation in their own occupation zone and, with so much conflicting intelligence,[71] were in no position to pursue any policy toward Dinaric Chetniks with confidence. In fact, Djujić's detachments were exhausted and of little use to anyone as an effective striking force. One of Mihailović's remaining representatives in the area, the former Belgrade attorney Lieutenant Colonel Mladen Žujević, reported in early August that the "Dinaric division was poorly formed, badly armed and disciplined," lacked "accurate registers of officers and troops," and could not field more than three thousand men. Djujić's "military command," he concluded, "which we read about this winter, is a pure figment of the imagination." [72]

In the extreme western part of Yugoslavia, Mihailović's delegate officers, the old collaborationists Jevdjević and Djujić, and the new group of civilian leaders who had succeeded Birčanin were all unable to revive the Chetniks. The Chetnik military formations were routed and scattered or, in the case of Djujić, rapidly declined, and almost all of Mihailović's efforts in 1943 to establish a solid political organization in the Dalmatian and Adriatic coast areas proved unsuccessful. For obvious reasons, the Italians were most suspicious of Chetnik political activities here. Moreover, since the spring military disasters, the recurrent tensions between

[68] For example, Comando XVIII, Corpo d'Armata/Ufficio Informazione to Comando 2. Armata, "Ribelli costituisi," 30 August 1943, *T-821*, roll 289, frame 11.

[69] Colonello Capo Ufficio (Carlà) to Comando XVIII. Corpo d'Armata, "Uccisione capo cetnico Plesic [sic]," 16 August 1943, *T-821*, roll 289, frame 23; Comando XVIII. Corpo d'Armata/Ufficio I to Comando 2. Armata, "Uccisione capo cetnico Plecas," 30 August 1943, *T-821*, roll 289, frame 21; Deakin, *Embattled Mountain*, p. 74.

[70] A letter of Djujić to the Italian command at Knin appears in Gizdić, *Dalmacija*, p. 522. It was dated sometime in early September.

[71] One report of early August even gave the Dinaric Chetniks a strength of twenty thousand and claimed they were increasing their strength rapidly with new recruits from Knin and Šibenik. Comando Div. "Zara"/Sezione Informazione to Comando 2. Armata, "N. 04/2895 del 9 agosto 1943," 9 August 1943, *T-821*, roll 290, frame 995.

[72] Mladen Žujević to Mihailović, 6 August 1943, in Gizdić, *Dalmacija*, entry for 6 August 1943.

the collaborationist local civilians, especially Jevdjević and Djujić, and Mihailović's agents came increasingly into the open.

Toward the end of the summer, in fact, nominal political leadership had passed almost by default to the anti-Jevdjević group of Professor Račić and the Orthodox cleric Urukalo. In August they took over the Chetnik political base, the Split National Committee, and, with the support of a few Montenegrin officers from General Djukanović's staff, began a blatantly Pan-Serb propaganda campaign.[73] The Split Chetniks apparently devoted the greater part of their brief activity to political squabbles with the pro-Maček Split Catholic Bloc and the Ustaši-dominated Croatian National Committee.[74] They lacked a military following and were not even supported by all pro-Mihailović elements in the area. Žujević, in his letter to Mihailović of 6 August, called the Račić-Urukalo group "a disgrace" and denounced the whole Split Chetnik organization as "a fatigued forum" and as "Greater Serbian politics which, in any other Yugoslav city, would be disgusting."[75] Needless to say, the Italians saw little use in the Split Chetniks and arrested the recently arrived Montenegrin officers in mid-August;[76] almost simultaneously, the Split Partisans succeeded, "despite all sorts of precautionary measures,"[77] in assassinating Račić. The Split Chetnik political leadership in Dalmatia thus collapsed almost as soon as it was formed. Indicative of the state of Mihailović's organization in this crucial sector on the eve of Italy's exit from the war is the fact that Račić's temporary successor was Mladen Žujević, a fierce critic of almost all the local Chetnik leaders and during most of the summer an Italian prisoner.[78]

Virtually everywhere in the western half of former Yugoslavia, the Chetnik rank and file, although not usually defeated militarily, were hopelessly dispersed, and the unit leaders, both officers and civilian, had lost control over their followings. The reverses suffered in Montenegro and Herzegovina were especially decisive. They upset the Chetniks' ef-

---

[73] Comando 2. Armata to Comando XVIII. Corpo d'Armata, "Dalmazia annessa-Preparativi dei nazionalisti," 15 August 1943, *T-821*, roll 289, frame 114; Comando XVIII. Corpo d'Armata, "Comitato Nazionalista Spalatino," 18 August 1943, *T-821*, roll 286, frame 593.

[74] Gizdić, *Dalmacija*, entry for 21 May, 1943; Comando 2. Armata/Ufficio I, "Dalmazia annessa—Comitato Nazionalista Croato di Spulato," 25 August 1943, *T-821*, roll 286, frame 587.

[75] Mladen Žujević to Mihailović, 6 August 1943, Gizdić, *Dalmacija*, entry for 6 August 1943.

[76] Comando XVIII. Corpo d'Armata to Intendenza 2. Armata/Ufficiale Prigionieri Guerra, "N. 9890 del 19.8.1943," 19 August 1943, *T-281*, roll 289, frame 225.

[77] Gizdić, *Dalmacija*, entry for 23 August 1943.

[78] Žujević, also called Acimović, had been arrested by the Italians at Split on 1 June. Comando XVIII. Corpo d'Armata to Comando 2. Armata, "N. 9325/I del 7.8.1943," 7 August 1943, *T-821*, roll 289, frame 242.

forts, which went back to Mihailović's arrival in Montenegro in June of 1942, to utilize Italian toleration and protection in order to put together a unified movement capable of dealing with both the Ustaši and Partisans before preparing for the expected Allied landing and guerrilla operations against the Axis occupation forces. Their foothold in Montenegro, Herzegovina, and Dalmatia lost, the Chetniks could no longer use their formations behind the central and southern parts of the Adriatic coast in conjunction with an Anglo-American operation in that sector.

After June of 1943 Mihailović was forced to fall back on the support of the civilian population of rump Serbia, which was militarily insignificant. Over the short term the prospects for reviving the organization with recruits from Serbia were hopeless. The few battle-worthy formations had already been brought to Montenegro, and most of the Chetniks in Serbia refused to violate what amounted to a truce with the Nedić administration. Those armed bands which continued to carry out "resistance" activities usually contained only a few hundred followers and could do little more than carry out individual acts of violence against uncooperative village heads, a certain amount of outright looting, and some agricultural sabotage.[79]

As a result of Partisan offensives, German raids, and shifts in Italian occupation policies, Mihailović on the eve of Italy's capitulation lost any chance to compete successfully with Tito for the allegiance of the anti-Axis civilians in western Yugoslavia. Yugoslavia was effectively divided into guerrilla spheres; Tito prevailed in the west, and Mihailović had to function as best he could in Serbia. This state of affairs was forced on Mihailović by internal events in Yugoslavia during the first half of 1943, but it was also sanctioned by the British in the course of their shift of support from the Chetniks to Tito.

[79] This brief characterization of the state of the Chetnik movement in Serbia in 1943 is based on sources which are, admittedly, rather dispersed: Generale Pieche to Ministero degli Affari Esteri, "Notizie della Serbia," 9 February 1943, *T-821*, roll 247, frames 647–48; Morava District Prefecture to chief of Serbian State Security, "N. 475/42 of April 1, 1943," *Dokumenti o Izdajstvu Draže Mihailovića*, no. 658; Valjevo District Prefecture to chief of Serbian State Security, "N. 1875/43 of June 4, 1943," *ibid.*, no. 661; Valjevo District Prefecture to chief of Serbian State Security, "N. 2009/43 of June 16, 1943," *ibid.*, no. 669; (?) to Mihailović, 10 August 1943, *ibid.*, no. 632; daily report of German liaison staff with Italian Second Army, "N. 764/43 of May 2, 1943," *Zbornik*, vol. 4, bk. 13, no. 152; OB Südost/Ia to OKW/WFSt, "Tagesmeldung," 1 June 1943, *T-311*, roll 175, frame 1360; OB Südost/Ia to OKW/WFSt, "Tagesmeldung," 3 July 1943, *T-311*, roll 175, frame 1256; OB Südost/Ia to OKW/WFSt, "Tagesmeldung," 5 July 1943, *T-311*, roll 175, frame 1252; OB/Südost/Ia to OKW/WFSt, "Tagesmeldung," 11 July 1943, *T-311*, roll 175, frame 1237; OB Südost/Ia to OKW/WFSt, "Tagesmeldung," 19 July 1943, *T-311*, roll 175, frame 1219; OB Südost/Ia to OKW/WFSt, "Tagesmeldung," 11 August 1943, *T-311*, roll 175, frame 1168; Comando Supremo/SIM to Centro SIM Albania-Montenegro, "Foglio Notizie N. 15," 10 August 1943, *T-281*, roll 287, frame 4; Mil. Bfh. Südost, "Tagesmeldung," 20 August 1943, *T-501*, roll 266, frame 1022.

The change in British policies toward the Yugoslav resistance reflected their new relationship with Russia after Stalingrad and their growing annoyance at the Chetniks' persistent collaboration with the Italians. Mihailović's attitude toward the British was somewhat like Tito's toward the Russians: he obviously felt that London had given him only symbolic support, and his anti-British remarks of 28 February at Kolašin, which Colonel Bailey immediately relayed to his superiors, bore that out. By the end of March Churchill was ready to send a note to the Jovanović émigré government threatening to withdraw British support from Mihailović if the Chetniks did not cease collaboration immediately.[80] The Yugoslav prime minister, in turn, broadcast these demands over Radio London in early April.[81] Intercepted and deciphered Chetnik messages make it clear that Mihailović was fully aware of Churchill's strong reaction but that for certain reasons, including faulty intelligence from Chetnik sympathizers in Belgrade, he chose not to take the ultimatum seriously.[82] Eden delivered another note to Jovanović on 7 May, this time using even more forceful language, and at the end of the month, or toward the close of Operation Schwarz, brought up the whole issue with Molotov. On 28 May the matter reached its first climax: the Deakin-Stuart group arrived at Tito's hard-pressed headquarters, and Bailey told Mihailović to move his forces to the Kapaonik Mountains in southwestern Serbia and to confine all further Chetnik operations to the area east of the Ibar River. He further informed Mihailović that henceforth the Allies would support him with supplies only in Serbia.[83] The spheres-of-influence arrangement was now a diplomatic as well as a military fact and had Churchill's blessing.

This arangement was at best a temporary expedient resulting from the civil war between Tito and Mihailović and the failure of the British to bring the two together. What is all the more striking is the fact that the Germans, and to some degree the Italians, were more impressed by London's efforts to bring about a Chetnik-Partisan truce than by the obvious

[80] Konstantine Fotich, *The War We Lost* (New York: Viking Press, 1948), p. 220; Dušan Plenča, *Medjunarodni Odnosi Jugoslavije u Toku Drugog Svjetskog Rata* (Yugoslavia's international relations during World War II); Belgrade: Institut Društvenih Nauka, 1962), pp. 176–80; Vojmir Kljaković, "Promjena Politike Velike Britanije prema Jugoslaviji u prvoj polovini 1943 godine" (Great Britain's change of policy toward Yugoslavia in the first half of 1943), *Jugoslovenski Istorijski Časopis* 3 (1969):52.

[81] High Command to Mihailović, 11 April 1943, in Oberkommando/I Abteilung/ Operationsbüro der Streitkräfte im Ostraum, "Abgehörte Funksprüche der Cetniks," 26 April 1943, *T-821*, roll 356, frame 168.

[82] Major Lalatović to Mihailović, 12 April 1943, in Der Deutsche General b. ital. Wehrmacht to Comando Supremo, "Abgehörte Funksprüche der Mihailović Bewegung," 26 April 1943, *T-821*, roll 467, frame 173.

[83] Aide memoire of British embassy to U.S. Department of State, 6 July 1943, *FRUS (1943)*, vol. 2: *(Europe)*, pp. 1009–10.

fact that the Chetnik organization in western Yugoslavia had been all but destroyed. The spheres-of-influence proposal was therefore taken by the occupation authorities to be the prelude to an alliance between Tito and Mihailović. A high-level intelligence report to Rome of late May, for example, warned, "it is certain that if London insists the efforts to unite all the anti-Axis forces will succeed." [84] By the end of the summer rumors were widespread that Mihailović and Tito were on the verge of joining forces in a general uprising. [85]

This misperception of events was typical rather than exceptional. The Axis Powers always tended to overestimate the influence of the Allies, especially the British, over the Yugoslav resistance, largely because their view of the situation in Yugoslavia was a function of their understanding of the probable course of events in the entire Mediterranean theater. Their attitude toward Mihailović was shaped far more by their persistent fear that the Allies would open up a second front in the Balkans than by their knowledge of the Chetniks' weakness and failure. [86] During May, Hitler began to think seriously of the occupation of the entire Balkan coastline by German troops, [87] and after the Allied invasion of Sicily the Germans hastened to prepare to protect the Adriatic. [88]

Seen in this context, even the shattered remains of the Chetnik organization in western Yugoslavia were a potentially dangerous resistance force which would revive as soon as the Allies arrived in the Balkans, either independently or in league with Tito. This assessment was not confined to German intelligence reports but was shared by Mihailović, who also dramatically overestimated the capabilities of the few officers and civilian supporters in the west. After the middle of July, therefore, Mihailović encouraged the fears and suspicions of the occupation authorities by sending out a whole series of directives calling for a coordination

[84] General Piechè to Ministero degli Affari Esteri, "Notizie della Serbia," 26 May 1943, *T-821*, roll 247, frames 644–45.

[85] For example, Comando 2. Armata/Ufficio Informazione, "Situazione politico-militare," 31 July 1943, *T-821*, roll 31, frame 247; Comando 2. Armata, "Accordi militari fra Mihailović e Tito," 21 August 1943, *T-821*, roll 286, frame 618; General Kommando XV. Geb. A.K./Ic, "Lagebericht 1.–31.8.1943," 1 September 1943, *T-314*, roll 559, frame 494.

[86] For example, John Ehrmann, *Grand Strategy* (London: Her Majesty's Stationery Office, 1956), 5: 61–62.

[87] Albert Garland and Howard McGraw Smith, *The Mediterranean Theater of Operations*, vol. 2, pt. 2 (*Sicily and the Surrender of Italy*) of U.S., Department of the Army, Office of the Chief of Military History, *The United States Army in World War II* (Washington, D.C.: U.S. Government Printing Office, 1965), p. 46; OKW/WFSt/Op., "Weisung Nr. 486," 19 May 1943, *Hitlers Weisungen für die Kriegführung*, p. 217; *Hitlers Lagebesprechungen*, entries for 19 and 20 May 1943 (with Keitel and V. Neurath).

[88] *KTB/OKW*, III, entries for 9–10, 13, and 17 July 1943; Comando 2. Armata/Informazione to Comando V. Corpo d'Armata, "N. I/19230 del 10.6.1943," 16 July 1943, *T-821*, roll 289, frame 589.

of strategy between the Chetniks and the Allies to prepare for an imminent Allied amphibious invasion.

According to Italian sources in late May Mihailović began to expect a major Allied action in the Balkans and was led to believe, although how is not certain, that the invasion would come in a month or two.[89] In June the date became more firm—1 August—and after the invasion of Sicily Chetnik headquarters in Serbia began calling for acts of sabotage against specific targets.

Thus Mihailović took his ostensibly most aggressive anti-Axis stand at a time when his subordinates were least capable of carrying out his directives. Moreover, almost all these orders went to the officers in the west, where, according to the "spheres" arrangement dictated by the British, only Tito was to receive Allied support. Chetnik headquarters in Serbia was out of touch with the situation in the area behind the Adriatic coast and clearly did not believe, as subsequent events would demonstrate, that the British were in the process of abandoning them.

If anything, Mihailović's actions had the effect of compromising rather than strengthening the position of the officers. Italian Second Army intelligence intercepted several of these directives, and on the day of the Sicilian invasion Robotti ordered all units to intensify vigilance and prepare for possible hostilities against the Chetniks.[90] On 19 July at Belluno Hitler took special care to impress on Mussolini and Ambrosio that Axis policies in the Balkans had to be based on a total struggle against all the armed bands.[91] On the same day O.K.W. ordered Belgrade to start a poster campaign offering a hundred thousand marks for information leading to Mihailović's arrest.[92]

Toward the end of July, immediately after Mussolini's fall, Mihailović, like everyone else, began to expect an Italian capitulation and issued instructions calling on his subordinates to prepare for attacks against Second Army garrisons.[93] More firmly convinced than ever that the Allied

---

[89] Comando 2. Armata/Ufficio Informazione to Comando VI. Corpo d'Armata, "N. I/14681 del 24.5.1943," 24 May 1943, *T-821*, roll 31, frame 245; Comando 2. Armata/Ufficio Informazione to Comando Supremo/SIM, "N. I/18681 del 4.7.1943," 4 July 1943, *T-821*, roll 286, frame 3.

[90] Comando 2. Armata to Comando V. Corpo d'Armata, "N. I/19593 del 14.7.1943," 14 July 1943, *T-821*, roll 289, frame 537; Comando 2. Armata/Ufficio Informazione to Comando Supremo/SIM, "N. I/19595 del 14.7.1943," 14 July 1943, *T-821*, roll 286, frame 10; Comando 2. Armata to Comando VI. Corpo d'Armata, "N. I/20232 del 20.7.1943," 20 July 1943, *T-821*, roll 289, frame 608.

[91] WFSt/Abt. Ausland to Aktensammelstelle Sud, "Relazione sopra le dichiarazioni del Fuhrer in occasione del incontro col Duce a Belluno . . . ," 1 August 1943, *T-821*, roll 347, frame 1041–42.

[92] The same price was placed on Tito's head. Benzler to Aus. Amt., "N. 720 vom 19.7.1943," 19 July 1943, *T-120*, roll 2908, frame 618H/E464518.

[93] Comando Supremo, "Situazione operativa e logistica degli Scacchieri Balcanici ed Egeo al 1 agosto 1943," 1 August 1943, *T-821*, roll 252, frame 64; Comando 2. Armata/

Balkan action was forthcoming and that the Italian troops would turn against their German allies, perhaps even before the capitulation, he went so far as to order Stanišić and Baćović to move their units close to the Adriatic and to proceed immediately to disarm the smaller Second Army garrisons.[94]

These instructions not only demonstrated that Chetnik headquarters in Serbia was making plans which were unrealistic and based on wishful thinking but also triggered a virtual revolt against Mihailović's command by the officers and civilian spokesmen in the west. The Chetniks who were supposed to disarm the Italians and sabotage the Germans' defensive measures in conjunction with an Allied landing were barely a factor in the confusing swirl of events between Mussolini's fall and the Italian capitulation. Baćović had practically no effective armed following; in late July Stanišić's troops numbered no more than three thousand;[95] the rest of the Montenegrin organization hardly existed. Jevdjević and Djujić barely escaped arrest by the Italians late in August,[96] and if General Robotti had not changed his mind at the last minute, Djujić probably would have been arrested by the Germans.[97]

With both the Germans and the Partisans moving up to the Adriatic, the Chetniks had all they could do to ensure their own survival. In mid-August Robotti ordered the Second Army command posts to inform the Chetniks that the Italians had full knowledge of Mihailović's plans and would resist any attempt by the officers' formations to approach Italian units.[98] At this point the Chetniks were trapped and revolted against Mihailović. Baćović, the leading officer outside of Montenegro, had been objecting since early August to Mihailović's orders for the disarmament of the Italians, and toward the middle of the month a number of local commanders joined the political spokesmen Jevdjević, Grdjić, Žujević,

Informazione to Comando V. Corpo d'Armata, "N. I/21596 del 2 agosto 1943," 2 August 1943, *T-821*, roll 289, frame 560; Oberkommando/I Abteilung/Operationsbüro der Streitkräfte im Ostraum, "Abgehörte Funksprüche der Cetniks," 6 August 1943, *T-821*, roll 356, frame 258.

[94] Oberkommando/I Abteilung/Operationsbüro der Streitkräfte im Ostraum, "Abgehörte Funksprüche der Cetniks," 12 August 1943, *T-821*, roll 356, frame, 262; Oberkommando/I Abteilung/Operationsbüro der Streitkräfte im Ostraum, "Abgehörte Funksprüche der Cetniks," 12 August 1943, *T-821*, roll 356, frame 264; Comando Supremo/SIM, "Novità Politico-Militare-ex-Jugoslavia," 25 August 1943, *T-821*, roll 247, frame 735.

[95] Baćović to Mihailović, 28 July 1943, in Der Deutsche General b. ital. Wehrmacht to Comando Supremo, "Abgehörte Funksprüche der Mihailović-Bewegung," 2 August 1943, *T-821*, roll 356, frame 256.

[96] Comando 2. Armata/Ufficio Informazioni to S.M.R. Esercito/R.I.E., "Promemoria di servizio per il Colonello Mordini," 29 August 1943, *T-821*, roll 285, frame 758.

[97] Comando VI. Corpo d'Armata to Comando 2. Armata, "N. 525 del 25.8.1943," 25 August 1943, *T-821*, roll 288, frame 383.

[98] Comando 2. Armata/Ufficio Informazione, "Colloquio tra il Ecc. Robotti e Petrucci . . . ," 11 August 1943, *T-821*, roll 31, frames 268–70.

and Djujić in admitting to the Italians that Mihailović had indeed given such directives and to promise that they would never carry them out.[99]

It is interesting to note that they disagreed with Mihailović over what their small units could do against the Italian garrisons but not over the prospect of the Allied Balkan landing. Baćović, for instance, although resolutely opposed to Mihailović's plan for beginning operations against the Italians before the capitulation, let it be known that he would turn against the Axis as soon as the British arrived in the Balkans.[100] Others even proposed collaboration with the Italians, believing that as soon as Italy capitulated the Second Army units would fight the Germans. In each instance, though, the key assumption was that the Allies would soon make a large commitment to the Balkan Peninsula. Thus Jevdjević, under Second Army house arrest until late August, proposed to the Italians earlier in the month that the Chetniks join the Italians to defend the Second Army occupation zone against the Germans until the Allies arrived.[101] Žujević argued for the same strategy in his letter to Mihailović of 6 August, in which he predicted that their "salvation will be the arrival of the Allies, because they will stop a fratricidal war in which we would be the weaker party."[102] Typically, the civilians were far more aware of the Chetniks' military weakness than were most of the officers and Mihailović and therefore were more inclined to rely on external support and diplomatic solutions. However, when Žujević speculated to Mihailović that "perhaps it is possible that the Allies will order the Italians to use their forces to maintain peace and order in the cities before their own arrival," he was as unrealistic as the Chetnik headquarters in Serbia.

On the eve of Italy's capitulation the Chetniks were still divided over whether they should seek the protection of the Second Army or disarm its units. Finding themselves caught between the Italians on the coast and the approaching Germans and Partisans to the east, their confusion and indecision was hardly surprising. The most uncertain factor, of course, was what the Italians would do when the capitulation was announced.

Comando Supremo, however, did virtually nothing to prepare their armed forces in Yugoslavia for the capitulation. During August they took measures for the removal of three divisions from the Second Army to Italy[103] but left Robotti in the dark about Rome's negotiations with

[99] Oberkommando/I Abteilung/Operationsbüro der Streitkräfte im Ostraum, "Abgehörte Funksprüche der Cetniks," 12 August 1943, *T-821*, roll 356, frame 262.

[100] SS. Frw. Geb. Div. "Prinz Eugen,"/Ia to Befh. d. dt. Truppen in Kroatien, "Verbindungsaufnahme mit ital. VI. Armeekorps," 13 August 1943, *T-314*, roll 566, frame 316.

[101] Oberkommando/I Abteilung/Operationsbüro der Streitkräfte im Ostraum, "Abgehörte Funksprüche der Cetniks," 10 August 1943, *T-821*, roll 356, frame 261.

[102] Gizdić, *Dalmacija*, entry for 6 August 1943.

[103] Giuseppe Castellano, *La Guerra Continua* (Milan: Rizzoli, 1963), p. 52; Leonardo Simoni, *Berlino: Ambosciata d'Italia, 1939–1943*, entries for 10 and 12 August 1943.

the Allies and how to deal with the Germans and both rebel groups when the armistice was announced.[104] This fact accounts for a good deal of the uncertainty of everyone else, Germans, Partisans, and Chetniks, about General Robotti's plans. As far as the Chetniks were concerned, Robotti had information on all their plans [105] but, because of the far more dangerous menace posed by the Germans and Tito, elected to use threats to keep the officers away from the coast without antagonizing them by resorting to severe reprisals.

Without specific instructions from Comando Supremo, the Second Army and Fourteenth Army Corps in Montenegro, with few exceptions, were overwhelmed by the Germans almost immediately after Eisenhower announced Italy's capitulation on 8 September.[106] Even army headquarters in Rome did not know about Badoglio's armistice talks until 3 September, and the only set of instructions intended to prepare the field commanders for hostilities against the Germans, General Roatta's "Memoria O. P. 44," was not written in final form until 2 September and probably did not reach the army commanders until a few hours before the proclamation of the armistice.[107] Rome's failure to prepare the Italians in Yugoslavia for the armistice [108] not only made things easier for the Germans but thwarted whatever small hopes the officers still had of obtaining even a temporary ally, some badly needed arms, and perhaps a few footholds along the coast.

Within about a week after the capitulation, almost the entire Italian command structure in Yugoslavia was broken up, and the Germans occupied most of the eastern shore of the Adriatic.[109] In some areas, like parts of Istria, the Croatian coastal region (Primorje), and parts of Dalmatia, Partisan formations, supported at times by popular uprisings, succeeded in disarming, according to current Yugoslav accounts, the lion's

[104] The best works dealing with Italy's negotiations with the Allies in August 1943 and the capitulation of the armed forces still operating ouside of he peninsula are the volumes by Smyth and Garland in the American official history and Ruggero Zangrandi, *1943 25 luglio–8 settembre* (Milan: Feltrinelli, 1964).

[105] For example, Comando Supremo, "Nuovi aspetti del movimento cetnico," 19 August 1943, *T-821,* roll 347, frames 617–18.

[106] Zangrandi, *1943,* p. 455.

[107] *Ibid.,* pp. 457-66.

[108] Zangrandi shows, for example, largely on the basis of interviews with former Italian generals in 1963 and 1964, that until the days of the capitulation Italian units in Albania, Montenegro, and Herzegovina had orders to turn over the airfields to the Germans in the event of an Allied attack on the Balkans. The command of Army Group East (Greece, Albania, Montenegro) also had instructions from Comando Supremo to defend Durazzo against the Allies in conjunction with the Germans.

[109] *KTB/OKW,* vol. 3, entries for 9 and 16 September 1943; Radoje Pajović, "Političke Prilike u Crnoj Gori u Vrijeme Kapitulacije Italije 1943" (The political situation in Montenegro at the time of Italy's capitulation in 1943), *Jugoslovenski Istorijski Časopis* 1 (1962), p. 54; Zangrandi, *1943,* pp. 527, 564–79.

share of four divisions.[110] Outnumbered by the Partisans and, of course, ineffective against German motorized units, the Chetniks lost out almost completely in the scramble for arms and strategic positions.

Only in the Sandžak and parts of Montenegro, and there only for a short while, were the officers' formations a competing factor. In the Sandžak, where the Chetniks had, according to Partisan sources, about three thousand men, the officers were able to "neutralize" and almost win over parts of the division "Venezia" and in early October came close to retaking Kolašin from the Montenegrin Partisans.[111] At nearby Priboj part of the Italian garrison joined and fought as temporary allies of the Chetniks.[112] These, however, were only local and temporary successes. In Montenegro and the Sandžak, the real contenders were the Germans and Partisans.

Only in those areas where the Chetniks were able to win over or somehow coerce isolated Italian units into a temporary alliance did the officers' bands achieve any results. Elsewhere in Montenegro Tito was clearly getting the upper hand by mid-October. In western Montenegro the federalist Popović's group completed its break with Mihailović by joining the German side almost immediately. General Djukanović, head of the Montenegrin National Committee, was given command of the Chetniks in Montenegro by Mihailović on 10 September but remained in Cetinje until the end of the month.[113] By the middle of October, Djukanović and a few hundred demoralized troops of Colonel Stanišić had moved to the Ostrog monastery near Nikšić, where they were surrounded and killed by the Partisans.[114] With Djukanović and Stanišić dead, the entire officer leadership in Montenegro had been removed one way or another, and Tito had completed what he set out to do during the anti-Chetnik offensive of March and April.

In the rest of western Yugoslavia the Chetniks played almost no role. Captain Ivanisević, Mihailović's former chief delegate in Dalmatia, some-

[110] Jovan Marjanović and Pero Morača, *Naš Oslobodilački Rat i Narodna Revolucija (1941–1945)* (Belgrade: Izdavacko Preduzecé, 1958), pp. 225–26.

[111] Second Shock Corps to Second Proletarian Division, 27 September 1943, *Zbornik,* vol. 3, bk. 5, no. 51; Second Shock Corps to commander of Italian "Venezia" Division, 27 September 1943, *ibid.,* no. 52; Second Shock Corps to Second Proletarian Divisions, 29 September 1943, *ibid.,* no. 59; Second Shock Corps to Vasojevici Battalion, 1 October 1943, *ibid.,* no. 67; Second Shock Corps to Vasojevici Battalion, 5 October 1943, *ibid.,* no. 74; Second Shock Corps to Italian "Venezia" Division, 8 October 1943, *ibid.;* Obrad Egić, *Ratni Dnevnik 2. Proleterske Dalmatinske Brigade* (Zagreb: Stvarnost, 1967), entries for 30 September, 1, 3, and 8 October 1943.

[112] Egić, *Ratni Dnevnik,* entries for 26–30 September 1943; Second Proletarian Brigade to Second Proletarian Division, 17 October 1943, *Zbornik,* vol. 1, bk. 16, no. 47.

[113] Lovčen Partisan Detachment to Supreme Staff of Montenegrin and Kotor National Liberation Units, 28 September 1943, *ibid.,* 3: 5, No. 56.

[114] Third Shock Division to Tenth Herzegovinian Brigade, 16 October 1943, *ibid.,* no. 114; Pajović, "Političke Prilike u Crnog Gori," p. 57.

how escaped to Italy on the eve of the armistice.[115] Shortly thereafter Jevdjević fled to Rijeka.[116] Djujić tried to delay through sabotage actions the German troop movements to the coast but with no success, and in late September he fled to evade arrest.[117] Major Baćović, the leading officer in the field, made brief contact with an Italian regiment in late September but dropped out of sight after that.[118]

The events of the fall were in a real sense anticlimactic for the officers' movement, for since the first military reversals in Herzegovina in March Mihailović's organization had been worn down steadily, although in different ways, by Tito, the Germans, and Robotti's headquarters. During the summer months, the Chetniks' enemies succeeded in eliminating or at least immobilizing the large bulk of the leadership cadres, so that by September, although the rank and file of the non-Communist Serb armed movement was probably about as numerous as in the spring, it lacked political cohesion and was totally ineffective as a military force.

Viewed from another perspective, the Mihailović movement had disintegrated not only because its headquarters and officers either lost control of the bands or were themselves removed but also because in a relatively short period of time the strength of their enemies increased dramatically. Between April and September the number of German divisions in former Yugoslavia went from six to thirteen,[119] and after the Italian capitulation the Partisans gained a large stock of arms and supplies and added perhaps as many as 80,000 troops to their ranks.[120] After May, when the Italians cut off aid to the officers, Mihailović had no way of coping with the German occupation or with Tito except through massive external support The Chetniks' persistent conviction that an Allied Balkan landing was imminent and that the British would back them politically, although unfounded and contrary to the obvious direction of London's policies, was psychologically understandable. In September, when the British announced a policy of equal support for both Tito and Mihailović, the illusion of exclusive Allied backing also collapsed.

[115] See the biographical note on Ivanisević in Gizdić, *Dalmacija,* entry for 25 April 1943.

[116] Ministero degli Affari Esteri to Sottosegretario di Stato agli Esteri, "Rapporto sintetico sul movimento cetnico e suoi emissari in Italia," 25 April 1944, *T-586,* roll 412, frame 005425.

[117] Generalkommando XV. Geb. A.K./Ic to 114 Jg. Division, "Cetnikführer Vojvode Djujić," 23 September 1943, *T-314,* roll 566, frame 790.

[118] Dušan Živković, *Boka Kotorska i Paštrovici u Narodnooslobodilačkoj Borbi* (Kotor and Pastrovici in the national liberation struggle) (Belgrade: Vojno Delo, 1964), p. 278.

[119] Marjanović and Morača, *Naš Oslobodilački Rat i Narodna Revolucije,* p. 224.

[120] Jozo Tomasevich, "Yugoslavia during the Second World War," in *Contemporary Yugoslavia,* ed. Wayne Vucinich (Berkeley, Calif.: University of California Press, 1969), p. 102.

VIII
COLLABORATION
AND DEFEAT

:

After the Italian capitulation, the Mihailović movement no longer represented a serious factor in occupied Yugoslavia with the limited exception of Serbia. As far as the Germans were concerned, the main battleground was still the western half of the country, where Tito's Partisans had seized the initiative and were soon to enjoy full Allied backing. In Nedić's Serbia the Partisans made no effective challenge for almost another year, and the remains of the Mihailović organization constituted at most a rather insignificant potential threat rather than an actual one. In most parts of Yugoslavia the demoralized Chetniks probably could have been destroyed completely by the Germans. Instead, many of them gained a lease on life by transforming themselves into German rather than Italian auxiliary forces and devoting their small strength to almost exclusively anti-Partisan ends.

All this was possible as a result of a certain shift, evident at the end of 1943, in the German attitude toward the Yugoslav resistance. By the end of the year, they finally began to adjust their policies toward the Chetniks and in some instances even brought about a revival of the officers' movements on a local basis. As long as the Partisan threat remained predominant, all projects for anti-Chetnik measures were first put off and then shelved altogether. In addition, the Allied decision to throw all their weight against the German Winterstellung in southern Italy in November 1943 helped to convince O.K.W. that no major amphibious operation against the western Balkans was imminent.[1] This fact, in conjunction with the tremendous successes of the Red Army in the Ukraine during the second half of 1943, led the Germans to foresee defending themselves in southeastern Europe against the Russians rather than the Anglo-Americans and made any future revival of the Mihailović organization appear out of the question.

Even so, the Germans did not decide to make an arrangement with Mihailović personally but rather sought to pick up the pieces of his organization in order to isolate further Chetnik headquarters from the remaining unit leaders and to win some badly needed native support for the anti-Partisan struggle. The basic thrust of their policies was to exploit the weaknesses and internal divisions of the officers' movement by tying individual armed bands to local German command posts and to convert them into anti-Partisan militia formations or, in the case of Montenegro, into armed detachments loyal to both the Germans and Nedić. Therefore, their growing willingness to arrive at accommodations with Chetnik bands had nothing to do with a "pro-Mihailović" reorientation of policy but was undertaken because they were finally convinced that Mihailović's influence over the anti-Communist armed formations was nonexistent or negligible.[2]

In many instances, the decision to use Serb nationalist forces against Tito was made by the German field commands immediately after the Italian capitulation and was implemented on the basis of the specific military situation in the area. In western Bosnia, for example, where the Partisan movement was spreading rapidly, many of Djujić's former troops came to terms with the Germans as early as October. A number of Djujić's followers had gone over to the Partisans or fled into the hills; those who began collaborating with the Germans could not have numbered more than a few thousand.[3] Djujić's own rehabilitation was not complete. Although he finally succeeded in having the Germans rescind

[1] As late as October 1943 the German High Command still thought that the invasion of southern Italy was possibly designed to establish a Mediterranean beachhead for later operations in the Balkan Peninsula. See, for instance, *KTB/OKW*, vol. 3, 2, entry for 1 October 1943; OKW/WFSt/Op.Abt., "N. 662411/43 vom 6.10.43," 6 October 1943, *T-78*, roll 329, frame 6285446; John Ehrmann, *Grand Strategy* (London: Her Majesty's Stationery Office, 1956), 5:75, 81, 82.

[2] Even Kasche was arguing that their treatment of the Chetniks should be "elastic" because Mihailović no longer posed a real challenge to the Germans and Pavelić. Kasche to Abwehrstelle Belgrad, "N. 46/43 vom 14.10.43," 14 October 1943, *T-501*, roll 265, frame 1160.

[3] See the undated report of the Chetnik Jovan Popović to Uroš Drenović in Drago Gizdić, *Dalmacija, 1943–45* (Zagreb: Epoka, 1962–64), p. 522.

their order for his arrest,[4] they never trusted him in large-scale anti-Partisan operations and used his troops only to protect the railway lines from Knin to the Adriatic coast.[5] Moreover, they avoided any written agreements with the Chetnik cleric and required all his followers to obtain identification passes from the occupation authorities in order to qualify for their meager dole of arms and munitions. In contrast with his earlier cooperation with the Italians, Djujić was now bargaining from a weak position in order to maintain what little remained of his own authority over a decreasing armed following. His contacts with Mihailović were ineffectual because the Germans had intercepted his radio ties with Chetnik headquarters in September.

Neither Djujić nor the other Bosnian Chetniks who submitted to the strictly controlled arrangements with the Germans had freedom of action. Djujić was forbidden to allow his Dinaric Chetniks to carry out actions in areas populated by Croats.[6] In western Bosnia, the formations of Uroš Drenović needed the close cooperation of nearby German units and were informed at the end of the year that Ustaši officers and administrators would return shortly to the Chetniks' old sphere.[7] In eastern Bosnia, the formerly anti-Axis Chetniks became so demoralized after repeated clashes with the occupation troops and the Partisans that by November at least some unit leaders finally agreed to cooperate with the Germans.[8]

In Montenegro, too, the shift in German policies saved the decimated Chetniks from a total collapse. By November, Lašić was the only leading officer remaining in the field, and his following probably numbered no more than five hundred men.[9] Together with other stragglers, the Montenegrin Chetniks' strength could not have exceeded a thousand; Lašić himself was almost killed by the Partisans near Podgorica, sent an urgent plea to one of his subordinates in November to get help from the Germans, and then reported that his position was menaced by "external and internal

[4] Gen. Kdo. XV. Geb. A.K./Ic to 114. Jg. Division, "Cetnikführer Vojvode Djujić," 11 October 1943, T-314, roll 566, frame 330.

[5] 114. Jg. Division/Ic to Chef. d. Generalstabes XV. Geb. A.K., "Überprüfung der Zusammenarbeit mit Cetnik-Verbände," 5 November 1943, T-314, roll 566, frames 337–40.

[6] 264. Inf. Div./Ia to Gen. Kdo. XV. Geb. A.K., "Lagebeursteilung," 7 December 1943, T-314, roll 555, frame 782.

[7] Drenović to Misić, 11 November 1943, Dokumenti o Izdajstvu Draže Mihailovića no. 173; Einheit Boeckl/Division Brandenburg to Pz. AOK 2/Ic, "Cetniks," 27 December 1943, T-314, roll 566, frames 228–30.

[8] 369 Kroat. Inf. Div./Ia to Gen. Kdo. XV. Geb. A.K., "N. 3589/43 vom 4.10.43," 5 October 1943, T-314, roll 556, frame 527; Mil. Bfh. Südost, "Tagesmeldung," 2 November 1943, T-501, roll 266, frame 844.

[9] Lašić to Vuksanović, 6 November 1943, Zbornik, vol. 3, bk. 6, no. 197.

enemies—that he was "disillusioned with everything" because "everyone [was] fleeing in all directions to save his own skin." [10]

Mihailović had been promising to send reinforcements from Serbia, but Lašić no longer believed him and added that "we hope Nedić sends strong units here to free this part of the country." As the Chetnik crisis deepened, the unit leaders were turning away from Mihailović and toward the Germans and Serb Quislings. Like Lašić in Montenegro, Drenović's group in western Bosnia also made an open appeal to Nedić.[11] At the same time Djujić was developing increasingly close ties with the pro-German and quasi-Fascist Ljotić Zbor movement and was sending false reports to Chetnik headquarters in order to circumvent Mihailović's influence. The Chetniks' movement toward collaboration in late 1943 was therefore undertaken without Mihailović's direction and worked to undermine even further the authority of Chetnik headquarters in Serbia.

At the end of the year, especially after the news of the pro-Tito decisions taken at Teheran, the swing to collaboration threatened to become a mass movement. Among Chetniks throughout Yugoslavia rumors circulated that King Peter II was traveling to Moscow to come to terms with Stalin and to dissolve officially the Mihailović organization; [12] Nedić had already reported that Chetnik officers were trying daily to offer their services to the State Guard authorities at Belgrade.[13] This movement received added impetus when the German Foreign Office plenipotentiary for the southeast, Hermann Neubacher, brought the recently captured Djurišić back to Belgrade and sponsored a treaty between a revived, pro-German Montenegrin Chetnik movement and Nedić.[14] Djurišić was ultimately able to rebuild his forces to a strength of about five thousand men,[15] to carry out anti-Partisan operations in southwestern Serbia, the Sandžak, and northern Montenegro; he was promised aid by Nedić's State Guard.[16] In Serbia several officers, including the important Mihailović agent Captain Kalabić, made local armistices, and some even agreed

[10] Lašić to Major Vojović, 25 November 1943, *Dokumenti o Izdajstvu Draže Mihailovića,* no. 87.

[11] Einheit Boeckl/Division Brandenburg to Pz. AOK 2/Ic, "Cetniks," 27 December 1943, *T-314,* roll 566, frames 228–30.

[12] Mil. Bfh. Südost, "Tagesmeldung," 31 October 1943, *T-501,* roll 266, frame 850; 114. Jg. Division/Ia to Gen. Kdo. XV. Geb. A.K., "Lagebeurteilung," 11 November 1943, *T-314,* roll 555, frame 746.

[13] Mil. Bfh. Südost, "Tagesmeldung," 17 October 1943, *T-501,* roll 266, frame 892.

[14] Hermann Neubacher, *Sonderauftrag Südost (1940–1945)* (Gottingen: Musterschmidt Verlag, 1957), pp. 123, 166; H. Mommsen, "Serbische Nationale Freiwilligenverbände," *Gutachten des Instituts für Zeitgeschichte,* vol. 2 (Stuttgart: Deutsche Verlags-Anstalt, 1966), p. 304.

[15] Boško Kostić, *Za Istoriju Naših Dana* (Toward a history of our times) (Lille: Jean Lausier, 1949), p. 137.

[16] Mil. Bfh. Südost, "Tagesmeldung," 15 November 1943, *T-501,* roll 266, frame 781.

to place their troops under German command for joint anti-Partisan operations.[17]

Toward the end of the year, then Nedić and the Germans had at least as much, if not more, influence over the behavior of the remaining Chetniks than Mihailović did. Every recent development, military and diplomatic, seemed to deepen the isolation of Chetnik headquarters in Serbia. At the same time, Tito launched his next major political offensive. He called the AVNOJ congress, at which the Partisans denounced the London government in exile and established their own political organs as the sole legitimate executive and legislative powers in Yugoslavia.[18] The Allies immediately agreed at Teheran to shift their support to Tito, and on 8 December General Wilson sent a virtual ultimatum to Mihailović, ordering the Chetniks to sabotage two bridges on the Belgrade-Saloniki railway line. When they refused to carry out the action, Churchill used the incident as an excuse for telling King Peter that the Allies had decided to back Tito exclusively and that Mihailović might have to be dismissed from the post of minister of war.[19] By the middle of December, the British had withdrawn their liaison officers from Chetnik headquarters and instructed them to join the Partisans.

At the beginning of 1944 Chetnik headquarters was all but completely cut off from the remaining handful of officers and civilian formation leaders; Mihailović was deprived of even partial Allied backing and issued bitter reports warning his Serb followers to "expect even stronger attacks on us from the British." [20] Lacking any military or diplomatic leverage, Mihailović's staff decided to shore up their position by making a dramatic domestic political gesture. In an attempt to counter Tito's pretensions to political command of postwar Yugoslavia and to offer a program which might induce the Allies (more likely the American) to revise their policies, Mihailović met with a group of Serb political figures in mid-December to lay the foundation for a strictly civilian and pro-Chetnik Yugoslav Democratic National Union (Jugoslovenski Demokrat-

---

[17] The treaty between Kalabić and the South-East High Command was signed on 27 November 1943 and is reproduced in Serbo-Croatian in *Dokumenti o Izdajstvu Draže Mihailovića*, no. 646.

[18] For a concise analysis of the most important decisions and significance of the AVNOJ assembly, see Jozo Tomasevich, "Yugoslavia during the Second World War," in *Contemporary Yugoslavia*, ed. Wayne Vucinich (Berkeley, Calif.: University of California Press, 1969), p. 103.

[19] Dušan Plenča, *Medjunarodni Odnosi Jugoslavije u Toku Drugog Svjetskog Rata* (Belgrade: Institut Društvenih Nauka, 1962), p. 221; Anthony Eden (Earl of Avon), *The Reckoning*.

[20] Ambassador to the Yugoslav government in exile (MacVeagh) to secretary of state, 31 December 1943, *FRUS (1943)*, vol. 2: *(Europe)*, pp. 1040–41; Command of Yugoslav Army in Homeland/Mountain Staff 60 to Paraćin Brigade, 4 January 1944, *Dokumenti o Izdajstvu Draže Mihailovića*, no. 733.

ski Narodni Zajednici).[21] The basic purpose was to broaden the Chetnik movement politically by setting up a program which, although forcefully anti-Communist, was sufficiently "democratic" to appeal to large numbers of Yugoslavs.

Mihailović and the officers were attempting to compete with the Partisans on issues they had long avoided. After attempting steadfastly to subordinate the Chetnik movement to a strictly military leadership, they now tried to create a civilian political arm. Instead of postwar political programs whose major goal was Greater Serbia, they turned to popular and democratic appeals. The result was the convocation of the congress of St. Sava's Day (which actually met from 12 to 16 January 1944) at the village of Ba in western Serbia.[22] The former leader of the Social Democrats and a civilian figure of a progressive stripe, Živko Topalović,[23] was chosen to preside over the meeting, which, according to a German source, was attended by about five thousand armed Chetniks, practically all from Serbia, and by almost three hundred civilian delegates.[24] Mihailović gave an address in which he repeatedly denied any dictatorial ambitions, and the congress ended approving a resolution which included a commitment of allegiance to both democratic and monarchic principles, an appeal to the Partisans to renounce political activities until the end of the war, and a plan for the creation of an enlarged and federally organized Yugoslavia.

The fruits of the congress did represent concessions, but several of the proposals were utterly unrealistic, and it is doubtful that the officers were in tune with the radicalized mood of the broad strata of the Yugoslav civilian population. Obviously, the most notable changes in the Chetnik position were the support for democratic political principles and the proposal for a federalized constitutional structure. Against this, though, must be balanced their refusal to moderate their position on

[21] Živko Topalović, *Pokreti Narodnog Otpora u Jugoslaviji, 1941–45* (Paris: n.p., 1958), p. 87.

[22] Aside from the account of the St. Sava Congress provided by its principal organizer Topalović (*ibid.*, pp. 81–87), the only other source which deals with it at length is a report by Neubacher. Deutsche Gesandtschaft Belgrad (Neubacher) to Auswärtig Berlin, "Der Sveti Sava Kongress der DM-Bewegung, 10 February 1943, *T-120*, roll 2908, frames 6183H/E464519–23.

[23] Topalović's own career anticipated both the democratic and the anti-Communist elements of the new Chetnik program. One of the founders of the left-leaning Yugoslav Socialist Workers' party in 1919, which joined the Third International, Topalović later stood out as one of the chief spokesmen of the party's reformist wing and was always a strong opponent of the Communists' revolutionary tactics. Pero Morača, *Istorija Saveza Komunista Jugoslavije* (History of the League of Yugoslav Communists) (Belgrade: Izdavačko Preduzeće Rad, 1966), pp. 17, 22.

[24] Nedić to Mil. Bfh. Südost, 22 February 1944, *T-501*, roll 256, frame 881.

the question of monarchy. Moreover, Mihailović's own firm denial that the officers intended to set up a military dictatorship reveals the considerable and understandable lack of confidence in them on the part of the civilians. Over the short term, the most significant outcome of the St. Sava Day congress was Mihailović's forceful refusal, at least for the time being, to join the drift toward collaboration.

The evidence indicates that Mihailović was at least partially successful in reasserting himself as the Chetniks' moral leader and that he did restrain temporarily the collaborationist tendencies among several of his former followers. By late January a noticeable and rapid deterioration of relations between the Chetniks and the Quisling formations, Nedić's Serb State Guard and Ljotić's Volunteer Corps, had set in; some of Mihailović's followers even attempted small-scale disarmament actions and sabotage activities against Nedić's units.[25] In February the situation in Serbia deteriorated even more rapidly. The officers' bands in some instances skirmished with Ljotić's troops, seized control of local administrative units, and denounced their treaties with the Germans.[26] Nedić was concerned enough to write to the German commanding general in Serbia threatening to resign if immediate action were not taken to curb Mihailović's growing influence among the Serb people and within the civil and military administration in Belgrade.[27]

Despite this temporary revival of limited resistance activity, it seems certain that Mihailović was still interested in long-range goals rather than risky immediate confrontations with the Germans. Practically all of the Chetniks over whom he had influence operated in parts of western and southern Serbia;[28] those formations which were active in early 1944 challenged the Quisling armed formations rather than the Germans. Mihailović, indeed, could hardly afford an armed struggle with the occupation forces, since he depended on them to resist Partisan intrusions into Serbia. He probably counted more on tightening up the Chetnik organization and preserving munitions to prepare for the seizure of power in Belgrade when the Germans withdrew from Yugoslavia. According to intercepted Chetnik radio messages, there is some evidence that in early March Mihailović tried to make an agreement with officers of the Bul-

[25] Mil. Bfh. Südost/Ia, "Kriegstagebuch, 1–29 Feb. 1944," 1 February 1944, *T-501*, roll 256, frame 003.

[26] Mil. Bfh. Südost/Ia, "Kriegstagebuch, 1–29 Feb. 1944," 3 and 10 February 1944, *T-501*, roll 256, frame 004; Mil. Bfh. Südost/Ia to Heeresgruppe F, "Tagesmeldung," 22 January 1944, *T-501*, roll 352, frame 927.

[27] Nedić to Mil. Bfh. Südost, 22 February 1944, *T-501*, roll 256, frames 878–86.

[28] Captain Burger to Mil. Bfh. Südost/Ia, "Verhalten gegenüber der DM-Bewegung," 2 February 1949, *T-501*, roll 256, frame 026.

garian occupation units in southern Serbia to ensure their cooperation in the event of a German withdrawal.[29]

Over the short term, the officers had to preserve somehow their enclave in Serbia. Accordingly, in late March, when the first large Partisan units attempted to force their way across the Drina River, the Chetniks in several instances joined ranks with Nedić and the Germans to stop them.[30] The force of military events made some form of collaboration almost a necessity if the Serb Chetniks were to survive, and Mihailović's anti-Axis appeals of January proved to be of only temporary significance.

By mid-April the Germans were again coming to believe that Mihailović's estrangement from the British was final. This assessment received added impetus when the Chetnik General Miroslav Trifunović let it be known that the officers were ready to provide fifty thousand troops against Tito in conjunction with the Germans.[31] Some of Mihailović's most important unit leaders, like Keserović, had already sent agents to Nedić's State Guard headquarters, and in May Ljotić took a first step towards smoothing over the extremely difficult relations with the officers when he conferred personally with General Trifunović at Gornji Milanovac in western Serbia.[32]

With the constant threat of Partisan raids into Serbia and an impending Soviet drive in the Balkans, all of the leaders of the native anti-Communist forces were thinking increasingly of closing ranks and forgetting past differences. Ljotić negotiated with the Chetnik officers, Nedić suddenly informed the Germans that he was no longer opposed to arrangements with Mihailović's agents,[33] and Mihailović himself, although avoiding active collaboration with the Germans as long as he could, did decide on a hands-off policy toward the occupation troops. In a message to one of his followers in south Serbia, Major Djurić, he summed up the situation by pointing out that

in the actions against Tito's bans on the Drina the Germans did not touch us. On the contrary many of our commanders were helped and enabled to avoid attacks made by the Communists from Bosnia. . . . As we have not sufficient munitions and forces, we cannot carry on fighting on two fronts. At present our most dangerous enemy are the Communists. Therefore, I order that every

---

[29] Kdr. d. Nachr. Aufkl. 4/Ic, "DM-Bewegung," 18 March 1944, *T-312*, roll 470, frame 8060326.

[30] See the testimony of General Milos Isaković (Bulgarian First Army Corps) in Belgrade on 5 September 1945 in *Dokumenti o Izdajstvu Draže Mihailovića*, no. 656.

[31] Mil. Bfh. Südost/Ia, "Kriegstagebuch—April 1944," 11 April 1944 (Anlage 45), *T-501*, roll 256, frame 458.

[32] Mil. Bfh. Südost/Ia to Heeresgruppe F, "N. 3187/44 vom 20.5.1944," 20 May 1944, *T-501*, roll 256, frame 769; Kostić, *Za Istoriju Naših Dana*, pp. 150–51.

[33] Mil. Bfh. Südost/Ia, "Kriegstagebuch—April 1944," 12 April 1944 (Anlage 46), *T-501*, roll 256, frame 460.

kind of armed action against the occupyer's armed forces cease but the occupyer will be attacked by propaganda.[34]

The Chetnik leadership as long as it could hovered between resistance and collaboration. Mihailović's subordinates in Serbia tried to come to terms with Nedić and Ljotić and even cooperated occasionally with the Germans against the Partisans, but Mihailović would go no farther than calling off hostilities against the Germans and officially maintained an anti-Axis stand. As a result most of the officers' formations received no appreciable aid from the Germans, and the movement remained militarily helpless throughout the summer of 1944. The German command in Belgrade continued to stress that the Chetnik "movement is and remains hostile" and prohibited measures contributing to "even the partial renewal of the Mihailović movement." Arms deliveries were to be made only "in very small quantities" and "on a purely local basis." [35]

Militarily, the Chetniks survived as a result of a truce with the Germans; politically, Mihailović's gestures had little impact, and he was reacting to events more than initiating them. In June the Germans failed to annihilate the Partisans in one daring strike, combining raids by motorized units and by about 650 paratroops, at Tito's headquarters at Drvar, Bosnia. Tito escaped in a Russian plane to Italy and discovered that Churchill had just had Mihailović removed as King Peter's minister of war.[36] Soon after, the Partisan leader took a major step toward breaking the political deadlock with the émigré government: the British agreed to sponsor the Tito-Subašić agreement, which guaranteed at least significant Communist participation in the postwar government.

Mihailović's response to his exclusion from the London government was to set up his own shadow administration, the Committee of Experts (Odbor Stručnjaka) in early July; it issued a denunciation of the Subašić "government" for its support of Communism and Croat separatism.[37] In late July the Odbor called a plenary session of the Central National Committee, originally established in the fall of 1941 at Ravna Gora, and at the meeting Subašić was called upon to resign.

In rejecting the London émigré government's compromise with Tito, Mihailović placed the Serb Chetniks in a position where they were almost forced to make common cause militarily with the Germans. In mid-July, a week after the formation of the Subašić government (7 July 1944), one of Mihailović's chief aides, Neško Nedić, held talks with the

---

[34] Fitzroy Maclean, *Disputed Barricades* (London: Jonathan Cape, 1957), pp. 264–65.
[35] Mil. Bfh. Südost/Ic, "Verhalten gegenüber der DM-Bewegung," 16 May 1944, *T-501*, roll 256, frames 754–55.
[36] Plenča, *Medjunarodni Odnosi*, pp. 250–55.
[37] *Ibid.*, p. 310.

head of the German South-East High Command, General Felber, in which he pledged that the Chetniks had broken completely with the British and requested arms and munitions for use exclusively against the Partisans. So forceful was Lieutenant Nedić's anti-British tirade that Felber reported to O.K.W. his "personal impression that this time the Chetniks' offer definitely should be taken seriously." [38]

General Felber's views were, however, not shared by Hitler. In late August, in fact, shortly after the Soviet liberation of Rumania, Hitler responded to the appeals of van Weichs of Army Group "F" for military collaboration with Mihailović; he approved weapons and munitions supplies to Chetnik groups only "for use in small tactical operations." [39] In any event, the military situation was hopeless for both the Germans and Mihailović, for Army Group "F" could at best manage only a temporary holding action against a Soviet invasion from Rumania and Bulgaria, and the Chetniks had to defend Serbia from a Partisan invasion from Bosnia without any reliable allies except a few of Nedić's and Ljotić's weak units.

Faced with the Partisan invasion of Serbia, Mihailović's headquarters continued to search for any possible ally. By mid-August rumors were circulating in Belgrade that the Chetniks had already lost over a thousand men against the Partisans in south Serbia,[40] and new efforts were made to get help from Nedic and Ljotic.[41] Mihailović's agent, Captain Predrag Raković, contacted Kostić and succeeded in inducing Nedić to agree to the immediate delivery of ten thousand rifles and twenty thousand uniforms, but before the month was over the Chetnik military position had completely disintegrated and word reached Belgrade that the Partisans had surrounded the troops of one of the leading officers, Major Keserović.[42]

In order to improve their chances of getting badly needed arms from Nedić and the Germans, Chetnik headquarters in the last week of August forbad the troops to attack German supply vehicles.[43] After all the countless turns and shifts of Mihailović's strategy, however, the German re-

---

[38] Mil. Bfh. Südost/Ic to OKW/WFSt, "DM-Bewegung in Serbien," 19 July 1944, *T-120*, roll 780, frames 371759–60; OKW/WFSt/Qu. 2 to Oberbfhb. Südost, "DM-Bewegung Serbien," 27 July 1944, *T-120*, roll 780, frame 371758.

[39] OKW/WFSt/Op (H) Südost to Ritter, "N. 0010269/44 vom 24.8.44," 24 August 1944, *T-120*, roll 3155, frame E518680.

[40] Neubacher to Aus. Amt, "N. S 88 vom 16.8.44," 16 August 1944, *T-120*, roll 780, frame 371754.

[41] Plenča, *Medjunarodni Odnosi*, p. 311; Kostić, *Za Istoriju Naših Dana*, pp. 155–56.

[42] Gerenza Affari Consolari in Belgrado to Ministero degli Affari Esteri, "N. 1359/809 del 26.8.44," 26 August 1944, *T-586*, roll 412, frame 5407.

[43] Neubacher to Ritter, "N. 1832 vom 28.8.44," 28 August 1944, *T-120*, roll 780, frame 371738.

sponse was still divided. While Felber and Neubacher favored collaboration, Hitler, according to Ribbentrop, continued to be suspicious of
"the real designs of Mihailović," [44] and in Belgrade the German police
intensified their hunt for Chetnik sympathizers, arresting about four
hundred in one day alone. [45]

With the Germans about to commence their slow withdrawal from the
Balkans [46] and Soviet and Partisan troops preparing for a march on Belgrade from the east and west, respectively, one may well ask what was
sustaining Mihailović's hopes. By then it was evident that he could not
depend on any appreciable support from the Germans, and the Chetniks'
declining prospects depended on holding their own somehow in Serbia
against Tito and on the Red Army remaining out of Yugoslavia. There
is, in fact, some evidence that Mihailović thought the Allies, especially
the Americans, were exerting their influence to prevent a Russian occupation of Belgrade.

Out of desperation as much as anything else, the Chetniks hoped for
some sort of spheres of influence arrangement between the Allies and
the Russians in which American opposition to Stalin's supposed designs
in the Balkans would override the earlier British support for Tito and
compel the Russians to accept a "mixed" political settlement in Yugoslavia. According to the British Colonel Bailey, the royal Yugoslav ambassador to Washington, the ferociously pro-Chetnik Konstantine Fotich,
had been encouraging Mihailović since early 1944 to think he could
play off the United States against the English. [47] Apparently, by the late
summer of 1944 American "policies" regarding the resistance movements
in Yugoslavia were so vague [48] and poorly coordinated that Mihailović
seized on every hint of a dramatic anti-Communist Allied political and/or
military intervention in Yugoslav affairs. Moreover, because Eisenhower's
headquarters would have nothing to do with military operations in the
Balkans, American activities there were confined exclusively to air and
O.S.S. intelligence operations. This last fact is significant, for it was
almost certainly the activities of American intelligence in Yugoslavia

[44] Ribbentrop to Neubacher, "N. 1905 vom 31.8.44," 31 August 1944, T-120, roll 780,
frame 371737.

[45] Gerenza Affari Consolari in Belgrado to Ministero degli Affari Esteri, "N. 1303/789
del 26.8.44," 26 August 1944, T-586, roll 412, frame 5411.

[46] O.K.W. ordered Army Group "E" to prepare for withdrawing its units from
Greece on 1 September.

[47] Ambassador to Yugoslav government in exile (Macreagh) to secretary of state,
21 February 1944, FRUS (1944), vol. 4: (Europe), p. 1349.

[48] According to Robert Murphy's account, Roosevelt's view of the situation in Yugoslavia immediately before the Cairo conference (November 1943) was that "we [the
Americans] should build a wall around those two fellows [Tito and Mihailović] and
let them fight it out, [then] we could do business with the winner." Diplomat among
Warriors (New York: Doubleday, 1964), p. 220.

which sustained Mihailović's expectations of an about-face in Allied policies in southeastern Europe.

The head of O.S.S., General William ("Wild Bill") Donovan, as early as January 1944 made clear his desire to preserve a flexible policy in Yugoslavia when he rejected a British request that American officers be sent at once to Tito's headquarters.[49] Soon after an O.S.S. officer proposed sending to Mihailović "a purely and confessedly intelligence officer,"[50] and when Donovan suggested the same idea to Hull, Roosevelt approved immediately.[51] Marine Corps Captain W. R. Mansfield arrived at Chetnik headquarters in March for the purpose, as Donovan explained it in a note of 31 March, of "infiltrating agents into Austria and Germany." He soon transmitted to Donovan's staff at Capri, Italy, a personal letter from Mihailović addressed to Eisenhower. Whatever the contents of this letter, Eisenhower's response was not very encouraging. Although he promised Donovan that "the proper staff sections will comb [it] for everything they can get," he felt compelled to add that "I should not attempt to answer directly the letter from General Mihailović."[52]

American intelligence operations with Chetnik headquarters in Serbia had at least two immediate and obvious goals: to secure the evacuation of several American pilots who had been shot down over Yugoslavia and retrieved by Mihailović's followers, and to use the Chetnik sanctuaries and their contacts with Belgrade to gain information on German plans in the Balkans. Aside from these aims, it appears certain that Donovan and the State Department representative for Mediterranean affairs, Robert Murphy, also hoped that the mission would maintain permanent contact with Mihailović and facilitate a later and decisive American political gesture in Yugoslavia. However, despite a certain anti-Tito mood in Washington, about which Hull hinted in July when he complained about the British "insistence on giving Tito politically and militarily a free hand for all Yugoslavia,"[53] Donovan's and Murphy's persistent efforts to influence their superiors got nowhere.[54]

O.S.S., then, acting independently, continued to pursue operations in

---

[49] Memorandum of the assistant secretary of state (Berle), 26 January 1944, *(1944)*, vol. 4: *(Europe)*, p. 1339–40.

[50] Ambassador to Yugoslav government in exile (Macreagh) to Hull, 21 February 1944, *ibid.*, pp. 1349–50.

[51] Donovan to Hull, 2 March 1944, *ibid.*, p. 1350, n. 53; memorandum prepared for mission to London of under secretary of state (Stettinius), 2 March 1944, *ibid.*, pp. 1353–54.

[52] Donovan's report is alluded to in Alfred D. Chandler, ed., *The Papers of Dwight D. Eisenhower: The War Years*, vol. 3 (Baltimore: The Johns Hopkins Press, 1970), p. 1815, n. 2.

[53] Secretary of state to counsellor of mission at Algiers, 8 July 1944, *FRUS (1944)*, vol. 4: *(Europe)*, p. 1387.

[54] Murphy, *Diplomat among Warriors*, p. 221.

Yugoslavia, and by the end of the summer its activities were obviously anti-Partisan. On 27 and 28 August, when Mihailović was sending out feelers for a more formal truce with the Germans, Colonel Robert H. McDowell, a former professor of Balkan history at the University of Michigan, arrived at Chetnik headquarters. According to Mihailović's testimony at his trial in 1946, McDowell told him that the Americans were not interested in his fighting the Germans and would prefer that he remain with his people.[55]

One might dismiss this statement as a clumsy effort by Mihailović, made during his final plea, to shift the blame for his actions to others were it not for the fact that there is reason to believe that McDowell did encourage the officers to think they had American backing for the pursuit of anti-Partisan projects. There is even strong evidence to suggest that McDowell led Mihailović to believe that the Russians would not enter Yugoslavia and that Mihailović took this as proof that at least part of the country would fall in the non-Communist "sphere." With that sort of external support, the Chetniks could make one last deal with the Germans, before they left the Balkans, in order to gain the upper hand in Serbia.

In early September Neubacher, who had good contacts with several Chetniks, reported that Mihailović, "with the full support of a small American staff who have arrived only recently, will fight against us [the Germans] under absolutely no circumstances" and that "the Americans have told him that Soviet Russia would be breaking the Teheran accords if they cross the Danube."[56] Next, Neubacher heard that the officers had been told by a certain colonel on Mihailović's staff, "a special agent of Roosevelt," that they could count on an "Anglo-American intervention" in the event of a Russian invasion of Serbia.[57] The officers made no secret of their calculations, and one of Mihailović's agents in Belgrade soon told Neubacher that they were sure "that in the last phase of the war, the Anglo-Americans would decide the fate of Serbia."[58] When Mihailović held an urgent meeting of his officers on 6 September he told them that the Red Army would not cross the Danube, for it would lead to a break with the Allies, and authorized the distribution of leaflets which asserted that the British and Americans had decided to cut off all

[55] Maclean, *Disputed Barricades*, p. 324; Plenča, *Medjunarodni Odnosi*, p. 312.

[56] Neubacher to Ritter, "N. 1864 vom 1.9.44," 1 September 1944, *T-120*, roll 780, frames 371731–32.

[57] Neubacher to Ritter, "N. 1868 vom 2.9.44," 2 September 1944, *T-120*, roll 780, frame 371729.

[58] Neubacher to Ritter, "N. 1882 vom 3.9.44," 3 September 1944, *T-120*, roll 780, frame 371726.

aid to Tito and were presently disarming Communist resistance groups in France and Italy.[59]

Only two days earlier, on 4 September, Neubacher felt ready to act and, judging that his "trump card [was] anti-Communism" and that the officers could not afford a simultaneous fight against the Germans and the Partisans, gave approval to "joint actions with the Chetniks." [60] The next day Mihailović instructed his subordinates to avoid conflicts with the Germans.[61] For the moment the way seemed clear for a collaboration between Chetnik headquarters and the Germans which, if born of mutual desperation and wild miscalculations, was collaboration nonetheless.

To a large degree, these illusions resulted from a double game Tito himself was playing with the western Allies and the Russians. Murphy, for example, was convinced after his talks with the Partisan leader in Italy on 31 August that "the Russians would not enter Serbia but would confine their activities along the Danube into Hungary, leaving Marshall Tito to deal with Serbian matters." [62] As late as 23 September, less than a week before the first Soviet units attacked the Germans in Serbia from Bulgaria, Maclean thought that Tito, who had left for Romania on the previous day, "would endeavor to persuade the Russians not to enter Yugoslavia." [63] Despite his statements to Maclean, Tito succeeded during his trip to Romania in working out the details for the supply of ten Partisan divisions and, more important, for the "Belgrade action," a Red Army invasion of Serbia.[64] On September 28, when the advance units of the Third Ukranian Front's 57th Army entered Yugoslavia, the Chetniks' desperate strategy fell apart completely. Shortly before this, Tito's troops overran the main body of Chetniks in western Serbia, came close to capturing Mihailović, and, according to some reports, seized his archives.[65]

By the end of September, the Partisan breakthrough in Serbia was complete, Mihailović's weak units were totally scattered, and Neubacher

[59] Kostić, *Za Istoriju Naših Dana,* p. 165.

[60] Neubacher to Ritter, "N. 1884 vom 4.9.44," 4 September 1944, *T-120,* roll 780, frame 371723.

[61] Plenč, *Medjunarodni Odnosi,* p. 312.

[62] Memorandum by U.S. political adviser on staff of supreme Allied commander, Mediterranean theater (Murphy), to assistant chief of Division of Southern European Affairs (Cannon), 8 September 1944, *FRUS (1944),* vol. 4: *(Europe),* p. 1404.

[63] U.S. political adviser on staff of supreme Allied commander, Mediterranean theater (Kirk), to Hull, 23 September 1944, *ibid.,* pp. 1410–11.

[64] Musheg M. Minasian, *Osvobozhdenie Narodov Yugyo-Vostochnoi Evropy* (The liberation of the peoples of southeastern Europe) (Moscow: Voennoe Izdatel'stvo Ministerstva Oborony SSSR, 1967), pp. 421–23.

[65] U.S. political adviser on staff of supreme Allied commander, Mediterranean theater (Kirk), to secretary of state, 16 September 1944, *FRUS (1944),* vol. 4: *(Europe),* pp. 1407–8. According to Kostić (*Za Istoriju Naših Dana,* p. 165), Mihailović owed his narrow escape to the support provided by one of Ljotić's Volunteer Corps detachments.

had lost all contact with Chetnik headquarters.[66] On 26 September a group of political figures on Mihailović's staff sent an appeal to the Allies through McDowell calling for help to stop the Bolshevik threat in Serbia,[67] but, by this time, the American attitude was irrelevant, and the final collapse of the Chetnik movement was beginning.

The hoped-for Allied intervention took the form, of course, of Churchill's famous "percentage deal" with Stalin on 9 October in which influence in Yugoslavia was vaguely sorted out on a fifty-fifty basis while Tito and the Russians pushed ahead toward Belgrade. The British and Americans were relying basically on the power of persuasion to stop or modify the civil war in Serbia; Churchill justified his arrangement with the Russians by the argument that the accord was intended to "produce a joint and friendly policy towards Marshal Tito, while ensuring that weapons furnished to him are used against the common Nazi foe rather than for internal purposes." [68] By 20 October, however, Belgrade had been liberated, and Tito soon felt secure enough to complain bitterly to Maclean about Colonel McDowell for "representing himself, or in any event . . . permitting himself to be represented as [the] official representative of [the] Govt. of the United States sanctioned by [the] Allied High Command on whose behalf H[ead] Q[uarters] promised support to Mihailović." At the end of October O.S.S. was assuring Washington that McDowell had been trying to get out of Yugoslavia for "over a month . . . [but had] met with many difficulties due to [the] increased tempo of fighting there." [69]

The spheres of influence arrangement bore no relation to military realities, and American "support" for Mihailović evaporated as quickly as it had appeared. The Chetniks were routed in their last bastion, and a number of the rank and file went over to the Partisans.[70] In November Donovan's staff, which had nourished so many of the officers' illusions, rejected a British request that they evacuate Mihailović on the grounds that "serious complications" would obviously result from such an action.[71]

During the rapid swirl of military events in the fall of 1944 virtually all the isolated and weak Chetnik formations which did not pass over to

[66] Neubacher to Ritter, "N. 2022 vom 26.9.44," 26 September 1944, *T-120*, roll 2955, frame E470218.

[67] Neubacher to Ritter, "N. 2032 vom 27.9.44," 27 September 1944, *T-120*, roll 780, frame 371718.

[68] Winston Churchill, *The Second World War, IV, Triumph and Tragedy* (Boston: Houghton Mifflin, 1953), p. 234.

[69] The quotation is from Maclean's report to General Wilson, in U.S. political adviser on staff of supreme Allied commander, Mediterranean theater, to secretary of state, 3 October 1944, *FRUS (1944)*, vol. 4: *(Europe)*, pp. 1415–16.

[70] See the remarks in Minasian, *Osvobozhdenie*, pp. 419–20.

[71] U.S. political adviser on staff of supreme Allied commander, Mediterranean theater, to secretary of state, 15 November 1944, *FRUS (1944)*, vol. 4: *(Europe)*, p. 1422.

the Partisans remained in the woods or disintegrated completely. Some of them skirmished with the rear of withdrawing German units,[72] but many remained close to Nedić's State Guard troops and avoided any military operations. With the loss of Serbia apparent to practically everyone, their only remaining options were to move their troops to the west toward the Adriatic or give up the fight altogether and join the German march to Slovenia and ultimately to Italy or Austria. Significantly enough, both options were based on the premise that the British and Americans were not prepared to sacrifice the anti-Tito cause completely and were willing to launch an amphibious operation against the Adriatic coast—or at least to thrust into northwestern Yugoslavia to save the Chetniks and various Quisling groups from Partisan vengeance.

The first plan, calling for a Chetnik exodus to Montenegro, Herzegovina, and Dalmatia, could succeed only in the event of an Allied show of force, carried out for anti-Partisan ends, along the Adriatic. It is revealing that several factions in the officers' camp, even including some persons who were disgruntled over Mihailović's leadership, continued to believe that an about-face in Allied policies toward the Yugoslav resistance was imminent. In Herzegovina, for example, Colonel Lukačević, who left Yugoslavia for Cairo in early 1944 and returned later to set up an anti-Axis Chetnik group free of Mihailović's authority, expected a British landing near Dubrovnik in September.[73] Kostić, too, relates that when he urged some of the officers to retreat to Slovenia along with the Volunteer Corps troops, he met strong opposition on the grounds that it would be wiser to move toward Dalmatia and Montenegro in order to act in conjunction with the Allied landing.[74] German intelligence reports suggest that Mihailović and the coterie of officers at his headquarters were thus deceived until very late in the war.[75]

Despite all the evidence to the contrary, there were signs toward the end of 1944 that sudden and dramatic shifts of Soviet and Anglo-American spheres of influence in the Balkans would leave the officers with a foothold in Yugoslavia, and Mihailović refused to capitulate. In part these expectations must have derived from the fact that by 12 November the last Red Army units had withdrawn from Yugoslav territory.[76] There is also some

---

[72] For example, in parts of western Serbia or in the area east of Sarajevo. Minasian, *Osvobozhdenie*, p. 420; Erich Schmidt-Richberg, *Der Endkampf auf dem Balkan* (Heidelberg: Scharnhorst-Buchkameradschaft, 1955) p. 55.

[73] See the interesting article by Radoje Pajović, "Formiranje Četničke Nezavisne Grupe Nacionalnog Otpora" (The formation of the Chetnik Independent Group of National Resistance), *Jugoslovenski Istorijski Časopis* 4 (1964): 53–70.

[74] Kostić, *Za Istoriju Naših Dana*, p. 173.

[75] See for instance the South-East High Command's "final report," Chef der Militärverwaltung Südost, "Abschlussbericht," n.d., *T-501*, roll 264, frame 242.

[76] Tomasevich, "Yugoslavia during the Second World War," p. 106.

reason to believe that Churchill's decisive intervention in Greece in December stiffened the officers' resolve to carry on the anti-Partisan struggle in the hope of Allied support. Djurišić, for example, was so impressed by British actions in Athens that he told one of Ljotić's delegates that he was considering a march through Albania to Greece to join with the English and Greek monarchist forces.[77] Finally, when news of the Churchill-Stalin "spheres" arrangement of October leaked out, some Chetniks thought its implementation would nullify Tito's earlier military victories. Thus Topalović wrote Mihailović from Italy on 3 November that "the governments of Great Britain and the Soviet Union have agreed to divide up Yugoslavia 50–50," which meant that "Tito will probably be given the upper hand in Croatia while we get Serbia east of the Drina River."[78]

By the end of 1944, however, when the Yugoslav "front" ran roughly from the Adriatic opposite Herzegovina to the Drava in the north, the Germans were no longer able to absorb the brunt of Partisan military pressures in the southern and eastern parts of the country, and the officers' bands were forced to move steadily north and west. The officers in Serbia had an extremely difficult time carrying out the evacuation; at the end of the year, in fact, German Army Group "E" refused an appeal from Mihailović's aide, General Trifunović. to allow the bands to cross the Drina into Bosnia.[79] By about mid-January, though, Mihailović had reached the area north of Sarajevo with a few thousand troops under his immediate command, but the retreating Germans still had orders to disarm the bands and resist their efforts to continue into central Bosnia.[80]

In order to prepare the way for as free a passage to the northwest as possible, Ljotić, Jevdjević, and Rupnik, the leader of the Slovene Quisling forces, all moved to Ljubljana, where they attempted for weeks to persuade the Germans and Ustaši to agree to let a large number of Mihailović's troops into Croatia and Slovenia. In November and December Pop Djujić was also urgently appealing for official permission for his battered Dinaric group to take refuge in Istria.[81] The Germans in Zagreb, especially Kasche, proved intransigent, and Ljotić had to go to Vienna personally in mid-December to speak to Neubacher before winning approval for the northward passage of the Dinaric Chetniks. Djujić's six

[77] Kostić, Za Istoriju Naših Dana, p. 200.

[78] Plenča (Medjunarodni Odnosi, pp. 261–62) found this letter in the Archives of the Military-Historical Institute at Belgrade.

[79] Schmidt-Richberg, Der Endkampf, p. 83.

[80] W. Bfh. Südost/Nach. Aufkl./Abt. 16, "N. 68/45 vom 10.1.45," 10 Jan. 1945, T-501, roll 266, frame 537; W. Bfh. Südost/Nach. Aufkl./Abt. 16, "Tito- und D.M.-Banden in chem. Jugoslawien," 18 January 1945, T-501, roll 266, frames 575–76.

[81] Kostić, Za Istoriju Naših Dana, p. 185.

thousand or so typhus-ridden followers made a slow journey to the Slovene coast, lost hundreds of men to the reprisals of nearby Ustaši,[82] and
in January were disarmed by the Germans.[83] Djujić, now without any
effective military strength, arrived at Ljubljana on 28 December to confer with the other Serb civilian anti-Communist leaders.

By early 1945, then, the Chetniks were splitting into two groups, with
the major civilian figures, Djujić and Jevdjević, in Slovenia and most
of the remaining officers in eastern Bosnia. The most important of the
Bosnian officers was Djurišić, whose following consisted of about seven
thousand troops and a few thousand civilian refugees; with him were
Ostojić and Račić, neither of whom had any following at all. By
February, after Djurišić's Montenegrins had arrived in the vicinity of
the other Chetnik formations in eastern Bosnia,[84] Mihailović had a force
of some twenty to twenty-five thousand,[85] including armed troops,
stragglers, and civilian refugees, under his nominal command. With
disaster approaching, however, he lost whatever remained of his moral
authority over the Chetniks, and in the movement's final weeks there was
a bitter falling out between the officers.

Djurišić was convinced that the only realistic course of action was an
immediate retreat to Slovenia, and he began sending radio messages to
Djujić that he negotiate the Montenegrins' safe passage to the northwest
through Nedić and Ljotić.[86] Toward the end of the month Djurišić
organized a meeting of the unit leaders, which Mihailović apparently did
not attend, and won general approval for a strategy of capitulation and
retreat.[87] The Montenegrin leader's proposals stimulated a movement
among the officers to desert the fight in the interior of the country and
join forces with the civilian group at Ljubljana. Ljotić encouraged this
trend in March by sending a delegation, headed by Kostić and the original chief figure in the Belgrade puppet administration, Milan Acimović,
to Mihailović's headquarters to convince the officers to throw in their

[82] W. Bfh. Südost/Nach. Aufkl./Abt. 16, "Tito- und D.M.-Banden in ehem. Jugoslawien," 9 January 1945, T-501, roll 266, frame 533.

[83] Kostić, Za Istoriju Naših Dana, pp. 198–200; W. Bfh. Südost/Nach. Aufkl. 4, "N.
188/44 vom 23.12.44," 23 December 1944, T-501, roll 260, frame 467; W. Bfh. Südost/
Nach. Aufkl./Abt. 16, "N. 6/45 vom 1.1.45," 1 January 1945, T-501, roll 266, frame
494; Obkdo. H. Gruppe F/Nach. Aufkl./Abt. 16, 5 January 1945, T-501, roll 266,
frame 512.

[84] Several of the Montenegrin Chetniks withdrew alongside and as auxiliary detachments of the German columns. This is evident from an eyewitness account of at
least one American pilot; he was shot down in July 1944 and was retrieved by the
Chetniks. (Major) James M. Inks, Eight Bailed Out (New York: W. W. Norton, 1954),
pp. 85ff.

[85] Tomasevich, "Yugoslavia during the Second World War," p. 167.

[86] Kostić, Za Istoriju Naših Dana, p. 202.

[87] Milan Basta, Rat posle Rata (The war after the war) (Zagreb: Novinarska Izda-
vačka Kuća Stvarnost, 1963), p. 125.

lot with the rapidly growing collection of Serb and Slovene anti-Communist forces gathering in Slovenia.[88] In order to present the "Slovene variant" in the most optimistic light, Kostić told Mihailović and his leading collaborators, Keserović, Kalabić, Račić, and Bacovic, that Ljotić was working out a plan to use a combined force of some twenty-five thousand Serb-Slovene fighters and Mihailović's twenty-five thousand troops as the basis for attempting a coup in Ljubljana, mobilizing thirty thousand more men, and securing Allied support. The goal was to keep Tito and the Russians out of the area long enough for King Peter to return to Slovenia.

Mihailović did not reject Ljotić's plan openly and even sent warm letters to Djujić and Jevdjević in Ljubljana, but he did refuse to move his own men to Slovenia. This, however, was enough to exacerbate further what was essentially a personal feud between Djurišić and Mihailović and brought about the final disintegration of the officers' movement. By early spring almost all the officers except Mihailović favored Djurišić's plan, and in late March they succeeded in establishing radio contact with the Ljotić-Djujić-Jevdjevic group.[89] In early April Djurišić's followers broke openly with Mihailović and began their march toward Slovenia.[90]

While Djurišić was negotiating with Pavelić for permission to move into the area just south of the Sava River, Mihailović was trying to restrain the massive exodus; he argued to Ljotić that there was "a considerable breakdown in the Communist ranks, especially in Serbia" and that they should not give up the struggle against Tito.[91] At this point, the more isolated and hopeless Mihailović's position became, the more extreme were his calculations. Although he probably had no more than ten thousand followers, he informed Ljotić that he would return to Serbia [92] and radioed Djujić on 11 April that his troops would join a popular uprising there against the Partisans.[93] Some evidence suggests that Mihailović had been planning a return to Serbia throughout early 1945. An intelligence report of the Ustaši High Command, dated 25 April 1945, explained that one of the reasons for the break between the Montenegrins and Chetnik headquarters was the fact that Djurisić was "opposed to the idea of participating in a march back to Serbia to start a national uprising." [94]

Mihailović's plan was, of course, suicidal, but as events turned out the

[88] Kostić, *Za Istoriju Naših Dana*, pp. 211ff.
[89] *Ibid.*, pp. 228-35.
[90] Basta, *Rat posle Rata*, p. 129.
[91] Mihailović to Ljotić, 1 April 1945, cited by Kostić, *Za Istoriju Naših Dana*, p. 238.
[92] Ljotić to Mihailović, 10 April 1945, cited in *ibid.*, p. 236.
[93] Mihailović to Djujić, 11 April 1945, cited in *ibid.*, p. 239.
[94] Cited by Basta, *Rat posle Rata*, p. 127.

schemes of the civilian collaborators and Djurišić were just as hopeless. At the end of the war, in fact, it was only a matter of who—the British, Ustaši, or Partisans—would dispose of each remaining Chetnik group. Djurišić, after setting out with approximately ten thousand followers, attempted to negotiate free passage through Croatia to Slovenia with the aid of the Montenegrin federalist Sekula Drljević, but quickly ran into trouble with the Ustaši government.[95] They were even attacked by Ustaši troops, but most must have survived because the British refused asylum to eight thousand left in Carinthia and sent them back to Maribor. There they were either "disarmed easily," according to the Titoist version,[96] or all murdered, as the former Nedić officer Karapandžić would have it.[97]

Perhaps one thousand of Djurišić's Chetniks and about five hundred of Jevdjević's troops somehow made it into Austria, but at the end of May the British moved them, along with thousands of Serb Volunteers, Slovene Homeguardsmen, and all sorts of collaborationist formations, back to Yugoslavia. As for the rest of the leaders, several simply disappeared, probably shot by the Partisans; others were later captured, tried, and executed; still others were able to save themselves by slipping into the Allied occupation zone. Ljotić, the last of the civilian ringleaders, was killed in an automobile accident in late April; Jevdjević, however, made his way to Italy and was fortunate enough to be removed by the British to Salerno.

Mihailović, of course, remained in eastern Bosnia until the close of the war and then, as planned, began to move his men back toward Serbia.[98] Around mid-May most of his following was destroyed in the area near the sources of the Drina and Neretva rivers. Mihailović escaped and was not captured until almost a year later, in March 1946. He was tried and convicted for high treason in Belgrade and was executed on 26 July 1946.

---

[95] *Ibid.*, p. 129.

[96] *Ibid.*, p. 133.

[97] Bor M. Karapandzić, *Kočevije—Tito's Bloodiest Crime* (Munich: Iskra, 1965), p. 44, n. 4.

[98] Tomasevich, "Yugoslavia during the Second World War," p. 111.

CONCLUSION

:

The preceding chapters have traced the development of an armed movement which was anti-Axis in its long-range goals and engaged in a marginal sort of resistance activity but which also carried out almost throughout the war a tactical or selective collaboration with the occupation order. This presents enormous problems for the historian, for there are perhaps no issues more charged emotionally than those of wartime collaboration and, its related topic, treason. Most of the literature, both popular and scholarly, prefers to examine resistance rather than collaboration; in the case of Yugoslavia during World War II, where a successful resistance group brought about a social and political revolution, this bias is especially marked. To place beside all the books and articles on Tito's Partisans there is only one serious study of the important and genuinely pro-Axis Croatian Ustaši.[1] But whereas Pavelić's treason and treachery were longstanding and immediately evident, General Nedić's collaboration with the Germans presents more complex problems, and Mihailović's behavior is even more difficult to characterize. Clearly, the Chetniks were in some sense both a resistance movement and collaborationists; there are also several degrees of collaboration, and each instance must be assessed on the basis of motives and surrounding circumstances. Writing

[1] Martin Broszat and Ladislas Hory, *Der Kroatische Ustascha Staat (1941–1945)*, Schriftenreihe der Vierteljahrsheft für Zeitgeschichte 8 (Stuttgart: Deutsche Verlags-Anstalt, 1964).

not long after the close of the war, Hugh Seton-Watson distinguished between at least five sorts of collaboration, and he probably did not exhaust all the possibilities.[2]

The officers' failure to undertake full-scale resistance obviously did not stem from pro-German or pro-Italian sympathies. It is probably more revealing to look at the Chetniks as a typical officer-led underground movement which for a whole variety of reasons proved abortive from the very beginning of the resistance. Their original plans were to build up an organization capable of seizing power immediately after a German withdrawal, to provide the Allies with information on the situation in the Balkans, to create diversions in the rear of the occupation troops in the event of a Balkan landing, and, in general, to act cautiously enough to avoid massive reprisals against the civilian population. Like officers in other defeated countries, their overriding loyalties were to the émigré government; as with several other non-Communist underground organizations, they felt uneasy about the immediate and postwar consequences of mass uprisings and tended to see their main function as providing information, carrying out acts of sabotage, and joining forces with conventional invasions by liberating troops.[3] In countries like France, Czechoslovakia, and Poland, clandestine groups of anti-Axis officers avoided open confrontations with the Germans until there was a real prospect of effective Allied aid and, in doing so, were pursuing what was probably the only sensible course of action.

In Yugoslavia, however, the strategy of carrying on underground irregular warfare, postponing aggressive resistance, and confining anti-Axis actions to isolated acts of sabotage and terror was not feasible, given the realities of the occupation order. The decisive facts about wartime Yugoslavia had to do with the system, or lack of system, of the occupation regime. Generally speaking, the Axis Powers made the mistake of imposing an incredibly brutal occupation and political settlement on the country without providing the force to back it up. Overall territorial arrangements were hasty makeshifts and satisfied neither the Italians and the Germans nor the Croatian Ustaši. The policies of terror and mass reprisals were virtually unrestrained and unique in their execution.

---

[2] *The East European Revolution* (New York: Praeger, 1951), pp. 106–7.

[3] For a comparative perspective on non-Communist resistance groups, there is a vast literature. A few recent studies which shed some light on the behavior of anti-Axis officers in other parts of occupied Europe are Hanns von Krannhals, *Der Warschauer Aufstand 1944* (Frankfurt am Main: Bernard u. Graefe Verlag, 1962); Vojtech Mastny, *The Czechs under Nazi Rule: The Failure of National Resistance, 1939–1942* (New York: Columbia University Press, 1971); Robert O. Paxton, *Parades and Politics at Vichy: The French Officer Corps under Marshal Pétain* (Princeton: Princeton University Press, 1966).

In the German sphere the army, rather than the Gestapo or S.S., was identified with the destruction of villages and mass deportations.[4] In Independent Croatia, the terrorist Ustaši held sway over the regular army, the assaults on the Serb villages of Bosnia and Herzegovina were part of an open civil struggle, rather than concentration camp killings, and everyone knew about them. The result was spontaneous revolt in practically all the predominantly Serb parts of Yugoslavia.

In some areas, like Serbia and Montenegro, by the end of 1941 the occupation forces were able to suppress the armed revolt and expel, although not destroy, the resistance leadership. This, however, did not alter the basic fact that, during most of the war the villages and outlying hilly areas throughout Yugoslavia lacked any permanent and effective authority. Here normalization was the exception and chaos and intermittent civil war were the rule. In rural Serbia the contending elements were the Germans, Nedić's Quisling armed forces, and a whole array of remote bands, all actual or potential supporters of Mihailović. In Montenegro the Italians gave up altogether and turned over large parts of the "protectorate" to separatist and pro-Mihailović officers. The most thoroughly anarchic situation was in Bosnia and Herzegovina, where the Italians, Germans, Ustaši, Serb nationalists, and Partisans competed for authority and spheres of influence. More than anywhere else, it was the ethnically mixed parts of Independent Croatia which gave the radical resistance a new life after the disasters of 1941 and sustained it throughout the war.

The unique facts about wartime Yugoslavia were, then, the weakness of the occupation system, the persistent failures of most attempts to impose a thoroughgoing pacification, and, consequently, a state of affairs characterized by anarchy and a largely unorganized and ongoing civil war. Stated more simply, there were actually three "wars" proceeding simultaneously: the resistance against the Axis occupation; the civil struggle between the Serbs on the one hand and the Croats and Muslims on the other; and a civil war within the anti-Axis camp which placed the Serb Chetniks against the Serb Partisans (large numbers of Croats joined Tito only in the latter part of 1943).

By choice and necessity, both Tito and Mihailović carried out civil wars in addition to anti-Axis resistance. The Partisans disputed with the officers, elected a strategy which invited continued reprisals, attacked Nedić's gendarmes and Pavelić's Ustaši troops, appealed for Muslim support against the extreme Serb nationalists, and in general led an anti-Chetnik struggle throughout the war. For Mihailović and the

<hr>

[4] Václav Král, *Prestuplenia protiv Evropy* (Crimes against Europe) (Moscow: Izdatel'stvo Mysl; 1968), p. 223.

officers, the dilemma created by the realities of the occupation was far worse since, unlike the Partisans, they had followed from the beginning a "wait-and-see" strategy. After the disaster in Serbia in late 1941, though, the focus of the Chetnik movement shifted to the west, and the officers had to rely on an already existing Serb nationalist armed movement which was bent on revenge and dominated by a local leadership. From then on, Mihailović's movement, despite its anti-Axis schemes and long-haul orientation, fought a basically civil war against the Partisans and the Muslim and Croatian civilian population.

The more involved the Serb nationalist movement became in the civil struggle, the more the officers had to place a priority on short-term goals. Although this certainly meant putting off anti-Axis resistance, it also meant that in order to fight Tito's Partisans, compete with the Ustaši, and wage border raids against the Sandžak Muslims, they could no longer remain an essentially underground organization. In order to carry out the policy of "parallel wars" against their domestic foes, the Serb nationalist leaders needed an armed movement, and this led to ongoing collaboration with the Italians.

The accommodations with the Italians made possible a temporary revival of the Chetniks in 1942, but it was precisely this sort of short-term success which ultimately proved fatal to the officers. Although the non-Communist Serb armed movement succeeded in many instances in adjusting itself to different occupation orders and local circumstances, it did so at the cost of becoming hopelessly dispersed and permanently dominated by civilian notables. Mihailović and his delegate-officers tried in vain in 1942 and 1943 to pull together the Chetnik formations under a firm military leadership and failed miserably. There was an almost permanent tension between the officers who were loyal to Mihailović and the formations' spokesmen, often civilians, who tended to be more responsive to the mood of their followers, took a more active part in negotiating with the occupation authorities, and therefore were more inclined toward collaboration.

Even where the officers played a predominant role, for example, in Montenegro, their reliance on external support undermined the usefulness of the armed formations. The Montenegrins divided influence with the Italians in their native province but could not operate freely anywhere else. In Serbia the officers survived by establishing a truce with and attaching themselves to the Nedić administration but in the process became militarily impotent. Virtually everywhere in the Serb parts of Yugoslavia, the nationalist movement came to depend on some form of support or toleration from the occupation powers, and the longer this state of affairs lasted the more they had to yield to pressures to conduct themselves as volunteer police detachments with exclusively anti-Partisan reponsibilities and strictly defined spheres of action.

As the war went on, the nationalist units had less and less freedom of maneuver, and Mihailović's staff had less influence with the formation leaders. Even at the end of 1942, during the high point of the Serb nationalist recovery, however, Mihailović could act decisively as the "leader" of the Chetniks only at the risk of arousing countermeasures from the Germans and Italians and sacrificing the gains and material aid which collaboration brought to the Serb spokesmen. By the middle of 1943, the Chetnik movement as a centrally directed and officer-led resistance organization capable of carrying on guerrilla warfare was a myth. In a more general sense, Mihailović's authority over the non-Communist armed movement and the military potential of the Chetniks were products of Allied wartime propaganda in 1941 and 1942 and of the Germans' persistent fear and mistrust of the Serb officers. The Chetniks in fact were local self-defense units, marauding bands of Serb villagers, anti-Partisan auxiliaries, forcibly mobilized peasants, and armed refugees, which a small groups of uncaptured Yugoslav officers was attempting without success to mold into an organized fighting force.

That the officers and civilian spokesmen failed in this effort does not alter the fact that the Serb nationalist movement, for all its shortcomings of leadership and strategy, did represent a very widespread response by Yugoslavia's largest national group to the experience of war, occupation, and civil anarchy. In a country as poorly organized and as politically divided as the Kingdom of Yugoslavia, a large part of the civilian population, including the Serbs, must have perceived the war in essentially local and ethnic-religious terms rather than in terms of postwar politics. The brutalities of the Axis occupation and Ustaši terror ignited national divisions but clearly did not create them, and what emerges from this study is a picture of a country which was politically, administratively, and culturally fragmented before the war and certainly even more so during it. Even the Partisans, so often credited, and with considerable justification, for pulling the country together, were an overwhelmingly Serb movement until well into 1943, and there is considerable evidence that they often expanded their ranks by appealing to national sentiments which had little to do with allegiance to the Yugoslav idea.

Also, it should be kept in mind that until the middle of the war the Partisans were in control of relatively large liberated areas only in parts of Bosnia and that their fighting effectives were probably no more numerous than the total of armed followers who made up the Serb nationalist movement. The overwhelming bulk of the Serb civilian population, mostly villagers and small independent peasants,[5] wanted security and armed protection and, in moments of overwhelming crisis, were willing to join an armed band, Partisan or Chetnik, for purposes of defense, plunder, or national revenge. Thus Herzegovinian and Montenegrin Partisans of 1941 appeared in the ranks of the Chetnik volunteer militia in 1942 and passed over to the Partisans again in 1943. Serb nationalist groups in Bosnia fought the Germans, Ustaši, and the Croat and Muslim civilians almost simultaneously and then were pacified or dispersed when the situation changed. Likewise, the Muslims of the Sandžak, hard pressed by both Serb and Montenegrin Chetniks, proved willing recruits for both the Germans and the Partisans.

Seen in this context, the failure of the officers and the Serb non-Communist armed movement was just one reflection of the thorough disintegration which Yugoslavia suffered during World War II. Toward the end of the war and after it, the Partisans made a heroic and remarkably successful effort to revive "Yugoslavia" on a new political basis, but their achievements in overcoming national hostilities almost certainly were not widely supported, due in large part to the fact that Serb, Croat, and Muslim particularist nationalism had no political outlet. World War II was of enormous significance to Yugoslavia not only because of the group it brought to power but also because of those it eliminated. Had Mihailović's officers and the Serb civilian nationalist leaders triumphed, with some sort of decisive Allied intervention on the Greek model, the restoration of the monarchy would surely have been accompanied by violent political purges and a reign of Serb vengeance.

[5] According to the 1931 census, Yugoslavia's population was over 76 percent rural and only 8.6 percent "industrial"; over 90 percent of the peasants were smallholders, owning ten hectares or less of land.

SELECTED
BIBLIOGRAPHY

:

I. PRIMARY SOURCES

A. UNPUBLISHED

This book rests primarily on three major bodies of unpublished source materials—the records of the Italian and the German occupation forces in former Yugoslavia and those of the German Foreign Office. Together, they constitute the documentary base for any understanding of occupation politics and the course of the resistance in Yugoslavia during World War II. Because so many Chetnik groups undertook negotiations of one sort or another or even established regular ties with the German and Italian authorities, these records are particularly useful for following the development of the Mihailović movement.

In 1955-56 a group of American scholars, known as the Committee for the Study of War Documents of the American Historical Association, undertook the major project of classifying, cataloging, and microfilming a massive collection of captured German documents, consisting for the most part of the records of the German armed forces and several Reich governmental agencies. These microfilm rolls, which can be purchased from the National Archives, are listed and described in the *Guides to German Records Microfilmed at Alexandria, Va.* (Washington, D.C.: National Archives, National Archives Records Service, 1958ff.). At the present time, these catalogues include the rolls of the microfilmed military records extending from the German High Command to theater headquarters, army groups, armies, corps, rear area commands, and some of the divisions.

For the purposes of this study, the most useful group of German military sources are contained in Microcopy T-501, Records of German Field Commands, Occupied Territories, and Others, where there is an extremely large amount of indispensable information, especially in rolls 250, 256, 264–68, 351, and 352, dealing with all aspects of the occupation and resistance movements from the headquarters of the Plenipotentiary Commanding General in Serbia (Bevollmächtigter Kommandierender General in Serbien), the German General in Zagreb (Deutscher General in Agram), and the Armed Forces Commander South-East (Wehrmachtbefehlshaber Südost).

The records of the Armed Forces and Army High Commands, although far less useful, are helpful in some instances. Microcopy T-77, Records of Headquarters, German Armed Forces High Command (Oberkommando der Wehrmacht/OKW), provides some interesting material, including intelligence reports on the Chetnik movement gathered by OKW/Amtsgruppe Ausland, in rolls 884–85. Daily reports of the South-East High Command (Oberbefehlshaber Südost) can be found in rolls 322 and 329 of Microcopy T-78, Records of Headquarters, German Army High Command (Oberkommando des Heeres/OKH).

The Records of German Field Commands, Army Groups, catalogued as Microcopy T-311, contain the records of Army Groups "E" and "F" (Heeresgruppen E, F) in rolls 175, 176, and 197, which were helpful for the latter part of the war. Similarly, the reports, war diary, and various communications of the Twelfth Army (AOK 12), which was later expanded to the South-East High Command and, finally, to Army Group "E," are essential to this study. These can be found in rolls 425, 452, 460, 461, 466, 469, and 470 of Microcopy T-312, Records of German Field Commands, Armies.

Below the army group and army level the usefulness of the military sources proved very uneven. The records of the 15th Mountain Corps (XV. Gebirgs Korps), rolls 554–57, 559, and 560 of Microcopy T-314, Records of German Field Commands: Corps, were only moderately helpful, but roll 1457 for the 18th Mountain Corps (XVIII. Gebirgs Korps), also in Microcopy T-314, contains all the documents pertaining to Mihailović's unsuccessful negotiations with the Germans in November 1941 and constitutes the basis of Chapter II.

Division-level sources produced practically no significant and new evidence. This holds true for the S.S. "Prinz Eugen" division (7. SS. Gebirgs Division), rolls 145–46 of Microcopy T-354, Miscellaneous S.S. Records, and for the 714th, 717th, and 718th Infantry Division (Infanterie Divisionen), rolls 2112, 2236–45, 2258, 2262, 2265–71, and 2281 of Microcopy T-315, Records of German Field Commands: Divisions. The Records of Reich Leader of the S.S. and Chief of the German Police (Reichsführer SS und Chef der Deutschen Polizei), catalogued as Microcopy T-175, does include some interesting reports on the Mihailović movement (roll 124) and information on developments in Serbia and within the Nedić government (rolls 126 and 140).

With the obvious exception of Serbia and, to a lesser degree, eastern Bosnia, the Italian military sources, catalogued in the three-volume *Guide to Records of the Italian Armed Forces* (Washington, D.C.: National Archives, National

Archives Records Service, 1967), are more helpful than the German records for evidence on the Chetniks' activities up to summer 1943. For the most part, the provenance of these records are the Italian High Command (Comando Supremo) and the Second Army Command (Comando 2. Armata). These sources are all classified as Microcopy T-821.

The most important microfilms of Comando Supremo records are rolls 21, 31, 125, 248, and 356, which include everything from summaries of high-level talks with the Germans on joint actions in Yugoslavia to reports on Italian sponsorship of the M.V.A.C. detachments and analyses of the Mihailović movement. The records of the Second Army Command, especially rolls 53, 54, 64, 66, 70, 285–90, 294, 297, 298, 395, 398–400, 410, 448, 474, 497, and 503, provided the foundation for the treatment of Italian policies in Yugoslavia in general and Italian relations with the Chetniks in particular.

Some of the Italian rolls are significant in rather special ways. Roll 232, for instance, consisting largely of Sixth Army Corps records, was invaluable for my understanding of the beginnings of the Serb armed resistance in Bosnia-Herzegovina in 1941. General Pieche's reports, important because Ambrosio usually read them, are mostly in rolls 247 and 347. Roll 347 is also valuable for a number of frames shedding light on Montenegrin Governor Pirzio Biroli's policies and attitudes toward the Chetniks. In addition, some of the Italian rolls have relevant German documents. An important German translation of an Italian summary of the Mihailović conference at Avtovac (July 1942) is in roll 252; a whole run of intercepted and decoded Chetnik radio messages, in German translation, appears in roll 356.

A separate body of Italian sources, the private papers of Mussolini, are classified as T-586. Rolls 405, 412, 488, 1019, 1285, and 1357, all containing records mainly from the Salò period, were of little use except for a few reports written in the fall of 1944 by Italian representatives in Belgrade on the disintegration of the Mihailović organization in Serbia.

Aside from the records of the Axis military authorities, the German Foreign Office sources, which are described in George O. Kent, *A Catalog of Files and Microfilms of the German Foreign Ministry Archives, 1920–1945* (Stanford, Calif.: Hoover Institution of Stanford University, 1966), vol. 3, are the major body of unpublished primary source materials. The microcopy number for all the German Foreign Office microfilm rolls is T-120.

Of these, the most useful, especially for German policies in Croatia, their relations with the Italians, Axis strategy for anti-Partisan warfare, and information on the Chetnik movement throughout the western half of former Yugoslavia, are the Kasche papers, found in rolls 1025, 1026, 1077, and 1088. These were supplemented by a large amount of pertinent diplomatic correspondence of the Foreign Office's state secretary (Staatssekretär) in rolls 197, 199, 200, 208, and 212, and the Ritter files, rolls 395, 402, 764, 780, and 2955. Occasionally, German intelligence and police reports, such as those found in rolls 348, 393, 1141, and 2908 (Abteilung Inland II) and roll 724 (Politische Abteilung I M), proved helpful.

Other papers bearing on Yugoslavia turned up in the records of the foreign minister (Reichsaussenminister) in roll 120, the under secretary of state (Unter-staatssekretär) in roll 1369, the Reich Chancellery (Reichskanzlei), roll 1374, and Politische Abteilung IV, roll 1687. In addition, the Foreign Office correspondence dealing with trade and economic matters, especially the records of the Commercial Policy Section (Handelspolitische Abteilung IVa), rolls 744, 1127, 1174, and 1178, includes materials on the activities of the Chetnik officers. The MacKensen papers, rolls 101 and 102, and the state secretary's files pertaining to relations with Italy, rolls 137, 140, and 141, are by and large of little help for my treatment of Italian policies in the Balkans.

B. PUBLISHED

1. Materials from the Chetnik Trials
Immediately after the war, Tito's government held a number of trials of major captured Chetniks, culminating in the Mihailović trial of the summer of 1946. Obviously, the most helpful publication coming from these trials is the collection of documentary evidence used against the general.

Yugoslavia. Državna Komisija za Utvrdjivanje Zločina Okupatora i njihovih Pomagaća. *Dokumenti o Izdajstvu Draže Mihailovića* (Documents on the treason of Draža Mihailović). Belgrade: Državna štamparija, 1945.

———. *Saopštena o Zločinima Okupatora i njihovih Pomagaća* (Report on the crimes of the Occupation Forces and their collaborators). Belgrade: Državna Štamparija, 1944–1946.

———. Supreme Court. Military Council. Belgrade. *The Trial of Dragoljub-Draža Mihailović—Stenographic Record and Documents from the Trial of D.D.M.* Belgrade: State Publishing House, 1946.

2. Memoirs and Diaries
A handful of these are quite useful for shedding light on the activities of the Chetniks, especially because none of the writers can be called "pro-Mihailović" in the full sense of that expression.

Dapčević, Peko. *Kako Smo Vodili Rat* (How we waged the war). Belgrade: Srpska Knjezina Zadruga, 1956.

Dapčević, one of Tito's leading generals, offers a penetrating analysis of Mihailović's failure to put together effective fighting units and contrasts this with the Partisans' development of guerrilla strategy and tactics.

Kostić, Boško. *Za Istoriju Naših Dana* (Toward a history of our times). Lille: Jean Lausier, 1949.

A fundamental source for Mihailović's relations with Nedić and Ljotić in 1944–45.

Maclean, Fitzroy. *Disputed Barricades*. London: Jonathan Cape, 1957.

As head of the British military mission with Tito from the fall of 1943 on, Maclean writes from a basically pro-Partisan point of view but does preserve a balanced attitude toward the Chetniks.

Neubacher, Hermann. *Sonderauftrag Südost, 1940–45*. Göttingen: Muster-schmidt Verlag, 1956.

Especially important for the German-sponsored arrangements with several of the Chetnik commanders, like Djurisić, in late 1943.

Roatta, Mario. *Otto Millioni di Baionette*. Milano: Mondadori, 1946.

Includes a justification of Roatta's policy of using Mihailović's troops against the Partisans despite the Italians' knowledge of the Chetniks' long-term anti-Axis aims.

Topalović, Živko. *Kako Su Komunisti Dograbili Vlast u Jugoslaviji* (How the Communists seized power in Yugoslavia). London: Izdanje Sindikalista, 1964.

―――. *Pokreti Narodnog Otpora u Jugoslaviji, 1941–45* (Movements of national resistance in Yugoslavia, 1941–45). Paris: n.p., 1958.

―――. *Srbija pod Dražom* (Serbia under Draza). London: Izdanje Budućnost, 1968.

Topalović, the principal organizer of Mihailović's Sa. Sava Day congress at Ba, not only knows a good deal about the Chetniks, especially in 1944 and 1945, but does not hesitate to expose the shortcomings of the movement, mainly pertaining to the officers' treatment of the Muslims and Croats.

The whole question of Italian policies in the Balkans, so important for the Mihailović movement, is supplemented by a number of published memoirs and diaries, although none of them say a great deal about the Chetniks except Roatta's account. The main ones consulted are:

Anfuso, Filippo. *Da Palazzo Venezia al Lago di Garda*. Rome: Capelli, 1957.

Badoglio, Pietro. *L'Italia nella Seconda Guerra mondiale*. Verona: Mondadori, 1946.

Bastianini, Giuseppe. *Uomini, Cose, Fatti*. Milan: Vitagliano, 1959.

Castellano, Giuseppe. *La Guerra Continua*. Milan: Rizzoli, 1963.

Cavallero, Ugo. *Comando Supremo: Diario 1940–1943 del Capo di S.M.G.* Bologna: Capelli, 1948.

Ciano, Galeazzo. *Diario*. Vol. 2 (1941–1943). Milan: Rizzoli, 1946.

―――. *L'Europa verso la Catastrofe*. Verona: Mondadori, 1948.

Favagrossa, Carlo. *Perchè perdemmo la Guerra*. Milan: Rizzoli, 1947.

Simoni, Leonardo [Baron Michele Lanza]. *Berlino: Ambasciata d'Italia, 1939–1943*. Rome: Migliaresi, 1946.

Zanussi, Giacomo. *Guerra e Catastrofe d'Italia*. Rome: Libraria Corso, 1945.

On the German side, the following supplement the material from the microfilmed diplomatic and military records:

Halder, Franz. *Kriegstagebuch*. Vol. 3: *Der Russlandfeldzug bis zum Marsch auf Stalingrad (22.6.1941–24.9.1942)*. Stuttgart: W. Koehlhammer Verlag, 1964.

Höttl, Wilhelm [Walter Hagen]. *The Secret Front—The Story of Nazi Political Espionage*. London: Weidenfeld and Nicolson, 1953.

Important for Tito's negotiations with the Germans in the spring of 1943.

Rendulic, Lothar. *Gekämpft, Gesiegt, Geschlagen*. Heidelberg: Verlag Welsermühl, 1952.

Rintelen, Enno von. *Mussolini als Bundesgenosse*. Tübingen: Reiner Wunderlich Verlag, 1951.

Includes a few interesting observations on the Italians' lack of preparation for the campaign of April 1941.

Several Partisans wrote memoirs but only a few of them have anything of significance to say about the Chetniks. In addition to Dapčević's previously cited account, which is exclusively military in focus, the most pertinent are:

Dedijer, Vladimir. *Dnevnik* (Diary). Vols. 1 and 2. Belgrade: Državni Izdavački Zavod Jugoslavije, 1945–46.
> Especially important for 1941 and 1942.

Egić, Obrad. *Ratni Dnevnik 2. Proleterske Dalmatinske Brigade* (War diary of the Second Proletarian Dalmatian Brigade). Zagreb: Stvarnost, 1967.
> Very good for the anti-Chetnik offensive of early 1943.

Gizdić, Drago. *Dalmacija, 1943–45* (Dalmatia, 1943–45). 2 vols. Zagreb: Epoka, 1962–64.
> This important work is actually a chronicle of all sorts of political and military events in Dalmatia and is particularly relevant to this study because it contains captured Chetnik documents.

Lola-Ribar, Ivan. *Uspomene iz Narodno-Oslobodilački Borbe* (Recollections from the national liberation war). Belgrade: Vojno Delo, 1961.

Events immediately before and during the April war are treated in:

Maček, Vladko. *In the Struggle for Freedom*. New York: Speller, 1957.

For British policy toward the resistance movements, which is treated in this book almost wholly on the basis of secondary works, one cannot overlook:

Churchill, Winston L. *The Second World War*. Vol. 5: *Closing the Ring*. London: Cassell, 1952.

The only American memoir which sheds any light on Roosevelt's policies, or lack of them, toward Tito and Mihailović is:

Murphy, Robert. *Diplomat among Warriors*. New York: Doubleday, 1964.

3. Official Publications, Military Records, and Correspondence
A number of other publications and collections provide indispensable information on both Axis and Allied policies in Yugoslavia and some material relating directly to the Chetniks.

Chandler, Alfred D., ed. *The Papers of Dwight D. Eisenhower: The War Years*. Vol. 3. Baltimore: Johns Hopkins University Press, 1970.
> This volume includes two messages from Eisenhower to General William Donavan, head of O.S.S. for the Mediterranean theater, which illustrate the former's lack of enthusiasm in 1944 for an overt American intelligence link with Mihailović.

Heibert, Helmut, ed. *Hitler's Lagebesprechungen*. Stuttgart: Deutsche Verlags-Anstalt, 1962.

International Military Tribunal. *Trial of the Major War Criminals (Proceedings)*. Vol. 10. Nuremberg: International Military Tribunal, 1946.
> This volume, which includes the interrogation of Ribbentrop in April 1946, supplements all the other evidence on the tensions between the Germans and the Italians in 1943 over the Chetnik question.

Kerekes, Lajos, ed. *Allianz Hitler-Horthy-Mussolini: Dokumente zur ungari-schen Aussenpolitik, 1933–1944.* Budapest: Akademiai Kiado, 1966.

Useful for following Hitler's short-lived scheme to give Croatia to Hungary in April 1941.

Les Lettres Secrètes Echangées par Hitler et Mussolini. Paris: Editions de Pavois, 1946.

This partial collection includes the correspondence between Hitler and Mussolini in February and March 1943 dealing with combined strategy for Operation Weiss.

Schramm, Percy E., et al., eds. *Kriegstagebuch des Oberkommandos der Wehr-macht.* 4 vols. in 7 parts. Frankfurt-on-Main: Bernard und Graefe Verlag, 1961–65.

An indispensable printed source for German military operations.

United States. Department of State. *Documents on German Foreign Policy (1918–1945.* Series D (1937–1945). Vols. 12 and 13. Washington, D.C.: U.S. Government Printing Office, 1962 and 1964.

These two last volumes of the German diplomatic record supplement the microfilmed Foreign Office documents for the period up to 11 December, 1941.

————. *Foreign Relations of the United States* (1943). Vol. 2: *(Europe)* and *(1944)*; vol. 4: *(Europe).* Washington, D.C.: U.S. Government Printing Office, 1964–66.

This collection includes documents which place in clearer perspective both American and British policies toward the resistance in Yugoslavia in the latter part of the war.

Yugoslavia. Jugoslovenska Narodna Armija. Vojnoistroijski Institut. *Zbornik Dokumenata i Podataka o Narodnooslobodilačkom Ratu Naroda Jugoslavije* (Collection of documents and acts on the national liberation war of the Yugoslav people). 13 vols. in 128 parts. Belgrade: Vojnoistroijski Institut, 1949–.

This series, organized regionally and, in some cases, topically, is much more than the basic source for the Partisan side of the war. Several of the docu-ments offer a great deal of information on Partisan clashes with Chetnik units, and some of these volumes reproduce Chetnik messages as well as Ustaši documents and Serbo-Croatian translations of Italian and German materials.

II. SECONDARY SOURCES

The literature on Yugoslavia during World War II is so vast that this survey of the secondary works necessarily is very selective and deals only with those items which proved of value for my treatment of the activities of the Mihailović movement and closely related themes. Also, in order to make the list more meaningful to the reader, this part of the bibliography is organized thematically rather than according to official histories, monographs, articles, etc.

A. GENERAL STUDIES

Countless surveys dealing with Yugoslavia during World War II are available in Serbo-Croatian and in Western languages. Among the more useful, either because of the strength of the research or the presentation of an overall argument, are:

Clissold, Stephen. *Whirlwind: An Account of Marshal Tito's Rise to Power.* London: Cresset Press, 1949.

One of the first accounts in English, but still a useful source for information; Clissold includes a short treatment of Tito's negotiations with the Germans in 1943 but, on the whole, is neither pro-Chetnik or pro-Partisan.

Dedijer, Vladimir. *Tito.* New York: Simon and Schuster, 1953.

Although hardly a history of World War II, this book must be mentioned because a good deal of it deals with the war. Dedijer was very close to Partisan headquarters in 1941 and 1942, and it was written as something of an "official" biography of Tito.

Djonlagić, Ahmet, et al. *Yugoslavia in the Second World War.* Translation by Lovett F. Edwards. Belgrade: Medjunarodna Stampa, 1967.

This English version is probably the best way for those who do not read Serbo-Croatian to examine a recent and intelligent exposition of the official Yugoslav point of view.

Johnson, Chalmers A. *Peasant Nationalism and Communist Power: The Emergence of Revolutionary China (1937–1945).* Stanford, Calif.: Stanford University Press, 1962.

Leaning on extensive study of Mao's strategic response to the Japanese occupation, Johnson argues that the Chinese Communists and (in his final, less well-researched chapter) Tito's Partisans succeeded mainly because they were successful in mobilizing a rural patriotic revolution which emerged as a result of particularly brutal occupation regimes. The problem is admittedly very complex, but my own impression is that one is treading on rather dangerous ground by employing a concept like "peasant revolution," with all that implies, to analyze the situation in Yugoslavia.

Lazitch, Branko. *Tito et la révolution Yougoslave (1937–1959).* Paris: Fasquelle, 1957.

Included here because it is one of the best-informed and probably the most balanced treatment to come from a Yugoslav émigré.

Marjanović, Jovan; and Morača, Pero. *Naš Oslobodilački Rat i Narodna Revolucija (1941–1945)* (Our war of liberation and the national revolution, 1941–1945). Belgrade: Izdavacko Preduzecé, 1958.

An excellent one-volume survey by two leading Yugoslav historians.

Matl, Josef. "Jugoslawien im Zweiten Weltkrieg." In *Jugoslawien,* edited by Werner Markert, pp. 99–119. Cologne: Bohlau Verlag, 1954.

A good short summary.

Shoup, Paul. *Communism and the Yugoslav National Question.* New York: Columbia University Press, 1968.

This book offers a solid analysis of a very important theme. There is some evidence, though, that at least in the first half of the war the Partisans had their share of problems recruiting successfully among Croats and Muslims, and I do not feel Shoup places proper emphasis on this.

Slabin, G. M. "Yugoslaviya." In *Antifashistkoe Dvizhenie Soprotivlenya v Stranakh Evropy v gody Vtoroi Mirovoi Voiny* (The anti-Fascist resistance movements in Europe during World War II, edited by V. P. Bondarenko, pp. 174–218. Moscow: Izdatel's stvo Sotsialno Ekonomicheskoi Literatury, 1962.

A concise Soviet treatment.

Tomasevich, Jozo. "Yugoslavia during the Second World War." In *Contemporary Yugoslavia*, edited by Wayne Vucinich, pp. 59–118. Berkeley, Calif.: University of California Press, 1969.

Despite its medium length, this is certainly the best treatment of the problem in English. Tomasevich, who uses unpublished German sources extensively, plans to publish a larger monograph on the same theme in the near future.

Tudjman, Franjo. *Okupacija i Revolucija* (Occupation and revolution). Zagreb: Institut za Historija Radničkog Pokreta, 1963.

This work includes some interesting details on the political activities of the western Bosnian Chetniks. From another perspective, it throws light on some of the tensions among Yugoslav historians of World War II by arguing a discernibly "Croatian" point of view on questions like the national composition of the Partisan movement.

B. DIPLOMATIC BACKGROUND AND AXIS INVASION

Among the works which helped fill in the background are:

Čulinović, Ferdo. *Dvadeset Sedmi Mart* (March twenty-seventh). Zagreb: Yugoslavenska Akademija Zvanosti, 1965.

The most complete treatment of the Belgrade coup, employing the unpublished diary of General Simović.

Fabry, Philipp. *Balkan Wirren (1940–41)*. Darmstadt: Wehr und Wissen Verlag, 1966.

Analyzes the role of Balkan affairs mainly in the context of German-Soviet relations and places a very strong emphasis on Stalin's designs in this area, which had a great deal to do with the erosion of Hitler's willingness to prolong the Non-Aggression Pact.

Hoptner, Jacob B. *Yugoslavia in Crisis (1934–1941)*. New York: Columbia University Press, 1962.

An exhaustive history of the Yugoslav diplomatic tangle preceding the Axis invasion, the book concludes that Prince Paul's policy of "appeasement for a price" was the only realistic course of action. Very critical, therefore, of the officers who led the coup of 27 March 1941.

Knejevitch, Radoje. "Prince Paul, Hitler and Salonika," *International Affairs* 27 (1951): 38–44.

Spells out in precise terms the possible advantages of an accommodation with the Axis Powers in 1940–41.

Salvemini, Gaetano. *Prelude to World War II*. London: Gallancy, 1953.
    Useful because of information on Mussolini's sponsorship of the Ustaši
    émigré group in Italy during the 1930s.

For a closer look at one aspect of the Axis invasion of April 1941, there is:

Hepp, Leo. "Die 12. Armee in Balkanfeldzug 1941," *Wehrwissenschaftliche
    Rundschau* 5 (1955): 199–216.
Tippelskirch, Kurt. "Der deutsche Balkanfeldzug 1941," *Wehrwissenschaftliche
    Rundschau* 2 (1955): 49–65.

C. THE AXIS POWERS AND YUGOSLAVIA DURING THE WAR

1. General

Deakin, Frederick William. *The Brutal Friendship: Mussolini, Hitler and the
    Fall of Italian Fascism*. New York: Harper and Row, 1962.
    Deakin, the most enthusiastically pro-Partisan of the British liaison officers
    in Yugoslavia during the war, has written an exhaustive history of Italo-
    German relations which is probably the best starting point for any study
    of particular issues confronting the Axis Powers.
Herzog, Robert. *Grundzüge der deutschen Besatzungverwaltung in den ost
    und südosteuropäischen Ländern während des Zweiten Weltkrieges*. Studien
    des Instituts für Besatzungsfragen in Tübingen 4. Tubingen: Institute fur
    Besatzungsfragen in Tübingen, 1955.
    Disappointing because Herzog confines himself exclusively to the terri-
    torial and jurisdictional aspects of the occupation administration without
    dealing with the substance of German policies.
Royal Institute of International Affairs. *Survey of International Affairs (1939–
    1946*. Vol. 4: *Hitler's Europe*. Edited by Arnold Toynbee and Veronica
    Toynbee. London: Oxford University Press, 1954.
    The article by Elizabeth Wiskemann on Yugoslavia gives a concise sum-
    mary of occupation politics.
Woescht, Johann. *Jugoslawien und das Dritte Reich*. Stuttgart: Seewald
    Verlag, 1969.
    The only detailed treatment of German policies in Yugoslavia. Unfor-
    tunately, this book, although full of information, proves little more than
    the length to which some Germans will go to find justifications for their
    actions in occupied Europe.

2. Special Problems

A handful of Yugoslav specialists have made scholarly contributions on the
Italian activities in Yugoslavia.

Kljaković, Vojmir. "Oslobodilački Rat Naroda Jugoslavije i Učešće Talijana
    u Ratu protiv Sovjetskog Saveza" (The Yugoslav people's war of liberation
    and the Italians' participation in the war against the Soviet Union). *Jugo-
    slovenski Istorijski Časopis* 4 (1964): 73–91.
    In a carefully written but not altogether convincing article, Kljaković
    advances the very official argument that the resistance compelled the Italians

to commit so many troops to Yugoslavia that Mussolini had to postpone repeatedly his plans for an even earlier and larger contribution to the war against the Red Army.

Leković, Miso. "Neki Aspekti Italijansko-Ustaškíh Odnosa i nijhov Odraz na Operacije NOC i POJ" (Some aspects of Italian-Ustaši relations and their impact on the operations of the National Liberation Army), *Jugoslovenski Istorijski Casopis* 4 (1965): 85–94.

A good example of the increasing willingness of Yugoslav historians to point out the very serious strains between the Italians and the Pavelić regime and their beneficial results for the Partisan movement.

Pajović, Radoje. "Političke Prilike u Crnoj Gori u Vrijeme Kapitulacije Italije 1943" (The political situation in Montenegro at the time of Italy's capitaulation in 1943), *Jugoslovenski Istorijski Časopis* 1 (1962): 47–62.

Provides background material on the disintegration of the Chetnik movement in Montenegro throughout 1943.

Sepić, Dragovan. "Talijanska Okupaciona Politika u Dalmaciji (1941–1943)" (Italian occupation policies in Dalmatia, 1941–1943, *Putovi Revolucije* 1 (1963): 215–42.

The only treatment of this theme.

Pavelić's Ustaši movement, which had so much to do with the growth of the Partisan and Chetnik revolts in Croatia, is treated in:

Broszat, Martin; and Hory, Ladislas. *Der Kroatische Ustascha Staat (1941–1945)*. Schriftenreihe der Vierteljahrshefte für Zeitgeschichte 8. Stuttgart: Deutsche Verlags-Anstalt, 1964.

This is the most serious study of the puppet Croatian state. Perhaps my only general criticism is that it leans too heavily on German primary sources and neglects the Italian side.

Kiszling, Rudolph. *Die Kroaten: Der Schichsalweg eines Südslawenvolkes.* Graz: Verlag Hermann Bohlaus Naehf, 1956.

Includes a lengthy discussion of the Ustaši period.

Paris, Edmond. *Genocide in Satellite Croatia (1941–1945)*. Chicago: American Institute for Balkan Affairs, 1961.

A startling account of the Ustaši's anti-Serb terror.

For the Nedić administration in Serbia and its relations with the Chetniks, there is very little except Kostić's memoirs. A few others to be mentioned are:

Martinović-Bajica, Petar. *Milan Nedić*. Chicago: First American Serbian Corporation, 1956.

A pro-Nedić view.

Mommsen, H. "Serbische Nationale Freiwilligen-Verbände," *Gutachten des Instituts für Zeitgeschichte.* Vol. 2. Stuttgart: Deutsche Verlags-Anstalt, 1966.

Illustrates how cautious the Germans were about arming and constituting Serb detachments regardless of how reliable the leaders were.

D. THE ALLIES AND THE RESISTANCE GROUPS IN YUGOSLAVIA

When discussing the role of British and American policies and military operations and their influence on events in Yugoslavia, I used secondary works very extensively, many of them official histories. Obviously, the literature on Allied strategy and military operations in the Mediterranean as well as on their policies toward the resistance movements is vast and often of very high quality. For military questions the major works are:

Ehrmann, John. *Grand Strategy.* Vol. 5. London: Her Majesty's Stationery Office, 1956.

Garland, Albert N.; and Smyth, Howard M. *The Mediterranean Theater of Operations.* Vol. 2: *Sicily and the Surrender of Italy.* United States Department of the Army. Office of the Chief of Military History. The United States Army in World War II. Washington, D.C.: U.S. Government Printing Office, 1965.

Leighton, Richard M. "Overlord Revisited: An Interpretation of American Strategy in the European War, 1942–1944," *American Historical Review* 68 (1963): 919–97.
    Includes a good analysis of American objections to operations in the eastern Mediterranean.

Playfair, Ian S. O. *The Mediterranean and Middle East.* Vol. 3. London: Her Majesty's Stationery Office, 1960.

The whole problem of the British shift of support from Mihailović to Tito in 1943 has been dealt with carefully in three articles in the Yugoslav historical journal *Jugoslovenski Istorijski Časopis:*

Deakin, Frederick W. "Britanija i Jugoslavija, 1941–1945" (Britain and Yugoslavia), *Jugoslovenski Istorijski Časopis* (1963): 43–58.

Kljaković, Vojmir. "Promjena Politike Velike Britanije prema Jugoslaviji u prvoj polovini 1943 godine" (Great Britain's change of policy toward Yugoslavia in the first half of 1943), *Jugoslovenski Istorijski Časopis* 3 (1969): 25–57.

Marjanović, Jovan. "Velika Britanija i Narodnooslobodilački Pokret u Jugoslaviji, 1941–1945" (Great Britain and the national liberation movement in Yugoslavia, 1941–1945), *Jugoslovenski Istorijski Časopis* 2 (1963): 31–42.

Deakin has recently published a work which carries ahead his research on Britain's relations with the Yugoslav resistance and leans heavily on the unpublished records of their liaison officers: *The Embattled Mountain.* New York: Oxford University Press, 1971. Also, mention should be made of Walter Roberts' recent *Tito, Mihailović and the Allies* (New Brunswick, N.J.: Rutgers University Press, 1972).

Other works which proved helpful are:

Meneghello-Dinčić, Kruno. "Les alliés et la résistance yougoslave," *Revue d'histoire de la Deuxième Guerre Mondiale* 2 (1962): 27–48.

Plenča, Dušan. *Medjunarodni Odnosi Jugoslavije u Toku Drugog Svjetskog*

Rata (Yugoslavia's international relations during World War II). Belgrade: Institute Drustvenih Nauka, 1962.

A very well-researched version of the official Yugoslav point of view. Plenča provides a great deal of useful information on the political activities of the Chetniks and the monarchic émigré government.

Woodward, Llewellyn. *British Foreign Policy in the Second World War.* London: Her Majesty's Stationery Office, 1962.

An equally official British survey.

E. MILAILOVIĆ AND THE CHETNIKS

Yugoslav historians have begun to do some serious work on the Milhailović movement, and, although they all adhere to the official line and the research in this area is still very spotty, some of their efforts merit serious consideration. Also, some of these articles and monographs use the Mihailović archives, which, of course, are unavailable to Western scholars.

Kačavenda, Petar. "Kriza Četničkog Pokreta Draže Mihailovića u drugoj polovini 1942 godine" (The crisis of Draza Mihailović's Chetnik movement in the second half of 1942), *Istorija Radničkog Pokreta* 1 (1965): 257–332.

Although Kačavenda makes a bit too much of the "crisis," this article is an excellent contribution, employing otherwise unavailable Chetnik messages.

Leković, Miso. "Planovi Draže Mihailovića za Uništenje Partizanske Države u Zapadnoj Bosni u drugoj polovini 1942 godine" (Draža Mihailovic's plans to crush the Partisan state in western Bosnia in the second half of 1942), *Jugoslovenski Istorijski Časopis* 1 (1966): 79–100.

Supplements Kačavenda's article and the evidence on Chetnik plans in 1942 from the unpublished Italian sources.

Mrazović, K. "NOP i Borda protiv Pokušaja Stvaranja Četničkih Oružanih Odreda u Slavoniji" (The national liberation movement's struggle against the Chetniks' attempt to establish armed units in Slavonia). In *Slavonija u Narodnooslobodilačkoj Borbi,* edited by Martin Kaminski, pp. 157–70. Slavonski Brod: Historijski Institut Slavonije, 1967.

The Chetniks failed to raise an armed movement in Slavonia more because Ustaši policies had practically eliminated the Serbs than because of competition from the Partisans.

Pajović, Radoje. "Formiranje Četničke Nezavisne Grupe Nacionalnog Otpora" (The formation of the Chetnik independent group of national resistance), *Jugoslovenski Istorijski Casopis* 4 (1964): 53–70.

A fascinating account, based largely on Lukačević's testimony at his trial in 1945, of the disintegration of the officers' movement in 1944 and the partial swing over to the Partisans.

F. REGIONAL STUDIES OF THE RESISTANCE

A staggering number of case and special studies on the resistance have appeared in Yugoslavia. By listing a handful of those which aided my treatment of the Chetniks, I am barely scratching the surface.

Basiljčić, Slobodan; and Marković, Dragan. *Delegat Vrhovnog Štaba* (Delegate from the Supreme Staff). Belgrade: Izdavačko Preduzeće Rad, 1968.
An account of Svetomar Vukmanović-Tempo's activities during the war, useful for the section on his eastern Bosnian mission of early 1942 where he confronted the Dangić Chetniks.

Three works on the Sandžak and Montenegro are helpful:

Cicmil, Obrad. *Durmitorski NOP Odred i njegova Područije* (The Durmitor National Liberation Detachment and its territory. Belgrade: Vojnoizdavački Zavod, 1966.
Čuković, Mirko. *Sandžak* (The Sandžak). Belgrade: Prosveta, 1964.
Živković, Dušan. *Boka Kotorska i Paštrovići u Narodnooslobodilačkoj Borbi* (Kotor and Paštrovići in the national liberation struggle). Belgrade: Vojno Delo, 1964.
Includes some information on the splits between the pro-Mihailović and Federalist Chetniks in western Montenegro.

The standard work on the beginnings of the resistance in Serbia in 1941, much of which discusses the Chetniks and which serves as an invaluable background for Chapter II of this book, is:

Marjanović, Jovan. *Ustanak i Narodnooslobodilački Pokret u Srbiji 1941* (The uprising and national liberation movement in Serbia in 1941). Belgrade: Institut Društvenih Nauka, 1963.

As Communist charges of Mihailović's collaboration and treason gained a wider audience, a number of pro-Chetnik figures rushed to his defense both before and after his trial. Among the more interesting apologies are:

Fotich, Konstantine. *The War We Lost*. New York: Viking Press, 1948.
Fotich was King Peter's ambassador to Washington during the war; an outspoken Greater Serbian and pro-Chetnik he attempted to influence American policy in an anti-Tito sense.

Hays, Arthur Garfield, Chairman. *Report of Commission of Inquiry of the "Committee for a Fair Trial for Draja Mihailovich."* New York: Committee for a Fair Trial for Draja Mihailovich, 1946.
Significant mainly because it includes the testimony of Colonel MacDowell.
Karadjordević, Peter II (King of Yugoslavia, 1941–45). *A King's Heritage: The Memoirs of King Peter II of Yugoslavia*. London: Cassel, 1955.
Knezević, Radoje L., ed. *Knjiga o Draži* (The book on Draza). 2 vols. Windsor, Canada: Srpska Narodna Odbrana, 1956.
A collection of first-hand accounts of Mihailović's subordinates. Particularly useful for the Chetnik point of view regarding strategy in Serbia in 1941.
Martin, David. *Ally Betrayed—The Uncensored Story of Tito and Mihailović*. New York: Prentice-Hall, 1946.
Wildly pro-Chetnik.
Plamenatz, John. *The Case of General Mihailović*. Gloucester, England: John Bellows, 1944.

Denies that Mihailović instructed his subordinates to collaborate with the Italians.

Trivanovitch, Vaso. *The Case of Draja Mihailovich.* New York: United Committee of South Slavic Americans, 1946.

For the sake of balance, I might mention two anti-Mihailović polemics, written from very different perspectives:

Adamic, Louis. *My Native Land.* New York: Harper and Brothers, 1943.
One of the first pro-Tito accounts, written by the major Partisan publicist in the United States.

Omarčanin, Ivo. *Istina o Draži Mihailovića* (The truth about Draza Mihailović). Munich: Logos Verlag, 1957.
A violently anti-Serb tract which gives the point of view of the Ustaši émigré community.

For Slovenia, see:

Škerl, France, *Poćeći Partizanskog Pokreta u Sloveniji* (The beginning of the Partisan movement in Slovenia). Belgrade: Vojnoizdavacki Zavod, 1956.
Unfortunately, this excellent work, which is based on extensive research in Italian documents, deals almost entirely with 1941 and says nothing about Mihailović's later efforts to gain a foothold in Slovenia through his delegate-officer Major Novak.

Developments in Albania and Kosovo-Metobija, as well as the Chetniks' fear that the Italians were playing the Albanian Muslims off against the Serbs in Montenegro, make more sense after reading:

Hadri, Ali. "Okupacioni Sistem na Kosovu i Metohiji, 1941–1944" (The occupation system in Kosovo-Metohija, 1941–1944), *Jugoslovenski Istorijski Časopis* 2 (1965): 39–60.

A fine supplement to the picture of the Herzegovinian revolt of the summer of 1941 presented by Italian Sixth Army Corps documents is:

Kovačević, B.; and Skoko, S. "Junski Ustanak u Hercegovini 1941" (The uprising in Herzegovina of June 1941), *Istorija Radničkog Pokreta* 1 (1965): 89–168.

G. THE FINAL PHASE OF THE WAR

A number of studies of military operations in 1944 and 1945 fill in the rather scanty German record on the collapse of the Chetnik movement at the end of the war:

Basta, Milan. *Rat Posle Rata* (The war after the war). Zagreb: Stvarnost, 1963.
The official Yugoslav interpretation of the anti-Chetnik measures employed by the Partisans, especially in Slovenia, in 1945.

Karapandžić, Bor, *Kočevje: Tito's Bloodiest Crime.* Munich: Iskra, 1966.
A pro-Chetnik version of the same events.

Schmidt-Richberg, Erich. *Der Endkampf auf dem Balkan.* Heidelberg: Scharnhorst Buchkameradschaft, 1955.

Provides some details on the retreat of a few scattered Chetnik groups.

Two Soviet accounts are helpful for operations in Serbia in September and October 1944:

Biriuzov, Sergei Semenovich. *Sovetskie Vooruzhennye Sily v Borbe za Os-vobozhdenie Narodov Iugoslavii* (The Soviet armed forces' struggle for the liberation of the Yugoslav people). Moscow: Voenizdat, 1960.

Minasian, Musheg Minasovich. *Osvobozhdenie Narodov Iugo-Vostochnoi Evropy* (The liberation of the peoples of southeastern Europe). Moscow: Voenizdat, 1967.

INDEX

:

THE JOHNS HOPKINS UNIVERSITY PRESS

This book was composed in Linotype Baskerville and Greco Bold display type by Port City Press, Inc., from a design by Susan Bishop. It was printed on S. D. Warren's 60-lb. 1854 regular paper and bound in Kivar 5 material by Universal Lithographers, Inc.